TASK-BASED LANGUAGE LEARNING

Peter Robinson, Editor

Blackwell Publishing was acquired by John Wiley & Sons in February 2007. Blackwell's publishing program has been merged with Wiley's global Scientific, Technical, and Medical business to form Wiley-Blackwell.

Registered Office
John Wiley & Sons Ltd, The Atrium, Southern Gate, Chichester, West Sussex, PO19 8SQ, United Kingdom

Editorial Offices
350 Main Street, Malden, MA 02148-5020, USA
9600 Garsington Road, Oxford, OX4 2DQ, UK
The Atrium, Southern Gate, Chichester, West Sussex, PO19 8SQ, UK

For details of our global editorial offices, for customer services, and for information about how to apply for permission to reuse the copyright material in this book please see our website at www.wiley.com/wiley-blackwell.

The right of Peter Robinson to be identified as the author of the editorial material in this work has been asserted in accordance with the Copyright, Designs and Patents Act 1988.

Library of Congress Cataloging-in-Publication Data

Task-based language learning / editor Peter Robinson.
   p. cm. – (The best of language learning series; 60:S2)
Includes index.
ISBN 978-1-4443-5023-4
1. Second language acquisition. 2. Language and languages–Study and teaching.
   I. Robinson, Peter
P118.2.T35 2011
418.0071–dc22

                              2011013219

A catalogue record for this book is available from the British Library.
Set in 9/10 Times NRPS by Aptara

01—2011

4/22/13

Task-Based Language Learning

Contents

Language Learning   ISSN 0023-8333

Task-Based Language Learning: A Review of Issues

Peter Robinson

Aoyama Gakuin University

Theoretically motivated, empirical research into task-based language learning has been prompted by proposals for task-based language teaching. In this review I describe early and more recent proposals for how task-based learning can stimulate acquisition processes and the theoretical rationales that have guided research into them. I also describe taxonomies of task characteristics that have been proposed and claims made about the effects of task characteristics on interaction, attention to input, and speech production. I then relate the issues raised to findings described in the five empirical studies in this issue concerning the effects of pedagogic task design on the accuracy, fluency, and complexity of learner language; the influence of individual differences in cognitive and motivational variables on task performance; the extent to which tasks, and teacher interventions, promote the quantity and quality of interaction that facilitate L2 learning; and the generalizability of task-based learning research in laboratory contexts to instructed classroom settings.

Keywords task characteristics; task complexity; task sequencing; taxonomic description; theoretical rationales; abilities; attention; conceptualization; interaction; speech production

Over the past 30 years, proposals for task-based language teaching (TBLT) have drawn on a variety of claims about—and prompted further research into—processes thought to promote successful second language acquisition (SLA). Many important contributions to task-based learning research addressing these claims have appeared in *Language Learning* throughout this period (see, e.g., Gass, Mackey, Alvarez-Torres, & Fernandez-Garcia, 1999; Platt & Brooks, 2002; Seedhouse, 2005; Skehan & Foster, 1999; Yule, Powers, & Macdonald, 1992). Certain of these claims for SLA processes that task-work can facilitate feature throughout the present review article and are the focus of the five recent empirical studies published in *Language Learning* that follow it:

Correspondence concerning this article should be addressed to Peter Robinson, Aoyama Gakuin University, 4-4-25 Shibuya, Tokyo 150-8366, Japan. Internet: peterr@cl.aoyama.ac.jp

- Tasks provide a context for *negotiating* and *comprehending* the meaning of language provided in task input, or used by a partner performing the same task.

- Tasks provide opportunities for *uptake of* (implicit or explicit) *corrective feedback* on a participant's production, by a partner, or by a teacher.

- Tasks provide opportunities for *incorporation of premodified input*, containing "positive evidence" of forms likely to be important to communicative success and that may previously have been unknown or poorly controlled.

- Tasks provide opportunities for *noticing the gap* between a participant's production and input provided and for *metalinguistic reflection* on the form of output.

- Task demands can focus attention on specific concepts required for expression in the second language (L2) and prompt effort to *grammaticize* them in ways that the L2 formally encodes them, with consequences for improvements in accuracy of production.

- Simple task demands can promote access to and *automatization* of the currently emerged interlanguage means for meeting these demands, with consequences for improved fluency of production.

- Task demands can also promote effort at *reconceptualizing* and rethinking about events, in ways that match the formal means for encoding conceptualization that L2s make available.

- Sequences of tasks can *consolidate memories* for previous efforts at successfully resolving problems arising in communication, on previous versions, thereby strengthening memory for them.

- Following attempts to perform simpler versions, complex tasks can prompt learners to attempt more ambitious, complex language to resolve the demands they make on communicative success, thereby stretching interlanguage and promoting *syntacticization*, with consequences for improved complexity of production.

- Additionally, all of the above happen within a situated communication context that can foster *form-function-meaning mapping* and can do so in ways that *motivate* learners to learn.

Research into task-based learning has followed a trajectory, with the first four of the above-listed SLA processes being explored by early research into the effects of the interactive demands of tasks on learning (e.g., Brown, 1991; Crookes & Gass 1993a, 1993b; Day, 1986; Doughty & Pica, 1986; Gass & Varonis, 1994; Long, 1983; Long & Porter, 1985; Pica & Doughty, 1985; Pica, Young, & Doughty, 1987; Swain & Lapkin, 1995). Research into task-based interaction has continued into the present (e.g., Alcon-Soler & Garcia Mayo, 2009; Gass, Mackey, & Ross-Feldman, this issue; Mackey, 1999, 2007; Mackey & Gass, 2006; Shehadeh, 2001), with the result that broad findings for the effects of interaction and corrective feedback have accumulated to the extent that meta-analyses showing the positive contributions of each to SLA are now available (Keck, Iberri-Shea, Tracy-Ventura, & Wa-Mbaleka, 2006; Mackey & Goo, 2007; Russell & Spada, 2006).

In contrast, the latter six above-listed SLA processes are the focus of more recent research into the cognitive demands and motivational impact of variously classified task characteristics and their effects on speech production, uptake, and longer term memory for input provided during task performance (e.g., Baralt, 2010; Bygate, Skehan, & Swain, 2001; Cadierno & Robinson, 2009; Dornyei & Kormos, 2000; Ellis, 2005; Gilabert, 2005, 2007; Gilabert, Baron, & Llanes, 2009: Ishikawa, 2007, 2008a, 2008b; Kim, 2008, 2009a, 2009b; Kuiken & Vedder, 2007a, 2007b; Michel, 2011; Nuevo, 2006; Revesz, 2009, 2011; Robinson, 2001b, 2007c; Robinson, Cadierno, & Shirai, 2009; Skehan & Foster, 1999, 2001; Tavakoli & Foster, this issue; Tavakoli & Skehan, 2005). No comprehensive meta-analyses of the effects of task characteristics in these areas of L2 production, uptake, and memory for input are available as yet, although syntheses of the accumulating findings about the effects of task characteristics contributing to their "complexity" on the accuracy, fluency, and complexity of L2 speech production are beginning to appear (Jackson & Suethanapornkul, 2010) and promise to go some way toward resolving competing claims made by Robinson (2001a, 2001b, 2005) and Skehan (1998, 2009b; Skehan & Foster, 2001) about the effects of simple versus complex task demands on each (these claims and rationales for them are described in more detail in a subsequent section of this article). Taken together, then, these early, and more recently researched, SLA processes constitute a large part of what has been called the "cognitive-interactionist" rationale for the effects of instruction on SLA (see Ortega, 2007) and, in particular, for the positive effects of TBLT on SLA. Although TBLT clearly calls upon much more than the SLA processes described earlier, it is these processes and their contribution to task-based language learning (TBLL) that are the focus of the empirical studies in the present issue.

Researchers exploring sociocultural rationales for language pedagogy (e.g., Lantolf & Thorne, 2006; Negueruela & Lantolf, 2006; Swain, 2000; Swain, Kinnear, & Steinman, 2010; Swain & Lapkin, 1995) also address many of the issues raised above about how TBLT can facilitate SLA processes. From a Vygotskian perspective, learning is a social, collaborative endeavor in which both "expert" and "apprentice" take part in a shared, goal-oriented activity. Task-work provides a context for such activity and for "interactional scaffolding" (Gibbons, 2009) of individual learners' attempts to use the L2, by another learner or by a teacher (see Toth, this issue). Task demands may also prompt effort at reconceptualization of events requiring linguistic expression in the L2, third language (L3), or other language being learned, leading learners to "think-for-speaking" in ways characteristic of native speakers of the language being learned (Han & Cadierno, 2010; Jarvis & Pavlenko, 2008; Odlin, 2008; Robinson, 2007d; Robinson & Ellis, 2008; Pavlenko, 2011; von Stutterheim & Nuese, 2003). This may be particularly so along those dimensions of L2 task complexity that have been proposed to direct learners' attention to the ways in which the conceptual and communicative demands of tasks are linguistically encoded (Cadierno & Robinson, 2009; Robinson, 2003b, 2005, 2007b; Robinson et al., 2009). Vygotsky argued that concepts are only internalized following a period of mediational support provided by experience of the concept—in conjunction with attempts to verbalize activities related to it with an interlocutor. Lantolf and Thorne (2006) have argued, drawing on Gal'perin's ideas for putting Vygotsky's ideas on concept development into L2 pedagogic practice, that "it is necessary to represent in a concrete material way the concepts to be internalized" (p. 305). Consequently, tasks (and material input to tasks) making conceptual demands on learners provide opportunities for verbalizing and internalizing concepts and for becoming aware of how their L2 scope and form of expression may differ from their L1 scope and linguistic encoding.

From TBLT to Task-Based Learning Research

Although SLA research has subsequently informed it, TBLT was, initially, a proposal for improving pedagogy with only a slight foundation in empirical research into the SLA processes listed earlier. Arising out of pedagogic proposals for a greater emphasis on communicative activities in language teaching (see, e.g., Brumfit & Johnson, 1979; Skehan, 2003; Valdman, 1978, 1980; Widdowson, 1978, for reviews), TBLT places the construct of "task" at the center of curricular planning. As Cook (2010) recently noted, TBLT "sees second language learning as arising from particular tasks that students do in the classroom.... In a sense it reconceptualizes communicative language teaching as tasks rather than the language or cognition-based syllabuses of communicative language teaching," and TBLT is the approach to language teaching "that has attracted most attention in the past decade" (p. 512). Although attention to proposals for TBLT still primarily comes from teachers and educational authorities charged with designing, implementing, and coordinating effective programs of language instruction at local, national, and international levels (e.g., Council of Europe, 2001; Leaver & Willis, 2004; Van den Branden, 2006; Willis & Willis, 2007), utilizing an increasing range of available instructional technologies (e.g., Thomas & Reinders, 2010), attention to TBLT has also come from SLA researchers concerned with explaining the effects of design features of tasks, and their implementation, on learning. SLA researchers often draw implications from their findings for classroom learning, testing, and program design. However, because much empirical SLA research into the effects of tasks on learning has been—and continues to be—done in experimental settings, there is a clear need to examine the generalizability of implications drawn from this research to actual classroom language performance on tasks, and the use of tasks for testing and syllabus design purposes. Kim (2009b) is an example of such needed bridging research, examining the generalizability of laboratory findings for the effects of task complexity on interaction-driven learning and development to EFL classroom contexts, with learners at different proficiency levels (see also Ellis, 1997; Gass, Mackey, & Ross-Feldman, this issue).

This important caveat aside, many of the current lines of inquiry that SLA research into task-based learning has pursued were originally prompted by the earliest pedagogic rationales for the use of tasks in language teaching. These were exploratory suggestions for connections between pedagogic practice and the acquisition processes they may stimulate. For example, in an article entitled "Towards Task-Based Language Learning" recapitulating points he had made earlier (Candlin, 1984), Candlin (1987) argued for:

> the introduction of *tasks* as the basis for classroom action . . . They serve as a compelling and appropriate means for realizing certain characteristic principles of communicative language teaching and learning, as well as serving as a testing-ground for hypotheses in pragmatics and SLA . . . task-based language learning is not only a means to enhancing classroom communication and acquisition but also the means to the development of classroom syllabuses. (p. 5)

What Candlin (1987) was arguing for was the adoption of "tasks" as the "units" of syllabus design rather than linguistic units such as grammatical structures, functional phrases, or vocabulary lists (see Long & Crookes, 1992; Long & Robinson, 1998; Robinson, 2009; White, 1988, for reviews of units of analysis for the purposes of syllabus design). Yet Candlin was also begging the question of whether classroom tasks (designed and operationally delivered in various ways) could also be shown to serve as constructs that confirmed theoretically motivated hypotheses about SLA processes and whether these hypothesized processes were prompted or inhibited by performing any *one* pedagogic task, in contrast to another, that differed along some dimension of its design features and/or features regarding their implementation. This argument is clearly still an issue at the heart of TBLL research (as the articles in this issue testify). Candlin then went on to say:

> Tasks must . . . be defined and their means of operationalisation explained. It will be necessary to offer ideas for their classification and their targeting. Above all their centrality to the syllabus cannot be taken for granted without evaluating how they can be selected and sequenced in a principled fashion. (p. 5)

This issue raised by Candlin (1987)—of selecting tasks to be performed *in sequences*—is also at the heart of much current SLA research (see Robinson, 2007b, 2010; Robinson & Gilabert, 2007), which promises both implications for program design and insights into the acquisition processes that task-based learning can promote, across the differing timescales that institutions and other authorities set for language instruction. The sequencing issue involves consideration not only of how differently designed *tasks* might affect opportunities for learning in different ways but also of how sequences of tasks—in the *different combinations* that sequencing decisions afford, and across the *different timescales* performing them requires—impact upon these learning opportunities.

Features of Tasks and Their Implementation

A necessary starting point for studying the influence of sequences of tasks on learning, however, is to study their isolated impact on learning: in order to analyze how these effects (if they are found) are subsequently multiplied (or not) by sequences in which different tasks, or versions of the same task, are performed. This agenda requires both experimental research into task effects on learning and parallel studies of these effects in language learning programs. With these issues in mind, Candlin (1987) offered one pedagogically-operational definition of "task" (for a summary of many other definitions that have subsequently been proposed, see Samuda & Bygate, 2008, pp. 62–70). A task, Candlin (1987, p. 19) wrote, is "one of a set of differentiated, sequencable, problem-posing activities involving learners and teachers." Then Candlin went on to describe certain key features of tasks that task designers should be able to accommodate and that teachers could provide, to optimally promote classroom learning:

- *Input.* This is the written, visual, or aural information that learners performing a task work on to achieve the goal of the task.
- *Roles.* These are the roles that learners have in performing a task, such as information-giver and information-receiver.
- *Settings.* These are the grouping arrangements in and outside of classrooms for which pedagogy prepares learners to communicate.
- *Actions.* These are the procedures to follow in performing the task or the various steps that learners must take along the road to task completion.
- *Monitoring.* This is the supervisory process of ensuring that the task performance remains on track.
- *Outcomes.* These are the oral, written, and/or behavioral outcomes in which the task is intended to result.
- *Feedback.* This includes evaluation of the whole or parts of a task performance by the teacher or other learners, including corrective feedback on language use as well as other helpful feedback.

Many of these features of tasks and their implementation—in the years since Candlin (1987) first described them—have been operationalized and studied with respect to their influence on task-based learning and performance. These include, for example, the following

- the facilitating effects of linguistically versus elaboratively modified *input* on comprehension (Yano, Long & Ross, 1994);
- the effects of task *role* (Yule & MacDonald, 1990) and *grouping arrangements* (Brown, 1991) on the amount of interaction;
- the effectiveness of different types of corrective *feedback* on uptake and development during task-based interaction (Mackey & Goo, 2007);
- the effects of task different task characteristics on spoken (Foster & Skehan, 1999) and written (Kuiken & Vedder, 2007a, 2007b) *outcomes.*

Tasks and the Designed Delivery of Instruction

However, what of the larger implications of the study of task effects on learning for decisions about instructional design and program development, implementation, and evaluation? Samuda and Bygate (2008, pp. 58–60) made a useful distinction between task-supported, task-referenced, and task-based approaches to the role of tasks in instructional design. On the one hand, tasks have been proposed as a useful means to *support* delivery of programs that follow a structural (Ellis, 1993) or lexical (Willis, 1996) syllabus. In this approach, tasks can be designed to focus on variously determined and sequenced grammar structures or lexical items (see Ellis, 2009, pp. 231–232; Toth, this issue), and "tasks are not necessarily used for assessment purposes and the syllabus itself may be defined by categories other than tasks" (Samuda & Bygate, 2008, p. 59).

In contrast, task-*referenced* approaches use tasks principally as a way of setting achievement targets and assessing the desired outcomes of a program of instruction, as in the case of the Australian Adult Migrant Language Program (AMEP; see Brindley & Slatyer, 2002) or the Common European Framework of Reference for Languages (Council of Europe, 2001). In most task-referenced approaches, decisions about the units of classroom instruction (however conceived) are made prospectively, bearing in mind progress toward outcomes of task achievement. However, Candlin (1984, 1987) thought tasks could be used as units of analysis for referencing, "retrospectively," what happened in classrooms over a course of instruction, with regard to what *language* was learned as a consequence of tasks performed, what *content* the tasks involved, and what *activities* the tasks led to for teachers and learners.

Writing at around the same time as Candlin (1984), Long (1985) described a different perspective on how the information about tasks and their influence on learning could be drawn on and integrated into "prospective" decisions about instructional program design. This is what Samuda and Bygate (2008) referred to as an example of the task-*based* approach to the use of tasks to organize program delivery and assessment. Essential to his proposals, Long distinguished between "target tasks"—what learners are expected to do on exit from instructional programs (identified via a needs analysis)—and "pedagogical tasks"—the tasks teachers and students work on in classrooms, which can be gradually increased in complexity so as to approximate target task demands. In contrast to a number of others who have subsequently argued for the important contribution that tasks can make to language pedagogy (e.g., Ellis, 2003; Skehan, 1998; Willis, 1996), Long (1985, 1998, 2005; Long & Crookes, 1992; Long & Norris, 2004) proposed that needs analysis was the necessary first stage in course design, allowing target tasks to be identified. Following this first stage, Long argued, target tasks should then be classified into task types, and following this, pedagogic versions of each task type should be designed. Subsequently, pedagogic tasks should be sequenced to form the syllabus, then performed in classrooms, and the extent to which they enable target task performance to be achieved should be evaluated with criterion-referenced, performance tests. Long's proposal for integrating research on task effects with other components of L2 program design, such as needs analysis, task sequencing, and evaluation outcomes, closely mirrored models proposed to guide educational decision making in English for specific purposes (ESP) programs in the 1970s and 1980s (e.g., Harper, 1984; Jupp & Hodlin, 1975; Munby, 1978) and in other domains of instruction following the generic ADDIE (Analysis, Design, Development, Implementation, Evaluation) model of instructional design (see Dick & Carey, 1996; Gagne, Wager, Golas, & Keller, 2005).

Recent Taxonomic Frameworks and Theoretical Rationales for Task-based Learning

Central to much recent task-based learning research are issues of the influence of task characteristics on learning and performance, the relative complexity of tasks having one or another of them, and the development of taxonomic models to facilitate prospective pedagogic decision making about sequencing tasks. These concerns aim to make instructional design decisions relevant for learners in L2 learning programs (Garcia-Mayo, 2007; Robinson, 2007b; Robinson & Gilabert, 2007). Essential to issues of program design to facilitate exit-program evaluations of success in learning are taxonomies of task characteristics (in any area of instruction) and rationales for how they can be used to implement classroom decisions about what task is presented to learners, at what point in an instructional program, and how such decisions can be validated (or not, and so changed) on the basis of exit-program evaluation procedures (see Clark & Elen, 2007; Merrill, 2007; Reigeluth, 1999; Reigeluth & Carr-Chellman, 2009).

Arising in part out of early speculations about what task characteristics may be influential on interaction and SLA (e.g., Candlin, 1984, 1987; Long, 1983; Prabhu, 1987) a number of increasingly elaborate *taxonomies* of task characteristics have been proposed as a basis for pedagogic task design (e.g., Pica, Kanagy, & Falodun, 1993; Prabhu, 1987; Robinson, 2007b; Skehan, 1998). Moreover, an increasing number of studies have operationalized characteristics of pedagogic tasks based on one or another of these taxonomic frameworks and have studied their effects (at different levels of complexity) on the amount of interaction they promote (Kim, 2009a, 2009b; Nuevo, 2006) and on the accuracy, fluency, and complexity of task outcomes (Gilabert, 2007; Tavakoli & Foster, this issue); language development (Collentine, 2010); and uptake of corrective feedback (Baralt, 2010; Revesz, 2009).

As with taxonomies of task characteristics, *theoretical rationales* motivating empirical research into task-based learning have also become more elaborate over this 30-year period, reflecting a development from the early emphasis on how task-based learning can facilitate comprehension of input through interaction and negotiation of meaning to more recent emphases on how task-based learning can facilitate attention to output and the development of increasingly targetlike speech production. Certain theoretical rationales have been offered for the predicted effects of tasks on learning, and specific taxonomic frameworks have been proposed for classifying task characteristics.

Theoretical Rationales for Task-Based Learning Research

The Procedural Syllabus

The first large-scale attempt to implement TBLT and to develop a theoretical rationale for it took place in India, between 1979 and 1984, and is described in Prabhu (1987). In his account of the theoretical motivation for the Bangalore Project and the task-based "procedural syllabus" it implemented, Prabhu argued that:

> task-based teaching operates with the concept that, while the conscious mind is working out some of the meaning-content, a subconscious part of the mind perceives, abstracts, or acquires (or re-creates as a cognitive structure) some of the linguistic structuring embodied in those entities, as a step in the development of an internal system of rules. The intensive exposure caused by the effort to work out meaning-content is thus a condition which is favorable to the subconscious abstraction—or cognitive formation—of language structure. (pp. 70–71)

Explicit instruction in grammar in the project was avoided because "teaching a descriptive grammar is likely—as has been pointed out at various times in the history of language pedagogy—to promote in learners an explicit knowledge of that grammar, rather than a deployable internal system" (pp. 72–73). Prabhu's cognitive rationale for TBLT is thus compatible with Krashen's (1982) claim that *comprehensible input* is necessary for learning and that "the effort to work out meaning-content" promotes incidental learning of tacit or implicit knowledge. Prabhu explained that the Bangalore Project "did not use group work in the classroom" because learner-learner interaction did not promote development of interlanguage (although see Adams, 2007, for evidence that it does), and may lead to fossilization:

The effect of learner-learner interaction will largely be a firming up of learners' [interlanguage] systems: each learner output will reinforce the internal systems of others without their being a corresponding process of revision. . . .The principle that interaction between the teacher and the learner, or between a text/task on paper and the learner, is more beneficial than interaction between one learner and another is thus part of the concept of learning which lies behind task-based teaching. (pp. 81–82)

The Interaction Hypothesis and Focus on Form

In contrast to Prabhu (1987), Long (1983, 1989) argued that the *interaction* task-work promotes *is* important because it not only provides one way in which input can be made comprehensible but additionally serves as a context for attending to problematic forms in the input and output during task-work. Such learner-driven attention to form, contingent on negotiation of meaning, can speed mapping of form-meaning relations and prompt interlanguage change in ways that respected each learner's own developmental trajectory (see Keck et al., 2006; Mackey, 2007). Consequently Pica et al. (1993) described a taxonomy of task characteristics in order to promote further research into which of these characteristics optimally promoted interaction work. Drawing on Schmidt's (1990; Schmidt & Frota, 1986) claim that attention to aspects of the surface structure of utterances, accompanied by the subjective experience of awareness or "noticing" them, was essential to learning, Long (1991, pp. 45–46) also argued that pedagogy could facilitate this process of attending to and noticing communicatively redundant, nonsalient features of the L2. This could be achieved by interventions that prompt a "focus on form" that "overtly draws students' attention to linguistic elements as they arise incidentally in lessons whose overriding focus is on meaning or communication." Doughty and Williams (1998) described a series of techniques, and proposals for research into them, for providing such additional "cognitive processing support" (p. 3) to learners. Decisions about focus on form could be made offline, proactively, leading, for example, to textual enhancement of problematic forms in the input to task performance, or could take place reactively, online, as in the case of recasts of selected forms in learners' output during task performance.

The Output Hypothesis

Swain (1995, pp. 125–126) argued that attention to output, whether this occurs in interaction between learners or not, has a facilitating role, because "in producing the target language. . . learners may notice a gap between what they want to say and what they can say, leading them to recognize what they do not know, or know only partially." Producing language also offers learners opportunities for testing hypotheses about well-formedness and for metalinguistic reflection on L2 form. Izumi (2003) and Kormos (2006) have described the stages of L2 speech production at which attention can operate to promote the three effects that Swain described, and current research is concerned with the extent to which the attentional demands of pedagogic tasks can be manipulated to lead learners to "push" their output.

A theoretical construct of interest here is the notion of attention as "capacity" and the related issues of how increasing the attentional demands of tasks affect the fluency, accuracy, and complexity of speech production (see Housen & Kuiken, 2009a, 2009b). Clearly, the human information processing system is limited in its ability to process and respond to information in the environment; but are breakdowns in performance caused by limits on attentional capacity? Skehan (1998, 2009) argued for this position, claiming that capacity limits on a single pool of attentional resources leads to decrements in the fluency, accuracy, and complexity of L2 speech when tasks are high in their attentional, memory, and other cognitive demands. In this view, capacity limits prevent learners attending to both accuracy and complexity of production on cognitively demanding tasks, leading learners to trade-off attention to one at the expense of the other. A contrasting position has been proposed by Robinson (2003a, 2007b), who argued that attentional capacity limits are an unsatisfactory, post hoc explanation for breakdowns in attention to speech. Following, in part, arguments made by Allport (1987), Neumann (1987), and Sanders (1998), Robinson (2003a, 2007d) suggested that breakdowns in "action-control," not capacity limits, lead to decrements in speech production and learners' failure to benefit from the learning opportunities attention directing provides. Consequently, increasing complexity along various dimensions of tasks, such as increasing the amount of reasoning a task requires, promotes greater effort at controlling production and more vigilant monitoring of output. This increased complexity leads to greater accuracy and complexity of L2 production when compared to performance on simpler task versions that require little or no reasoning.

The Limited Capacity Hypothesis
Schmidt (1990, p. 143) noted that "Task demands are a powerful determinant of what is noticed" in experimental settings "and provide one of the basic arguments that what is learned is what is noticed. . . The information committed to memory is essentially the information that must be heeded in order to carry out a task." The extent to which this is true of L2 learning tasks in classrooms is an important issue for the design of materials and instruction. Because much

TBLL research has taken place in experimental settings, the relevance of findings from these studies to instructional decision making in diverse classroom settings, and for diverse populations of learners, require generalizability studies, as Gass, Mackey and Ross-Feldman (this issue) have described. Skehan (1998) provided the first extended psycholinguistic rationale for the effects of certain aspects of task demands on attention, "noticing," and speech production, focusing in particular on the extent to which having time to plan a task led to increases in the accuracy, fluency, and complexity of speech produced when compared to performance on tasks for which planning time was not available. Skehan's limited capacity hypothesis (p. 97) proposed that more demanding tasks "consume more attentional resources... with the result that less attention is available for focus on form": Therefore, sequencing tasks from less cognitively demanding to more demanding optimizes opportunities for attentional allocation to language forms. In Skehan's view, task design is a means to promote "balanced language development" in the areas of accuracy, fluency, and complexity of production. This process can be facilitated because certain task characteristics "predispose learners to channel their attention in predictable ways, such as clear macrostructure towards accuracy, the need to impose order on ideas towards complexity, and so on" (Skehan, 1998, p. 112; cf. Tavakoli & Foster, this issue). However, due to limitations in attentional resources, tasks can lead either to increased complexity or accuracy but not to both—so learners must "trade-off" attention to one aspect of production to the detriment of the other. Tasks should therefore be sequenced by choosing those tasks with characteristics that lead to each, at an appropriate level of difficulty, as determined by three factors: (a) *Code complexity* is described in "fairly traditional ways," as in descriptions of structural syllabuses, or developmental sequences (Skehan, 1998, p. 99); (b) *cognitive complexity* is the result of the familiarity of the task, topic, or genre, and the processing requirements; information type, clarity, and organization; and amount of computation required; and (c) *communicative stress* involves six characteristics, including time pressure, number of participants, and opportunities to control interaction.

The Cognition Hypothesis
The cognition hypothesis provides a theoretical rationale for the effects of task demands on language learning that differs from Skehan's proposal. This rationale is rooted in claims by Cromer (1973, 1991) that conceptual development creates the conditions for first-language (L1) development, and in claims by Slobin (1993) that parallels in L1 and L2 development (as revealed in data reported in Perdue, 1993a, 1993b) are evident because adult L2 learners

initially attempt to linguistically encode concepts that emerge earliest during child development. In this view, learners adopt, by default, the ontogenetically determined order of meaning (concept)-form (language) mapping in attempts to produce the L2 (see Robinson, 2005). For instructed SLA, the fundamental pedagogic claim of the cognition hypothesis is that in task-based syllabi, pedagogic tasks should be sequenced solely on the basis of increases in their cognitive complexity, which mirror the sequences in which children are able to meet the cognitive demands of tasks during L1 acquisition, and that such sequences provide optimal support for L2 learners in their attempts to use accurate and complex language at the level needed to meet real-world target task demands (Robinson, 2001a, 2005). In this account, learners do not trade-off attention to accuracy against attention to complexity of production: Rather, on some dimensions of task demands (described below), increasing complexity is argued to promote more accurate, grammaticized production *and* more complex, syntacticized utterances. Referring to Givon's (1985) distinction between pragmatic and syntactic modes of production, Robinson (1995, 2003b) has argued that simple task demands elicit the pragmatic mode (characterized by loose coordination of clauses and little use of grammatical morphology) in contrast to complex task demands. Complex task demands lead to greater effort at conceptualization and elicit the morphologically richer and structurally more complex syntactic mode, in line with Givon's (2009, p. 12) claim that "More complex mentally-represented events are coded by more complex linguistic/syntactic structures."

To guide research into these claims, and also pedagogy, Robinson (2007b) proposed an operational taxonomy of task characteristics. This taxonomic, Triadic Componential Framework (TCF) distinguishes three categories of task demands implicated in real-world task performance. Task *condition* refers to interactive demands of tasks, including participation variables (e.g., open vs. closed tasks) and participant variables (e.g., same vs. different gender). Characteristics of tasks distinguishing the demands made by task conditions thus include many of the factors described in Pica et al.'s (1993) taxonomy. A second category of task *difficulty* concerns individual differences in learner factors, such as working memory capacity, which can affect the extent to which learners perceive task demands to be difficult to meet. These factors explain why two learners may find the same task to be more or less difficult than each other, and, broadly speaking, these individual difference factors may combine to result in "aptitudes" for certain kinds of task performance and task-based learning. Task *complexity* refers to the intrinsic cognitive complexity of tasks, such as their reasoning demands. Robinson distinguished three different kinds of reasoning demands: (a) spatial reasoning, as involved in navigating through, and giving directions about, places like cities while driving, or giving instructions on how to back a car into a small parking space; (b) causal reasoning, involved in understanding and explaining why a natural or mechanical event occurred (why a bridge fell down in a storm, why exchange rates fluctuate); and (c) intentional reasoning, as involved when explaining behavior with reference to the intentions, beliefs, and desires of others (why Tom suddenly left the party, why Jill has stopped speaking to Mary, etc.).

The TCF distinguishes task features affecting the cognitive complexity of tasks along two dimensions. Resource-*directing* dimensions of complexity affect allocation of cognitive resources to specific aspects of L2 code. For instance, tasks that increase in their intentional-reasoning demands require linguistic reference to the mental states of others. These demands should therefore direct learners' attention to forms needed to meet them during communication, such as psychological state terms in English (e.g., *believe, wonder*). These forms may be currently known but not well controlled, or if they are unknown, then attempts to complete the task may make them salient and "noticeable." By increasing complexity along these dimensions, initially *implicit* knowledge of the L1 concept-structuring function of language (see Talmy, 2000) becomes gradually *explicit* and available for change during L2 production. In contrast, resource-*dispersing* dimensions do not do this: Making a task complex by removing planning time does not direct the learner's attention to specific aspects of L2 code but rather disperses attention over many linguistic and other features. Increasing task demands along these dimensions has the effect of gradually removing processing support (such as planning time) for access to current interlanguage; thus, practice along them requires, and should encourage, faster and more automatic L2 access and use. Based on this resource-directing/dispersing distinction and the TCF, Robinson (2010) proposed two *operational principles* for sequencing tasks in a task-based syllabus: (a) Sequencing should be based only on increases in cognitive complexity, (b) increase resource-dispersing dimensions of task complexity first (to promote access to current interlanguage), then increase resource-directing dimensions of complexity (to promote development of new form-function mappings, and destabilize the current interlanguage system).

Task Demands and Stages of Speech Production
Theoretical rationales for the influence of task demands on writing and both reading and listening comprehension currently lag behind rationales for their effects on speech production in articulating linkages between rationales proposed

and explanatory psycholinguistic mechanisms. With respect to the latter, both Skehan (2009a, 2009b; cf. Tavakoli & Foster, this issue; Tavakoli & Skehan, 2005) and Robinson (1995, 2005) have drawn on Levelt's model of speech production in their psycholinguistic rationales for how task demands should affect L2 speech performance, as have others who have been more generally concerned with identifying the mechanisms involved in producing L2 speech and responding to negative feedback on it (e.g., Bygate, 1999; Doughty, 2001; Izumi, 2003; Kormos, 2006, 2011; see also de Bot, 1996, 1998). Levelt's model of speech production identifies stages in which speech is assembled for production, beginning with a *conceptualization* stage, leading to preparation of the preverbal message, followed by stages of *lexical and grammatical encoding, articulation,* and (optionally, possibly individually initiated or coconstructed) *monitoring* of utterances following production (which can lead to self-repair, see Gilabert, 2005, 2007; Kormos, 1999; Swain & Lapkin, 1995). Levelt's model is a stage model (for arguments against stage models in general, see Larson-Freeman & Cameron, 2007; and see Dell, 1986, and Dell, Juliano, & Govindjee, 1993, for alternative spreading activation models of speech production), but preparation of speech at the stages Levelt described is proposed to be performed in parallel, and processing is incremental, so all stages of speech production are simultaneously active, with feed-forward and feedback operations connecting these stages.

Drawing on Levelt's model (1989; Levelt, Roelofs, & Meyer, 1999) of speech production, Robinson (1995) argued that increasing the conceptual demands of tasks (naturally) leads to greater effort at conceptualization and "macroplanning" at the stage of message preparation, thus "creating the conditions for development and re-mapping of conceptual and linguistic categories" (Robinson et al., 2009, p. 537), during subsequent "microplanning" and the lexicogrammatical encoding stage into which macroplanning feeds. In Levelt's model, the conceptualization stage generates a "preverbal message": "the message should contain the features that are necessary and sufficient for the next stage of processing—in particular for grammatical encoding" (Levelt, 1989, p. 70). Therefore, greater effort at conceptualization during message preparation, induced by conceptually demanding tasks, should lead to what Dipper, Black, and Bryan (2005, p. 422) called "paring down" of conceptual information into a "linguistically relevant representation" for subsequent encoding, at the microplanning stage, with positive consequences for accurate and complex performance.

Skehan (2009a, 2009b) has recently proposed a fine-grained analysis of how some aspects of task demands that make them more difficult (what

Skehan, 2009a, calls "complexifying/pressuring" influences) or less difficult (what Skehan calls "easing/focusing" influences) are related to the stages of speech production that Levelt (1989) described. Skehan (2009a) argued that it is the connections he proposes between task demands and their influence on stages of speech production that cause the effects of task demands on the accuracy, fluency, and complexity of spoken performance. For example, where a task requires dynamic relations between task elements to be described (as when describing how cars were moving prior to the occurrence of a traffic accident), then this will lead to more complex language performance, compared to describing concrete, static information (e.g., the arrangement of furniture in a room). In this case, the locus of differences in performance on the two tasks is attributed to differences at the conceptualization stage of message preparation. In contrast, monologic tasks lead to more complex spoken performance than dialogic tasks, but this is attributed to differences at the formulation stage and subsequent lexicosyntactic encoding procedures. Skehan, then, basically argued that different task characteristics (either intrinsic to their design or characteristics of their implementation) have effects on spoken performance that are caused by more or less effort at the conceptualization stage versus task characteristics that result in effects caused by processing for speech production at the lexical and syntactic encoding and formulation stages. What is valuable about Skehan's proposal is its attempt to ground discussion of task characteristics, and their effects on learning and performance, in a model of speech production mechanisms, thereby providing a psycholinguistic rationale for the effects of what has been metaphorically referred to in the SLA literature as "pushed" output. Much more theory and research in this area is needed and is likely to be forthcoming.

Taxonomies of Task Characteristics

For TBLL research to produce cumulative findings, with application to pedagogy, a taxonomy of task characteristics is needed. A major aim of task-based learning research is to establish such a taxonomy. The benefits of an agreed taxonomic framework for research into task effects are clear. On the one hand, a taxonomy describes a *finite* list of task characteristics and categories of them. This can serve as a focus for concerted research into the effects of those characteristics on learning, when used to deliver different kinds of task content, and with learners at different levels of proficiency, or with different task aptitude or other profiles, thus enabling the generalizability of findings for the characteristics and their effects to be charted. On the other hand, a taxonomy with instructional relevance identifies characteristics of pedagogic tasks that can be used to approximate the demands made by a wide variety of real-world target-task performance objectives. There are thus constraints that an operational taxonomy of task characteristics should satisfy if it is to be both useful for coordinating research and with application to pedagogy. Two *pedagogic* constraints that a taxonomy must meet are (a) that it is *detailed* enough in its listing of characteristics to allow a wide variety of target-task performances to be approximated and (b) that the characteristics it identifies must be *feasible*, allowing task designers in different programs using the taxonomy to make similar decisions about how to operationalize the characteristic. An additional *theoretical* constraint is (c) that the taxonomy is motivated by what is currently known about SLA processes and development. A final hybrid *theoretical-pedagogic* constraint is that (d) it should be possible to use the taxonomy to classify and sequence tasks, following some metric for combining task characteristics in sequences and in ways that are hypothesized to lead to language learning.

For extensive reviews of the many task characteristics, and categories of them, that have been proposed, see Ellis (2003), Nunan (1993, 2004), Robinson (2001a, 2007b), and Samuda and Bygate (2008). Three taxonomies in particular continue to predominate in task-based language research. The earliest of these was proposed by Pica et al. (1993), who described a typology of "communication tasks," each with different configurations of activity (the role relationships between participants, and direction of information flow between them) and goal (the outcomes the task was expected to result in). They further analyzed the goals and activities tasks that could result in terms of the opportunities they provided for learning. For example, where task goals are the same or convergent, then they claimed it was "expected" that the task would lead to (a) comprehension of input, (b) feedback on production, and (c) interlanguage modification. In contrast, where interactants have divergent goals, then each of these was only "possible," therefore providing fewer opportunities for learning. The task types that Pica et al. identified were Jigsaw, Information-gap, Problem-solving, Decision-making, and Opinion exchange. Pica et al.'s typology therefore expands on the three types of task that the Bangalore Project used and that Prabhu (1987, pp. 46–47) had ordered from Information gap, to Reasoning gap, to Opinion gap in terms of the demands these task types made on learners. This taxonomy satisfies the *feasible* constraint described previously and also the *theoretical* constraint (with respect to interactionist rationales for SLA), but it fails to meet the first constraint because it lacks sufficient *detail* (consisting of only five task types) and it also fails to meet the fourth constraint because it provides no information about how task types can be sequenced optimally for learners.

Skehan's (1998, 2003; Skehan & Foster, 2001) taxonomy, described earlier, consists of categories of task characteristics that contribute to code complexity, cognitive complexity, and communicative stress and builds on Candlin's (1987) proposals for factors that may influence task performance and learning. For example, the vocabulary load a task involves affects its code complexity, the clarity and sufficiency of information provided affects its cognitive complexity, and the number of participants and time limits affect its degree of communicative stress (see Kuiken & Vedder, 2007b, for discussion). In more recent work, Skehan (2009a, 2009b) has maintained a focus on how task characteristics can *complexify* (e.g., by requiring greater quantities of information to be expressed) and *pressure* task performance (by imposing tight time constraints), and as observed above, Skehan has linked complexifying/pressuring task characteristics to Levelt's (1989) model of stages in speech production, which cause their effects on the accuracy, fluency, and complexity of learners' language. Skehan's taxonomy is *theoretically motivated*, not with respect to interactional influences on learning (as is the case with Pica et al.'s [1993] taxonomy) but with respect to the effects of tasks on the psycholinguistic processes causing variation in speech production. The characteristics that Skehan described are also *feasible* because task designers should consistently be able to manipulate time pressure, quantities of needed information, and so forth. However, as with Pica et al.'s taxonomy, the characteristics described lack sufficient *detail* to link pedagogic versions to a wide variety of real-world task performances (although Skehan has been clear that his model is not intended to address how pedagogic tasks can be used to do this), and no metric is offered for sequencing the characteristics described.

Robinson's (2001a, 2007b) TCF, described earlier (and see the Appendix), combines elements from both Pica et al.'s (1993) and Skehan's (1998, 2003) proposals. Following the rationale described previously, the category of task characteristics contributing to their cognitive complexity are proposed to affect speech production in different ways along resource-directing and dispersing dimensions. The category of task characteristics describing the different participation, and participant factors involved in task performance, are proposed to affect the extent of interaction in different ways. The third category of task difficulty in the TCF involves learner factors, which may influence performance and learning on tasks having characteristics distinguishing their interactive or cognitive demands (see Albert & Kormos, this issue). For example, along the ± single task dimension of task complexity, individuals high in working memory capacity and in the ability to switch attention between task demands may find dual tasks (requiring two things to be done simultaneously, such as answering a phone call while monitoring a TV screen in the office) to be less difficult than those lower in these abilities. Similarly, when the solution to a task learners are performing is indeterminate and not fixed (+ open) as opposed to determinant and fixed (+ closed), then individual differences in measures of emotional control, such as openness to experience and tolerance of ambiguity (Costa & McCrae, 1985; Furnham & Ribchester, 1995), may predict more, or less, successful engagement in task participation to meet these goals (with those more open to experience and more tolerant of ambiguity adapting better to participation in open tasks, and vice versa). It is not yet clear what the ability and affective factors are that contribute to perceptions of task difficulty, and so both promote and mitigate successful performance on the simple and complex task characteristics listed under the category of Task Complexity in the appendix or affect performance under different interactional Task Conditions listed there. Research into individual differences in affective and ability factors and the extent to which they affect task performance is much needed (see Albert & Kormos, this issue, for one example) because if these links can be established through research, they could be used to operationalize batteries of individual difference measures that can be used to profile "task-aptitudes"—with the twin aims of matching learners to tasks that optimize their opportunities for successful L2 learning and performance and of supporting them when their ability and affective profiles are not well matched to the demands tasks make on them (see Robinson, 2007a, 2007a; Snow, 1994).

In summary, with regard to the criteria that task taxonomies should meet in order to be pedagogically useful and acquisitionally optimal, the TCF is more *detailed* than Pica et al.'s (1993) or Skehan's (1998) taxonomies while being equally *feasible* and *theoretically motivated*. It has the advantage too, of an associated *sequencing metric* described earlier, particularly, that (a) sequencing pedagogic versions of target tasks should be based only on increases in cognitive complexity and that (b) resource-dispersing dimensions of task complexity should first be increased (to promote access to current interlanguage) and then resource-directing dimensions of complexity should be increased (to promote development of new form-function mappings and destabilize the current interlanguage system). Whether this sequencing procedure (intrinsically linked to the TCF taxonomy) is optimal for promoting successful task performance and language learning is, as yet, empirically unresolved, because research into it has only recently begun (e.g., Romanko & Nakatsugawa, 2010).

The Articles in This Issue

The articles in this issue all describe careful empirical studies, selected from recent issues of *Language Learning* because they address one or another of the issues about TBLL raised earlier. The first two articles, by Tavakoli and Foster and by Albert and Kormos, dealt centrally with the effects of tasks on outcome measures of speech production. Tavakoli and Foster began by observing that research into the effects of tasks on production is important because it can "illuminate the proposition that task performance in itself drives interlanguage change by causing learners to attend to and retain information about the target language as they use it" (p. 38). Additionally, research identifying "features of tasks that impact on a learner's processing" may help provide "empirically sound principles for classroom materials design" (p. 38) and inform decisions about which tasks to choose to "guide a learners focus of attention to particular aspects of the language being learned" (p. 38). Drawing on Skehan's (1998, 2009a, 2009b) limited capacity hypothesis—that given finite attentional resources, learners will "prioritize one aspect of performance, such as being accurate, over another, such as being suitably fluent or complex" (p. 41)—they hypothesized that two characteristics of narrative tasks (loose vs. tight *structure*, and storyline *complexity*) will have these effects. Their hypotheses are that (a) narratives with tight structure will lead to more accurate language, whereas those with loose structure will lead to greater fluency; and (b) compared to less cognitively complex narratives that only foreground events, more complex narratives that both foreground and background events will lead to more syntactically complex and lexically diverse language but have no effects on accuracy. The research found that in narrative performance on the task that has tight structure (and so is simple on what Robinson (2003a) called this resource-dispersing dimension of cognitive demand) and that has two storylines (and so is simultaneously complex on this resource-directing dimension of task demands in Robinson's framework), there is greater accuracy, fluency, and complexity, as the cognition hypothesis predicts. However, other findings, such as performance on a narrative with loose structure and two storylines, appear to confirm Skehan's predictions, because it appears that the higher fluency and complexity this narrative elicits is traded off against lower accuracy. Tavakoli and Foster also argued that their results for greater accuracy on narrative tasks with tight structure can be interpreted as support for Skehan's claim that some effects task characteristics have on production are caused (as in this case) by the extent to which they free up attention at the conceptualization stage of speech production. Tight structure frees up attention because it reduces the need for effort at macroplanning of coordinated narrative event descriptions during conceptualization, and attention freed up from effort at conceptualization is, in turn, allocated to the formulation stage, resulting in greater accuracy.

Albert and Kormos also studied the effects of narrative task performance on the accuracy, fluency, and complexity of production. However, they are principally interested in the extent to which individual differences in creativity can influence task performance. Building on Carroll's (1993) three-stratum theory of cognitive abilities and his observation that one common higher order ability factor is idea production and drawing also on Guilford's (1967) distinction between divergent and convergent thinking, Albert and Kormos proposed that divergent thinking contributes to three facets of creativity that may affect idea production on L2 tasks: creative fluency, flexibility, and originality. They argued that these facets of creativity should be particularly influential on certain tasks, "especially open-ended ones like narrative tasks, for which there is no correct solution, but a large number of solutions are possible" (p. 82). In other words, they argued, creativity thus measured should contribute positively to performance on open versus closed tasks. They hypothesized that creativity (operationalised and measured using a test developed by Barkoczi & Zetenyi) should be particularly influential on the quantity of talk produced (as evident in the number of idea units) as well as lexical variety and the variety of narrative structure. They found that creative fluency and originality were related to the amount of talk produced, and the complexity of narrative structure attempted but had no effect on accuracy of production.

The articles by Tavakoli and Foster and by Albert and Kormos are complementary with respect to their focus on narrative task production. However, the attempt by Albert and Kormos to identify individual differences contributing to the difficulty learners experience in meeting narrative task demands is particularly important. Tasks, and characteristics of them that designers and researchers manipulate, are unlikely to have effects on production and learning independently of the abilities different learners bring to the context of task performance. All learning is the result of complex interactions between task demands contributing to their intrinsic cognitive *complexity* (so a less cognitively complex task should always meet with more success for any one learner than its more intrinsically complex counterpart) and the cognitive abilities and affective dispositions learners have, which affect their experience of how *difficult* tasks are and so contribute to variation in levels of success reached by any two learners on the same task (see Robinson, 2001a, 2001b, 2003a, 2007a; Shuell, 1980; Skehan, 1989; Snow, 1989, 1994; Sternberg, 2002). To what extent, therefore, might Tavakoli and Foster's findings for the effects of the design characteristics of narrative tasks on speech production been different if they had used measures of participants' creative fluency and originality as covariates in their analyses—as Albert and Kormos demonstrate that both of these affect the nature of learners responses to narrative task demands?

The following two articles each explore the extent to which tasks can be used to support vocabulary or grammar instruction. In Long's terms (1991; Doughty & Williams, 1998; Long & Robinson, 1998) the researchers address how tasks can be used to focus attention on forms selected and sequenced for instruction following a lexical or grammatical syllabus. In her article, Kim operationalizes Hulstijn and Laufer's (2001) motivational-cognitive construct of task-induced involvement in order to examine whether certain tasks are more effective than others in promoting L2 vocabulary acquisition. After reporting previous findings concerning the effects of task characteristics on vocabulary acquisition, such as de la Fuente's (2002) finding that tasks involving negotiation plus output led to greater receptive and productive learning than exposure to words provided in premodified input to tasks, Kim cited Hulstijn and Laufer's (p. 542) claim that "the more effective task required a deeper level of processing of the new words than the other task." Hulstijn and Laufer's involvement load hypothesis is an attempt to operationalize differences in the *depth of processing* that tasks can encourage, whereby greater involvement in task demands causes greater depth of processing, which, in turns, leads to better retention of vocabulary than does lower involvement in task demands. The motivational *need* component of involvement load is driven by the desire to comply with task requirements, whereas *search* and *evaluation* are cognitive components that affect the extent to which attention is paid to form-meaning relationships when encountering vocabulary during the task. In two experiments, Kim found, first, that a writing task, with a higher involvement load index compared to tasks involving reading with comprehension activities or gap fill activities, led to more effective initial learning and better retention of new words. Second, she found that different tasks (writing a composition vs. writing sentences containing words) that had the same level of involvement load were effectively equivalent in promoting initial learning and retention of words.

In his article, Toth presented a rich, quantitative and qualitative assessment of the extent to which learner led discourse (LLD) and teacher led discourse (TLD) during tasks designed to maximize meaningful language use of, and attention to, the target of an (one semester) earlier instructional episode (in which learners were explicitly taught metalinguistic information about the Spanish anticausative clitic *se*) facilitated their subsequent learning of it. Toth's study is

most clearly an example of task-*supported* approaches to instruction, following a predetermined (in this case, following course book-prescription) order for
grammar teaching. Additionally, his study used closed, two-way information
gap tasks to deliver the LLD treatment but open topic discussion for eliciting
the effects of TLD on learning, in order to promote "scaffolded feedback given
to facilitate form-meaning mapping" (p. 148). Although the tasks used to deliver LLD and TLD treatments were very different in their participation and
participant structure this was the difference Toth sought to investigate. Toth
found that TLD, and the participant/participation (see the Appendix) task conditions it was delivered through, was more effective at promoting development
of the grammatically targeted, and previously practiced, forms than was LLD
in two-way information exchange tasks.

The final article in this issue begins by summarizing the earliest theoretical
rationales for the benefits of task-based interaction—and the opportunity for
metalinguistic reflection on output it provides, that is, "the twofold potential
of negotiation—to assist L2 comprehension and draw attention to L2 form—
[which] affords it a more powerful role in L2 learning than has been claimed
so far" (Pica, 1994, p. 508), and that "under certain task conditions, learners
will not only reveal their hypotheses, but reflect on them, using language to do
so" (Swain, 1995, p. 132). Gass, Mackey, and Ross-Feldman then reviewed a
number of claims that have been made (e.g., by Foster, 1998, and Nunan, 1991)
that experimental conditions operationalized in studying these issues may well
not reflect the interactional patterns typical of classroom language learning
contexts. They pointed out that although "there is not a prototypical classroom,
any more than there is a prototypical laboratory" (p. 193), researched findings in
the latter settings must demonstrate their generalizability to classrooms. Gass,
Mackey, and Ross-Feldman went on to show that findings for interactional
patterns in the experimental and classroom contexts they studied suggest few
differences between them while revealing—in both settings—differences in
interactional patterns that depended on the *type* of task the learners carried
out. This issue of demonstrating the *generalizability* of findings from empirical
research into the influence of task demands on learning to *classrooms*, in diverse
institutional contexts and with diverse populations, is one that must continue to
mediate between all of the theoretical claims and empirical findings described
in this issue, and claims about their instructional relevance, as Bygate, Norris,
and Van den Branden (2009) have pointed out:

> Underpinning this empirical impetus is the imperative for research to
> focus on how TBLT works within the context of ongoing programs. Hence

the TBLT enterprise will not be able to rely on individual case studies of learners conducted outside the context of programs of instruction, or on laboratory studies, nor on studies carried out in host classrooms in which the use of tasks is investigated without relating their use to the teaching of the ongoing program. Such work provides a valuable contribution—in a sense it might be seen as a form of piloting—for the empirical grounding of TBLT. However, more widespread pedagogically contextualized research is clearly needed. (p. 497)

Revised version accepted 10 January 2011

References

Adams, R. (2007). Do second language learners benefit from interacting with each other? In A. Mackey (Ed.), *Conversational interaction in second language acquisition* (pp. 29–51). Oxford: Oxford University Press.

Alcon-Soler, E., & Garcia-Mayo, M. P. (Eds.). (2009). Interaction and language learning in foreign language contexts [Special issue]. *International Review of Applied Linguistics, 47*(3–4).

Allport, D. A. (1987). Selection for action: Some behavioral and neurophysiological consequences of attention and action. In H. Heuer & A. Sanders (Eds.), *Perspectives on perception and action* (pp. 395–419). Hillsdale, NJ: Erlbaum.

Baralt, M. (2010). *Task complexity, the Cognition Hypothesis and interaction in CMC and FTF environments.* Unpublished doctoral dissertation, Georgetown University, Washington, DC.

Brindley, G., & Slatyer, H. (2002). Exploring task difficulty in ESL listening assessment. *Language Testing, 19,* 369–394.

Barkoczi, I., & Zetenyi, T. (1981). *A kreativitas vizsgalata* [The examination of creativity]. Budapest: Orszagos Pedagogiai Intezet.

Brown, R. (1991). Group work, task differences and second language acquisition. *Applied Linguistics, 12,* 1–12.

Brumfit, C., & Johnson, K. (1979). *The communicative approach to language teaching.* Oxford: Oxford University Press.

Bygate, M. (1999). Task as a context for the framing, reframing and unframing of language. *System, 27,* 33–38.

Bygate, M., Norris, J., & Van den Branden, K. (2009). Understanding TBLT at the interface between research and pedagogy. In K. Van den Branden, M. Bygate, & J. Norris (Eds.), *Task-based language teaching: A reader* (pp. 496–499). Amsterdam: Benjamins.

Bygate, M., Skehan, P., & Swain, M. (Eds.). (2001). *Researching pedagogic tasks: Second language learning, teaching and testing.* New York: Longman.

Cadierno, T., & Robinson, P. (2009). Language typology, task complexity and the development of L2 lexicalization patterns for describing motion events. *Annual Review of Cognitive Linguistics, 6,* 245–277.

Candlin, C. (1984). Syllabus design as a critical process. In C. Brumfit (Ed.), *General English syllabus design* (pp. 29–46). Oxford: Pergamon.

Candlin, C. (1987). Towards task-based language learning. In C. Candlin & D. Murphy (Eds.), *Language learning tasks* (pp. 5–22). London: Prentice Hall.

Carroll, J. B. (1993). *Human cognitive abilities: A survey of factor-analytic studies.* New York: Cambridge University Press.

Clark, R., & Elen, J. (Eds.). (2007). *Handling complexity in learning environments: Theory and research.* Oxford: Elsevier.

Collentine, K. (2010). Measuring complexity in task-based synchronous computer-mediated communication. In M. Thomas & H. Reinders (Eds.), *Task-based language learning and teaching with technology* (pp. 105–130). London: Continuum.

Cook, V. (2010). Linguistic relativity and language teaching. In V. Cook & A Bassetti (Eds.), *Language and bilingual cognition* (pp. 509–518). New York: Psychology Press.

Costa, P., & McCrae, R. (1985). *The NEO Personality Inventory manual.* Odessa, FL: Psychological Assessment Resources, Inc.

Council of Europe (2001). *Common European framework of reference for languages.* Cambridge: Cambridge University Press.

Cromer, R. (1973). The development of language and cognition: The cognition hypothesis. In B. Foss (Ed.), *New perspectives in child development* (pp. 184–252). Harmondsworth, UK: Penguin.

Cromer, R. (1991). *Language and thought in normal and handicapped children.* Oxford: Blackwell.

Crookes, G., & Gass, S. (Eds.). (1993a). *Tasks in a pedagogical context: Integrating theory and practice.* Clevedon, UK: Multilingual Matters.

Crookes, G., & Gass, S. (Eds.). (1993b). *Tasks and language learning: Integrating theory and practice.* Clevedon, UK: Multilingual Matters.

Day, R. (Ed.). (1986). *Talking to learn: Conversation in second language acquisition.* Rowley, MA: Newbury House.

de Bot, K. (1996). The psycholinguistics of the output hypothesis. *Language Learning, 46,* 529–555.

de Bot, K. (1998). Does the Formulator know its LFG? *Bilingualism: Language and Cognition, 1,* 25–26.

de la Fuente, M. (2002). Negotiation and oral acquisition of L2 vocabulary: The roles of input and output in the receptive and productive acquisition of words. *Studies in Second Language Acquisition, 24,* 81–112.

Dell, G. (1986). A spreading activation theory of retrieval in sentence production. *Psychological Review, 93,* 283–321.

Dell, G., Juliano, C., & Govindjee, A. (1993). Structure and content in language production: A theory of frame constraints in phonological speech errors. *Cognitive Science, 14*, 179–221.

Dick, W., & Carey, L. (1996). *The systematic design of instruction* (4th ed.). New York: Harper Collins.

Dipper, L., Black, M., & Bryan, K. (2005). Thinking for speaking and thinking for listening: The interaction of thought and language in typical and non-fluent comprehension and production. *Language and Cognitive Processes, 20*, 417–441.

Dornyei, Z., & Kormos, J. (2000). The role of individual and social variables in oral task performance. *Language Teaching Research, 4*, 275–300.

Doughty, C. (2001). Cognitive underpinnings of focus on form. In P. Robinson (Ed.), *Cognition and second language instruction* (pp. 206–257). Cambridge: Cambridge University Press.

Doughty, C., & Pica, T. (1986). "Information gap tasks": An aid to second language acquisition? *TESOL Quarterly, 20*, 305–325.

Doughty, C., & Williams, J. (1998). Issues and terminology. In C. Doughty & J. Williams (Eds.), *Focus on form in classroom second language acquisition* (pp. 1–11). New York: Cambridge University Press.

Ellis, R. (1993). The structural syllabus and second language acquisition. *TESOL Quarterly, 27*, 91–113.

Ellis, R. (1997). *SLA research and language teaching*. Oxford: Oxford University Press.

Ellis, R. (2003). *Task-based language teaching and learning*. Oxford: Oxford University Press.

Ellis, R. (Ed.). (2005). *Planning and task performance in a second language*. Amsterdam: Benjamins.

Ellis, R. (2009). Task-based language teaching: Sorting out the misunderstandings. *International Journal of Applied Linguistics, 19*, 222–246.

Foster, P. (1998). A classroom perspective on the negotiation of meaning. *Applied Linguistics, 19*, 1–23.

Foster, P., & Skehan, P. (1999). The influence of source of planning and focus of planning on task-based performance. *Language Teaching Research, 3*, 215–247.

Furnham, E., & Ribchester, T. (1995). Tolerance of ambiguity: A review of the concept, its measurement and applications. *Current Psychology, 14*, 179–199.

Gagne, R. M., Wager, W. W., Golas, K. C., & Keller, J. M. (2005). *Principles of instructional design* (5th ed.). Belmont, CA: Thomson, Wadsworth.

Garcia-Mayo, M. P. (Ed.). (2007). *Investigating tasks in formal language learning*. Clevedon, UK: Multilingual Matters.

Gass, S., Mackey, A., Alvarez-Torres, M. J., & Fernandez-Garcia, M. (1999). The effects of task repetition on linguistic output. *Language Learning, 49*, 549–581.

Gass, S., & Varonis, E. (1994). Input, interaction and second language production. *Studies in Second Language Acquisition, 16*, 283–302.

Gibbons, P. (2009). *English learners, academic literacy and thinking: Learning in the challenge zone.* Portsmouth, NH: Heinemann.

Gilabert, R. (2005). *Task complexity and L2 oral narrative production.* Unpublished doctoral dissertation, University of Barcelona, Barcelona, Spain.

Gilabert, R. (2007). The simultaneous manipulation along the planning time and +/- Here-and-Now dimensions: Effects on oral L2 production. In M. P. Garcia Mayo (Ed.), *Investigating tasks in formal language learning* (pp. 44–68). Clevedon, UK: Multilingual Matters.

Gilabert, R., Baron, J., & Llanes, M. (2009). Manipulating task complexity across task types and its influence on learners' interaction during oral performance. *International Review of Applied Linguistics, 47,* 367–395.

Givon, T. (1985). Function, structure, and language acquisition. In D. Slobin (Ed.), *The crosslinguistic study of language acquisition* (Vol. 1, pp. 1008–1025). Hillsdale, NJ: Erlbaum.

Givon, T. (2009). *The genesis of syntactic complexity.* Amsterdam: Benjamins.

Guilford, J. P. (1967). *The nature of human intelligence.* New York: McGraw-Hill.

Han, Z., & Cadierno, T. (Eds.). (2010). *Linguistic relativity in SLA: Thinking for speaking.* Bristol, UK: Multilingual Matters.

Harper, R. (1984). *ESP for the university. ELT Documents.* Oxford: Pergamon.

Housen, A., & Kuiken, F. (Eds.). (2009). Complexity, accuracy and fluency (CAF) in second language acquisition research [Special issue] *Applied Linguistics, 30*(4).

Hulstijn, J., & Laufer, B. (2001). Some empirical evidence for the involvement load hypothesis in vocabulary acquisition. *Language Learning, 51,* 539–558.

Ishikawa, T. (2007). The effects of increasing task complexity along the -/+ Here-and-Now dimension. In M. P. Garcia Mayo (Ed.), *Investigating tasks in formal language learning* (pp. 136–156). Clevedon, UK: Multilingual Matters.

Ishikawa, T. (2008a). The effect of task demands of intentional reasoning on L2 speech performance. *Journal of Asia TEFL, 5,* 29–63.

Ishikawa, T. (2008b). *Task complexity, reasoning demands and second language speech production.* Unpublished doctoral dissertation, Aoyama Gakuin University, Tokyo.

Izumi, S. (2003). Comprehension and production processes in second language learning: In search of the psycholinguistic rationale for the output hypothesis. *Applied Linguistics, 24,* 168–196.

Jackson, D., & Suethanapornkul, S. (2010). *The Cognition Hypothesis: A synthesis and meta-analysis of research on second language task complexity.* Unpublished manuscript.

Jarvis, S., & Pavlenko, A. (2008). *Crosslinguistic influence in language and cognition.* New York: Routledge.

Jupp, T., & Hodlin, S. (1975). *Industrial English: An example of theory and practice in functional language teaching.* London: Heinemann.

Keck, C., Iberri-Shea, G., Tracy-Ventura, N., & Wa-Mbaleka, S. (2006). Investigating the link between task-based interaction and acquisition: A meta-analysis. In J.

Norris & L. Ortega (Eds.), *Synthesizing research on language learning and teaching* (pp. 91–132). Amsterdam: Benjamins.

Kim, Y. (2008). The contribution of collaborative and individual tasks to the acquisition of L2 vocabulary. *Modern Language Journal, 92,* 114–130.

Kim, Y. (2009a). The effects of task complexity on learner-learner interaction. *System, 37,* 254–268.

Kim, Y. (2009b). *The role of task complexity and pair grouping on the occurrence of learning opportunities and L2 development.* Unpublished doctoral dissertation, Northern Arizona University, Flagstaff.

Kormos, J. (1999). Monitoring and self-repair in L2. *Language Learning, 49,* 303–342.

Kormos, J. (2006). *Speech production and second language acquisition.* Mahwah, NJ: Erlbaum.

Kormos, J. (in press). Speech production and the Cognition Hypothesis. In P. Robinson (Ed.), *Second language task complexity: Researching the Cognition Hypothesis of language learning and performance.* Amsterdam: Benjamins.

Krashen, S. (1982). *Principles and practice in second language acquisition.* New York: Pergamon.

Kuiken, F., & Vedder, I. (2007a). Cognitive task complexity and linguistic performance in French L2 writing. In M. P. Garcia Mayo (Ed.), *Investigating tasks in formal language learning* (pp. 117–135). Clevedon, UK: Multilingual Matters.

Kuiken, F., & Vedder, I. (2007b). Task complexity and measures of linguistic performance in L2 writing. *International Review of Applied Linguistics, 45,* 241–260.

Lantolf, J., & Thorne, S. (2006). *Sociocultural theory and the genesis of second language development.* Oxford: Oxford University Press.

Larsen-Freeman, D., & Cameron, L. (2007). *Complex systems and applied linguistics.* Oxford: Oxford University Press.

Leaver, B., & Willis, J. (Eds.). (2004). *Task-based instruction in foreign language education: Practices and programs.* Washington, DC: Georgetown University Press.

Levelt, W. J. M. (1989). *Speaking: From intention to articulation.* Cambridge MA: MIT Press.

Levelt, W. J. M., Roelofs, A., & Meyer, A. S. (1999). A theory of lexical access in speech production. *Behavioral and Brain Sciences, 22,* 1–38.

Long, M. H. (1983). Native speaker/non native speaker conversation and the negotiation of comprehensible input. *Applied Linguistics, 4,* 126–141.

Long, M. H. (1985). A role for instruction: Task-based language teaching. In M. Pienemann & K. Hyltenstam (Eds.), *Modeling and assessing second language acquisition* (pp. 77–99). Mahwah, NJ: Erlbaum.

Long, M. H. (1989). Task, group, and task-group interactions. *University of Hawai'i Working Papers in ESL, 8,* 1–25.

Long, M. H. (1991). Focus on form: A design feature in language teaching methodology. In K. de Bot, R. Ginsberg, & C. Kramsch (Eds.), *Foreign language research in cross-cultural perspective* (pp. 39–52). Amsterdam: Benjamins.

Long, M. H. (1998). Focus on form in task-based language teaching. *University of Hawai'i Working Papers in ESL, 16,* 49–61.

Long, M. H. (Ed.). (2005). *Second language needs analysis.* Cambridge: Cambridge University Press.

Long, M. H., & Crookes, G. (1992). Three approaches to task-based syllabus design. *TESOL Quarterly, 26,* 27–56.

Long, M. H., & Norris, J. (2004). Task-based teaching and assessment. In M. Byram (Ed.), *Routledge encyclopedia of language teaching and learning* (pp. 597–603). New York: Routledge.

Long, M. H., & Porter, P. (1985). Group work, interlanguage talk, and second language acquisition. *TESOL Quarterly, 19,* 207–228.

Long, M. H., & Robinson, P. (1998). Focus on form: Theory, research, and practice. In C. Doughty & J. Williams (Eds.), *Focus on form in classroom second language acquisition* (pp. 15–41). New York: Cambridge University Press.

Mackey, A. (1999). Input, interaction and second language development: An empirical study of question formation in ESL. *Studies in Second Language Acquisition, 21,* 557–587.

Mackey, A. (Ed.). (2007). *Conversational interaction in second language acquisition.* Oxford: Oxford Unversity Press.

Mackey, A., & Gass, S. (Eds.). (2006). Interaction research: Extending the methodological boundaries [Special issue]. *Studies in Second Language Acquisition, 28*(2).

Mackey, A., & Goo, J. (2007). Interaction research in SLA: A meta-analysis and research synthesis. In A. Mackey (Ed.), *Conversational interaction in SLA* (pp. 407–451). Oxford: Oxford University Press.

Merrill, M. D. (2007). Hypothesized performance on complex tasks as a function of scaled instructional strategies. In R. Clark & J. Elen (Eds.), *Handling complexity in learning environments: Theory and research* (pp. 265–282). Oxford: Elsevier.

Michel, M. (2011). *Cognitive and interactive aspects of task-based performance in Dutch as a second language.* Unpublished doctoral dissertation, University of Amsterdam, Amsterdam.

Munby, J. (1978). *Communicative syllabus design.* Cambridge: Cambridge University Press.

Negueruela, E., & Lantolf, J. (2006). Concept-based instruction and the acquisition of L2 Spanish. In R. Salaberry & B. Lafford (Eds.), *The art of teaching Spanish: Second language acquisition from research to praxis* (pp. 79–102). Washington, DC: Georgetown University Press.

Neumann, O. (1987). Beyond capacity: A functional view of attention. In H. Heuer & A. Sanders (Eds.), *Perspectives on perception and action* (pp. 361–394). Berlin: Springer.

Nuevo, A. (2006). *Task complexity and interaction: L2 learning opportunities and interaction*. Unpublished doctoral dissertation, Georgetown University, Washington, DC.

Nunan, D. (1991). Methods in second language classroom research: A critical review. *Studies in Second Language Acquisition, 13,* 249–274.

Nunan, D. (1993). Task-based syllabus design: Selecting, grading and sequencing tasks. In G. Crookes & S. Gass (Eds.), *Tasks in a pedagogical context: Integrating theory and practice* (pp. 55–68).Clevedon, UK: Multilingual Matters.

Nunan, D. (2004). *Task-based language teaching*. Cambridge: Cambridge University Press.

Odlin, T. (2008). Conceptual transfer and meaning extensions. In P. Robinson & N. Ellis (Eds.), *Handbook of cognitive linguistics and second language acquisition* (pp. 306–340). London: Routledge.

Ortega, L. (2007). Meaningful practice in foreign language classrooms: A cognitive-interactionist perspective. In R. DeKeyser (Ed.), *Practice in a second language* (pp. 180–207). New York: Cambridge University Press.

Pavlenko, A. (2011). Thinking and speaking in two languages: Overview of the field. In A. Pavlenko (Ed.), *Thinking and speaking in two languages* (pp. 237–262). Bristol, UK: Multilingual Matters.

Perdue, C. (Ed.). (1993a). *Adult language acquisition: Cross-linguistic perspectives: Vol. 1. Field methods*. Cambridge: Cambridge University Press.

Perdue, C. (Ed.). (1993b). *Adult language acquisition: Cross-linguistic perspectives: Vol. 2. The results*. Cambridge: Cambridge University Press.

Pica, T. (1994). Research on negotiation: What does it reveal about second language learning conditions, processes and outcomes? *Language Learning, 44,* 493–527.

Pica, T., & Doughty, C. (1985). The role of group work in classroom second language acquisition. *Studies in Second Language Acquisition, 7,* 233–248.

Pica, T., Kanagy, R., & Falodun, J. (1993). Choosing and using communication tasks for second language teaching and research. In G. Crookes & S. Gass (Eds.), *Tasks and language learning: Integrating theory and practice* (pp. 1–34). Clevedon, UK: Multilingual Matters.

Pica, T., Young, R., & Doughty, C. (1987). The impact of interaction on comprehension. *TESOL Quarterly, 21,* 737–758.

Platt, E., & Brooks, F. B. (2002). Task engagement: A turning point in foreign language development. *Language Learning, 52,* 365–400.

Prabhu, N. S. (1987). *Second language pedagogy*. Oxford: Oxford University Press.

Riegeluth, C. (Ed.). (1999). *Instructional-design theories and models: A new paradigm of instructional theory* (Vol. 2). Mahwah, NJ: Erlbaum.

Reiguluth, C., & Carr-Chellman, A. (Eds.). (2009). *Instructional-design theories and models: Building a common knowledge base* (Vol. 3). New York: Routledge.

Revesz, A. (2009). Task complexity, focus on form and second language development. *Studies in Second Language Acquisition, 31,* 437–470.

Revesz, A. (in press). Task complexity, focus on L2 constructions, and individual differences: A classroom-based study. *Modern Language Journal, 95*(4).

Robinson, P. (1995). Task complexity and second language narrative discourse. *Language Learning, 45,* 99–140.

Robinson, P. (2001a). Task complexity, cognitive resources, and syllabus design: A triadic framework for investigating task influences on SLA. In P. Robinson (Ed.), *Cognition and second language instruction* (pp. 287–318). Cambridge: Cambridge University Press.

Robinson, P. (2001b). Task complexity, task difficulty, and task production: Exploring interactions in a componential framework. *Applied Linguistics, 22,* 27–57.

Robinson, P. (2003a). Attention and memory during SLA. In C. Doughty & M. H. Long (Eds.), *The handbook of second language acquisition* (pp. 631–678). Oxford: Blackwell.

Robinson, P. (2003b). The Cognition Hypothesis, task design and adult task-based language learning. *Second Language Studies, 21*(2), 45–107. Retrieved from http://www.hawaii.edu/sls/uhwpesl/21(2)/Robinson.pdf

Robinson, P. (2005). Cognitive complexity and task sequencing: Studies in a componential framework for second language task design. *International Review of Applied Linguistics, 43,* 1–32.

Robinson, P. (2007a). Aptitudes, abilities, contexts and practice. In R. M. DeKeyser (Ed.), *Practice in second language learning: Perspectives from applied linguistics and cognitive psychology* (pp. 256–286). New York: Cambridge University Press.

Robinson, P. (2007b). Criteria for classifying and sequencing pedagogic tasks. In M. P. Garcia Mayo (Ed.), *Investigating tasks in formal language learning* (pp. 7–27). Clevedon, UK: Multilingual Matters.

Robinson, P. (2007c). Task complexity, theory of mind, and intentional reasoning: Effects on L2 speech production, interaction, uptake and perceptions of task difficulty. *International Review of Applied Linguistics, 45,* 193–214.

Robinson, P. (2007d). *Rethinking-for-speaking and L2 task demands: The Cognition Hypothesis, task classification and task sequencing.* Plenary address given at the 2nd International Conference on Task-Based Language Teaching, University of Hawai'i, September. Retrieved from http://www.hawaii.edu/tblt2007/PP/presentations.htm

Robinson, P. (2009). Syllabus design. In M. H. Long & C. Doughty (Eds.), *Handbook of second language teaching* (pp. 294–310). Oxford: Blackwell.

Robinson, P. (2010). Situating and distributing cognition across task demands: The SSARC model of pedagogic task sequencing. In M. Putz & L. Sicola (Eds.). *Cognitive processing in second language acquisition: Inside the learner's mind* (pp. 243–268). Amsterdam: Benjamins.

Robinson, P., Cadierno, T., & Shirai, Y. (2009). Time and motion: Measuring the effects of the conceptual demands of tasks on second language production. *Applied Linguistics, 28,* 533–554.

Robinson, P., & Ellis, N. C. (2008). Conclusions: Cognitive linguistics, second language acquisition and L2 instruction—Issues for research. In P. Robinson & N. C. Ellis (Eds.), *Handbook of cognitive linguistics and second language acquisition* (pp. 489–546.) New York: Routledge.

Robinson, P., & Gilabert, R. (Eds.). (2007). Task complexity, the Cognition Hypothesis and second language instruction [Special issue]. *International Review of Applied Linguistics, 45*(3).

Romanko, R., & Nakatsugawa, M. (2010). Task sequencing based on the Cognition Hypothesis. *Language Teacher, 34*(5), 9–11.

Russell, J., & Spada, N. (2006). The effectiveness of corrective feedback for the acquisition of L2 grammar: A meta-analysis of the research. In J. Norris & L. Ortega (Eds.), *Synthesizing research on language learning and teaching* (pp. 133–164). Amsterdam: Benjamins.

Samuda, V., & Bygate, M. (2008). *Tasks in second language learning.* London: Palgrave Macmillan.

Sanders, A. (1998). *Elements of human performance.* Mahwah, NJ: Erlbaum.

Schmidt, R. (1990). The role of consciousness in second language learning. *Applied Linguistics, 11,* 127–158.

Schmidt, R. (2001). Attention. In P. Robinson (Ed.), *Cognition and second language instruction* (pp. 1–32). Cambridge: Cambridge University Press.

Schmidt, R., & Frota, S. (1986). Developing basic conversational ability in a second language: A case study of an adult learner of Portuguese. In R. Day (Ed.), *Talking to learn: Conversation in second language learning* (pp. 237–322). Rowley, MA: Newbury House.

Seedhouse, P. (2005). "Task" as a research construct. *Language Learning, 55,* 533–570.

Shehadeh, A. (2001). Self- and other-initiated modified output during task-based interaction. *TESOL Quarterly, 35,* 433–457.

Shuell, T. (1980). Learning theory, instructional theory and adaptation. In R. Snow, P. Federico, & W. Montague (Eds.), *Aptitude, learning and instruction: Vol. 2. Cognitive process analyses of learning and problem solving* (pp. 277–302). Mahwah, NJ: Erlbaum.

Skehan, P. (1989). *Individual differences in second language learning.* London: Arnold.

Skehan, P. (1996). A framework for the implementation of task-based instruction. *Applied Linguistics, 17,* 38–62.

Skehan, P. (1998). *A cognitive approach to language learning.* Oxford: Oxford University Press.

Skehan, P. (2003). Task-based instruction. *Language Teaching, 36,* 1–14.

Skehan, P. (2008). Language instruction through tasks. In E. Hinkel (Ed.), *Handbook of research in applied linguistics* (pp. 289–301). New York: Routledge.

Skehan, P. (2009a). Models of speaking and the assessment of second language proficiency. In A. Benati (Ed.), *Issues in second language proficiency* (pp. 203–215). London: Continuum.

Skehan, P. (2009b). Modelling second language performance: Integrating complexity, accuracy, fluency and lexis. *Applied Linguistics, 30,* 510–532.

Skehan, P., & Foster, P. (1999). The influence of task structure and processing conditions on narrative retellings. *Language Learning, 49,* 93–120.

Skehan, P., & Foster, P. (2001). Cognition and tasks. In P. Robinson (Ed.). *Cognition and second language instruction* (pp. 183–205). Cambridge: Cambridge University Press.

Slobin, D. (1993). Adult language acquisition: A view from child language study. In C. Perdue (Ed.), *Adult language acquisition: Crosslinguistic perspectives: Vol. 2. The results* (pp. 239–252). Cambridge: Cambridge University Press.

Snow, R. (1987). Aptitude complexes. In R. Snow & M. Farr (Eds.), *Aptitude, learning and instruction: Vol. 3. Conative and affective process analysis* (pp. 11–34). Hillsdale, NJ: Erlbaum.

Snow, R. (1989). Cognitive-conative aptitude interactions in learning. In R. Kanfer, P. Ackerman, & R. Cudeck (Eds.), *Abilities, motivation and methodology: The Minnesota symposium on learning and individual differences* (pp. 435–474). Hillsdale, NJ: Erlbaum.

Snow, R. (1994). Abilities in academic tasks. In R. Sternberg & R. Wagner (Eds.), *Mind in context: Interactionist perspectives on human intelligence* (pp. 3–37). New York: Cambridge University Press.

Sternberg, R. (2002). The theory of successful intelligence and its implications for language aptitude testing. In P. Robinson (Ed.), *Individual differences and instructed language learning* (pp. 13–44). Amsterdam: Benjamins.

Swain, M. (1995). Three functions of output in second language learning. In G. Cook & B. Seidlhoffer (Eds.), *Principle and practice in applied linguistics: Studies in honor of H. G. Widdowson* (pp. 125–144). Oxford: Oxford University Press.

Swain, M. (2000). The output hypothesis and beyond: Mediating acquisition through collaborative dialogue. In J. Lantolf (Ed.), *Sociocultural theory and second language learning* (pp. 97–114). New York: Oxford University Press.

Swain, M., Kinnear, P., & Steinman, L. (2010). *Sociocultural theory in second language education: An introduction through narratives*. Bristol, UK: Multilingual Matters.

Swain, M., & Lapkin, S. (1995). Problems in output and the cognitive processes they generate. *Applied Linguistics, 16,* 370–391.

Talmy, L. (2000). *Toward a cognitive semantics: Vol. 1. Concept structuring systems.* Cambridge, MA: MIT Press.

Tavakoli, P., & Skehan, P. (2005). Strategic planning, task structure and performance testing. In R. Ellis (Ed.), *Planning and task performance in a second language* (pp. 239–276). Amsterdam: Benjamins.

Thomas, M., & Reinders, H. (Eds.). (2010). *Task-based language learning and teaching with technology.* London: Continuum.

Valdman, A. (1978). Communicative use of language and syllabus design. *Foreign Language Annals, 11,* 567–578.

Valdman, A. (1980). Communicative ability and syllabus design for global foreign language courses. *Studies in Second Language Acquisition, 3,* 81–96.

Van den Branden, K. (Ed.). (2006). *Task-based language education.* Cambridge: Cambridge University Press.

von Stutterheim, C., & Nuese, R. (2003). Processes of conceptualization in language production: Language specific perspectives and event construal. *Linguistics, 41,* 851–888.

White, R. (1988). *The ELT curriculum: Design, management, innovation.* Oxford: Blackwell.

Widdowson, H. G. (1978). *Teaching language as communication.* Oxford: Oxford University Press.

Willis, D. (1990). *The lexical syllabus: A new approach to language teaching.* London: Collins.

Willis, D., & Willis, J. (Eds.). (2007). *Doing task-based teaching.* New York: Oxford University Press.

Willis, J. (1996). *A framework for task-based learning.* London: Longman.

Yano, Y., Long, M. H., & Ross, S. (1994). The effects of simplified and elaborated texts on foreign language reading comprehension. *Language Learning, 44,* 189–219.

Yule, G., & MacDonald, D. (1990). Resolving referential conflicts in L2 interaction: The effect of proficiency and interactive role. *Language Learning, 40,* 539–556.

Yule, G., Powers, M., & MacDonald, D. (1992). The variable effects of some task-based learning procedures on L2 communicative effectiveness. *Language Learning, 42,* 249–277.

Appendix

The Triadic Componential Framework for Task Classification—Categories, Criteria, Analytic Procedures, and Design Characteristics

Task complexity (cognitive factors) (Classification criteria: cognitive demands) (Classification procedure: information-theoretic analyses)	Task condition (interactive factors) (Classification criteria: interactional demands) (Classification procedure: behavior-descriptive analyses)	Task difficulty (learner factors) (Classification criteria: ability requirements) (Classification procedure: ability assessment analyses)
(a) Resource-directing variables making cognitive/conceptual demands	(a) Participation variables making interactional demands	(a) Ability variables and task-relevant resource differentials
± Here and now	± Open solution	h/l Working memory
± Few elements	± One-way flow	h/l Reasoning
± Spatial reasoning	± Convergent solution	h/l Task-switching
± Causal reasoning	± Few participants	h/l Aptitude
± Intentional reasoning	± Few contributions needed	h/l Field independence
± Perspective-taking	± Negotiation not needed	h/l Mind/intention-reading
(b) Resource-dispersing variables making performative/procedural demands	(b) Participant variables making interactant demands	(b) affective variables and task-relevant state-trait differentials
± Planning time	± Same proficiency	h/l Openness to experience
± Single task	± Same gender	h/l Control of emotion
± Task structure	± Familiar	h/l Task motivation
± Few steps	± Shared content knowledge	h/l Processing anxiety
± Independency of steps	± Equal status and role	h/l Willingness to communicate
± Prior knowledge	± Shared cultural knowledge	h/l Self-efficacy

Adapted from Robinson 2007b, by permission of Multilingual Matters. Reproduced with permission of the publisher, Multilingual Matters.

Language Learning   ISSN 0023-8333

Task Design and Second Language Performance: The Effect of Narrative Type on Learner Output

Parvaneh Tavakoli

London Metropolitan University

Pauline Foster

St. Mary's University College

This article reports on a detailed empirical study of the way narrative task design influences the oral performance of second-language (L2) learners. Building on previous research findings, two dimensions of narrative design were chosen for investigation: narrative complexity and inherent narrative structure. Narrative complexity refers to the presence of simultaneous storylines; in this case, we compared single-story narratives with dual-story narratives. Inherent narrative structure refers to the order of events in a narrative; we compared narratives where this was fixed to others where the events could be reordered without loss of coherence. Additionally, we explored the influence of learning context on performance by gathering data from two comparable groups of participants: 60 learners in a foreign language context in Teheran and 40 in an L2 context in London. All participants recounted two of four narratives from cartoon pictures prompts, giving a between-subjects design for narrative complexity and a within-subjects design for inherent narrative structure. The results show clearly that for both groups, L2 performance was affected by the design of the task: Syntactic complexity was supported by narrative storyline complexity and grammatical accuracy was supported by an inherently fixed narrative structure. We reason that the task of recounting simultaneous events leads learners into attempting more hypotactic language, such as subordinate clauses that follow, for example, *while, although, at the same time as*, etc. We reason also that a tight narrative structure allows learners to achieve greater accuracy in the L2 (within minutes of performing less accurately on a loosely structured

---

This article reports part of a larger study funded by the Economic and Social Research Council of the United Kingdom (award reference: RES-000-22-1155). A presentation of the results was made at PacSLRF 2006 at the University of Queensland, Brisbane.

Correspondence concerning this article should be addressed to Pauline Foster, St. Mary's University College, Waldegrave Road, Twickenham, Middlesex, TW1 4SX, UK. Internet: fosterp@smuc.ac.uk

narrative) because the tight ordering of events releases attentional resources that would otherwise be spent on finding connections between the pictures. The learning context was shown to have no effect on either accuracy or fluency but an unexpectedly clear effect on syntactic complexity and lexical diversity. The learners in London seem to have benefited from being in the target language environment by developing not more accurate grammar but a more diverse resource of English words and syntactic choices. In a companion article (Foster & Tavakoli, 2009) we compared their performance with native-speaker baseline data and see that, in terms of nativelike selection of vocabulary and phrasing, the learners in London are closing in on native-speaker norms. The study provides empirical evidence that L2 performance is affected by task design in predictable ways. It also shows that living within the target language environment, and presumably using the L2 in a host of everyday tasks outside the classroom, confers a distinct lexical advantage, not a grammatical one.

Keywords second language performance; task effects; narrative structure; storyline complexity; processing capacity; limited-attention model; multiple-pool model

If anyone ever builds a corpus of academic writing on the subject of second language acquisition (SLA), it is fair to speculate that the word *task* and its derivatives will be among the most common items found therein. One reason for the frequency of *task* or *task-based* in SLA journal articles, book titles, and conference proceedings is that the construct (in various guises) has been the focus of great interest in both second language (L2) pedagogy and L2 research for more than 20 years. This interesting and not uncontroversial state of affairs appears to have come about for three partly overlapping reasons. First, research promises to illuminate the proposition that task performance in itself drives interlanguage change by causing learners to attend to and retain information about the target language as they use it (Ellis, 2001; Swain, 1995). From this angle, exploring SLA through task performance is interesting for its own sake and is not necessarily directed toward pedagogic applications. Where, when, and why learners acquire knowledge of L2 forms during task performance are questions of greater interest than how this phenomenon can be harnessed in class. Second, and more pedagogically, if research identifies the catalyzing features of tasks that impact on a learner's language processing, it provides empirically sound principles for classroom materials design (Bygate, 1999) rather than the more intuitive reasoning drawn upon currently. Finally, research can explore the claim that task design and performance conditions can be chosen deliberately by a teacher to guide a learner's focus of attention to particular aspects of the language being learned. Knowing how a particular kind of task is likely to be done opens up the possibility of closely manipulating learner performance in predictable ways, thereby promoting learning opportunities and developing proficiency (Candlin, 1987; Skehan, 1998; Samuda, 2001).

As noted earlier, task-based research into SLA is not without controversy. Locating the task characteristics that might support SLA progress is, in some quarters, taken to bolster the case for a language teaching approach that uses *only* tasks, with the claim that language learning is more efficient this way than, say, through explicit instruction of grammatical rules (Long & Robinson, 1998; Willis & Willis, 1996). For many this is several steps too far. Swan (2005) pointed out that a classroom focus on explaining grammatical structures (which is not a task as we define it later) is not necessarily the waste of time that it is occasionally dismissed as (cf. also, Sheen, 2003). In fact, in classroom situations where time and resources are lacking, it might rightly be the methodology of choice. It is not, however, our intention in this article to explore the ideal balance between a task-based or grammar-based diet in language classrooms. Our starting point is that task-based L2 performance is an interesting subject in itself and worthy of empirical investigation, but as tasks are widely used in language teaching and in language exams, learning more about their impact should have practical value. At the very least, research in this area can contribute to improving a state of affairs where some pedagogic choices might have to be made on the basis of what is intuitively appealing or currently popular.

Given then that research into task-based L2 performance is important, active, and potentially very useful to both L2 theorists and L2 practitioners, we concede at once that a completely satisfactory definition of the word "task" remains elusive in SLA studies (see Bygate, Skehan, & Swain, 2001, pp. 9–12). Some of the definitions offered are either very broad (e.g., Carroll, 1993; Long, 1985) or else too narrow to capture all of the applications for which it might be wanted (Bachman & Palmer, 1996). Long, for example, defined the word very neatly but unhelpfully as "the hundred and one things that people do in everyday life." Bachman and Palmer restricted it to "an activity that involves individuals in using language for the purpose of achieving a particular goal or objective in a particular situation," thereby excluding a conversational interaction for which there might not be any particular purpose or situation.

In this article we hesitate to add another definition of task to the list, but for our purposes, the most suitable definition is something of a distillation of Nunan (1989) and Skehan (1998). We take as a task anything that classroom language learners do when focusing their attention primarily on what they want to say to others or what others are trying to say to them. Language tasks closely resemble what learners do in their first language when they are, for example, telling stories, making plans, discussing problems, or explaining information, and as such, they are very common in communicative L2 teaching. This definition of task will answer most purposes and certainly covers the activities described as tasks in the research we review and the research we undertake.

Motivated by a practical concern either to understand how teachers might teach more effectively and learners learn more effectively or by a more theoretical interest in how tasks themselves uncover the processes of SLA, researchers have looked at a wide variety of task features and task effects. This work is located mostly (but not exclusively) within a cognitive paradigm of SLA and a limited-capacity model of L2 processing. Briefly, this takes language learning as essentially the mental process of acquiring systems of knowledge through processing, storing, and retrieving linguistic information. Limited capacity for such activity means that the learner's mind must divide its attention between the message being conveyed and the formal aspects of language (its grammar, phonology, and vocabulary) needed for the message to be successfully formulated. Tasks engage the learner in a primary focus on expressing and understanding meanings, but at the same time they have the potential to prompt a timely shift of attention to form in productive and predictable ways.

The task features explored in this paradigm include the following: participant structure (Long, 1983; Pica, 1996); direction of information exchange (Pica, 1994); diversity of task outcomes (Duff, 1986); opportunities for focus on form (Doughty & Williams, 1998; Swain, 1991); the effects of pretask planning (Ellis, 1987; Mehnert, 1998); online planning (Yuan & Ellis, 2003) and of posttask activities (Bygate, 1996); the impact of cognitive complexity (Brown, Hudson, Norris, & Bonk, 2002; Plough & Gass, 1993; Robinson, 2000, 2001); and the effects of task repetition (Bygate, 2001; Lynch & Maclean, 2001). These studies variously report the following: learners are more likely to engage actively in a task if they are in a dyad rather than in a group; having to act as giver and receiver of information supports interaction, especially of negotiation of meaning kind; tasks can draw learners' attention to formal aspects of the language they are using; planning time before a task is a supportive influence on the accuracy, fluency, and complexity of the language attempted[1]; repeating a task leads to increased accuracy and increased ambition in the language attempted; the more cognitively demanding a task is, the greater the syntactic complexity it entails. All of these various investigations suggest that tasks are not neutral vehicles for language practice or display and that their type, content, design, sequence, and implementation conditions are all matters of some consequence for performance.

Relevant here is Levelt's (1989, 1993) serial model of language processing, which attempts to show how a speaker moves from intending to say something to articulating this message in a stream of speech. There are three processing components in this model: The Conceptualizer works prelinguistically to generate the intended message, the Formulator encodes the intended message into the requisite grammatical and phonological forms, and the Articulator uses the phonological encodings to execute the speech plan. Ideally, to avoid irritating pauses, the Formulator operates on partially complete information as the Conceptualizer continues to feed in what is to be said rather than waiting for the Formulator and Articulator to catch up with it. Indeed, for native speakers, parallel processing of ideas and articulated speech can be achieved because the necessary grammatical and phonological encoding draws on automatized linguistic knowledge, which can be accessed and executed very fast, thanks in part to a huge store of ready-made language chunks (Pawley & Syder, 1983). Such automatized knowledge and lexical processing shortcuts are, however, beyond the scope of a language learner, resulting in slow speech or even silence as her Conceptualizer, Formulator, and Articulator compete for limited attentional resources. Whereas it appears that in any competition for attentional resources the Conceptualizer will win (VanPatten, 1990), some of the research noted earlier (Bygate, 2001; Ellis, 1987; Foster & Skehan, 1996; Lynch & Maclean, 2001; Mehnert, 1998) has suggested that it is possible to increase attentional resources for the Formulator and Articulator through planning time and task repetition, presumably because an initial performance of the task, or planning time before the task, takes care of the Conceptualizer's attentional needs and there is now more capacity for linguistic encoding and articulation. In turn, this should provide the speaker with greater capacity for attention to L2 forms.

The idea of human attention as a limited resource has a long pedigree in the psychology of learning (e.g., Cheng, 1985; Schneider & Shiffrin, 1977; Shiffrin & Schneider, 1977). It argues that a new skill initially requires much attention to execute, and so we are not able to give simultaneous attention to other things. Juggling flaming torches for the first time, for example, will probably require our entire attention and make it impossible to carry on a conversation with anyone watching. However, as we automatize the necessary hand-eye coordination through repeated practice, its capacity demands will decrease and we will be able to afford attention to what someone might be saying. Skehan (1998) applied this model to L2 processing, arguing that performing in an imperfectly learned L2 imposes a large burden on the learner's attention and causes the learner to make choices: to prioritize one aspect of performance, such as being accurate, over another, such as being fluent or suitably complex. This model of L2 performance has, however, been challenged by Robinson (2001, 2003, 2005). He drew on Givón's work (1985, 1989), for whom the functional complexity of a task is matched by the structural complexity of the language needed to express it. This means that the more demanding a task is deemed to be in terms of its content, the more complex the language a learner will attempt when transacting it: Form and content are not in competition, but in league with one another. Robinson (2001) cited more recent work in psychology (such as Navon, 1989, and Neumann, 1996) that rejects limited capacity processing, and he proposed a model of attention in which language learners can access multiple attentional pools that do not compete. As depletion of attention in one pool has no effect on the amount remaining in another, language learners can prioritize both form *and* meaning and both accuracy *and* complexity.

Clearly, much more research will have to be undertaken before we are in a position to say which of these competing models is the most convincing. The research undertaken here is not specifically designed to test a limited-attention model against a multiple-resource model. We start from a position of support for Skehan's (1998) limited-attention model, but we will need to consider our results in the light of Robinson's (2001) alternative. Therefore, in the research reported here, we explore further how the demands of the task being carried out affect the allocation of a learner's limited attentional resources and impact on language performance, as displayed by its fluency, accuracy, complexity, and lexical diversity. Our particular interest is in two narrative task types that previous studies have suggested impact on performance: number of storylines and inherent structure.[2]

Storyline Complexity

The consideration of "foreground and background" information as a significant characteristic of narratives is not new. Polanyi-Bowditch (1976) and Hooper and Thompson (1980) both saw *foreground* as the material that supplies the main points of discourse (such as in a narrative), whereas *background* is the part that merely assists, amplifies, or comments on it. Tomlin (1984) argued that foreground information describes those propositions in the story that are more important or central to the development of the overall theme, whereas background information is used to describe ideas that elaborate or explicate the foreground information. Similar accounts are given by Bardovi-Harlig (1992), Dry (1983), Reinhart (1984), and von Stutterheim (1991).

From a more language teaching perspective, Bardovi-Harlig (1998) described foregrounded events in a narrative as those that generally move time forward, whereas background elements are there to elaborate on, explain, or evaluate the events in the foreground. It stands to reason that a narrative in which there are only foreground events asks less of the story teller than one in which background events need to be incorporated, presumably at moments at which some kind of elaboration or explanation is required before the main foreground story can be moved on. Tavakoli and Skehan (2005) in a post hoc analysis of their L2 narrative task data used this foreground/background feature to account for unexpected complexity scores in two of the tasks they used. Unlike the other tasks, these had dual storylines, and a close inspection of the transcripts pinpointed increased syntactic complexity at moments where the participants were trying to connect the two.

This chimes with Matthiessen and Thompson (1988), who noted that in English subordinate clauses usually signal a condition, reason, purpose, cause, setting, manner or means and with Harris and Bates (2002), for whom narrative background is usually described (again, in English) with syntactic subordination. It follows therefore that learners of English, doing a narrative task in which they are expected to connect background events to the main storyline, are going to be prompted to formulate subordinate clauses to achieve their purpose.

Task Structure

The second variable we wish to investigate is also suggested by previous research findings. Two studies (Foster & Skehan, 1996; Skehan & Foster, 1997) explored the extent to which cognitive complexity, operationalized as familiar and unfamiliar task content, would impact on task performance. In general, the results went as predicted: that talking in an L2 about well-known information (oneself and one's life) entailed a more fluent and accurate performance, whereas talking about new and unfamiliar information (certain crimes and punishments) entailed a performance that was less fluent and less accurate but more complex. Whereas the conclusion could be confidently drawn that familiar information requires less attention to process and thus a more fluent and accurate L2 performance can be achieved, a post hoc analysis of the data from the two studies together showed rather strikingly that a variable other than familiarity of content might be also operating on the data. The most fluent performance was observed from one task in the first study and another in the second study, even though these did not have the same degree of familiar information. With the addition of planning time (another variable under investigation), the two tasks returned the most accurate performance. A plausible interpretation is that the key variable here is structure: Both of these tasks dealt with events that had a clear time sequence from beginning to middle and end, and this had eased the processing burden and enabled greater attention to accuracy and fluency in performance. This was tested by Skehan and Foster (1999) and upheld. A narrative task with a tightly structured storyline was significantly associated with greater fluency than a narrative lacking such clear structure. Greater accuracy was again associated with a combination of tight narrative structure and planning time. Thus, the processing burden of telling a story in an L2 appears to be eased if the narrative comprises episodes that are very obviously sequenced from beginning to middle and end, but the burden is increased if the episodes are not susceptible to this neat kind of ordering.[3]

The Research Study

The aims of the present study were to develop a greater understanding of the way task structure can influence the oral language performance of nonnative speakers, especially in terms of their L2 accuracy, fluency, complexity, and lexical diversity. It seeks to replicate the impact found for tight narrative structure on accuracy and fluency (as reported by Skehan and Foster, 1997), to test out the post hoc finding of Tavakoli and Skehan (2005) that two storylines provoke greater syntactic complexity. It also sought to investigate a new angle: whether intersecting storylines would be associated with greater lexical diversity. There is no existing research to suggest that this is the case, but it can be argued that if two storylines need to be woven together in a single narrative, this will involve learners in using more diverse vocabulary than they would need for a single storyline.

Participants

These were in two groups. In one group were 40 learners of English based in London. They were mostly female and between 19 and 47 years of age. They came from a wide variety of mother-tongue backgrounds. In an Oxford Placement test, all had been scored as "intermediate" (i.e., band 4 on a scale of 0–9). In the other group were 60 learners of English based in Teheran, Iran. These were all female, between 19 and 45 years of age. All had Farsi as a mother tongue. In the locally administered placement test of English proficiency, they had achieved scores that put them in an "intermediate" category.[4]

Having participants from two language learning settings (inside and outside the target language environment) enabled us to use a grouping variable to see if the results obtained from matched groups of participants from London and Teheran replicated each other. It also enabled us to look at the possible effects of the learning environment on L2 proficiency. The learners in London were in typically communicative classrooms in which they had plenty of speaking and listening activities. The learners in Teheran also were in classrooms where speaking and listening activities were common and where they were not allowed to use Farsi.

Hypotheses

Taking the two variables of narrative task structure and complexity of storyline, plus the variable of learning environment, the following five research hypotheses were formulated:

H1: Compared to narratives with only foreground events, those in which both foreground and background information need to be described will be associated with learners producing more complex language.

H2: Compared to narratives with a loose structure, those with a tight structure will be associated with learners producing more accurate language.

H3: Compared to narratives with a loose structure, narratives with a tight structure will be associated with learners producing more fluent language.

H4: Compared to narratives with only foreground events, narratives with both foreground and background events will be associated with greater lexical diversity.

H5: Similar patterns of results for H1–H4 will be obtained for learners based within the target language environment (London) and those based outside it (Teheran). We take the null hypothesis here, as we have no reason to suppose there will be any difference.

Design

The study had a 2 × 2 factorial design shown in Figure 1. Each participant was asked to tell aloud two narratives, each comprising a series of six cartoon frames (Heaton, 1966; Jones, 1980; Swan & Walter, 1990) (see the Appendix). The 100 participants were given either *Journey* and *Football* ($n = 50$) or *Walkman* and *Picnic* ($n = 50$). This design allowed for a within-subjects comparison for inherent narrative structure and a between-subjects comparison for the presence or absence of background events.

The variable of tight/loose narrative structure was operationalized by choosing two narratives (*Journey* and *Walkman*) in which the events could be reordered without compromising the story and two other narratives (*Football* and *Picnic*) for which this was impossible. The variable of background events was present in the *Walkman* and *Picnic* narratives and absent in the *Football* and *Journey* narratives.

Story events	Inherent narrative structure	
	Loose	Tight
+ foreground − background	Journey story $n = 50$	Football story $n = 50$
+ foreground + background	Walkman story $n = 50$	Picnic story $n = 50$

Total $N = 100$. Participants did *either* journey and football tasks, *or* walkman and picnic tasks. The task order was counterbalanced.

Figure 1 Research design.

Procedures

Permission was granted by the two colleges for students to volunteer for the research project. Volunteers were told that they would be recorded while narrating stories in English from cartoon prompts. It was stressed that the recordings would be confidential and anonymous, that this was not a test, and that no proficiency score would ever be calculated. Apart from age and first language (L1) background, no personal information was sought.

For each recording, the participants met individually with one of the researchers in a quiet room. They were asked first to look over a cartoon story for up to 3 min to check that they understood its contents. They were then recorded as they told the story. When the first narrative was complete, a second story was presented and told in the same way. The order of the stories was counterbalanced to control for any practice effect.

Transcription, Coding, and Analysis

The digital recordings were downloaded to a Goldwave Digital Editor and transcribed as Word documents using Soundscriber software. In order to complete an analysis of lexical variety, the transcripts were further transferred to CHAT format to be readable by the CLAN software of the CHILDES program. The transcripts were coded for the following dependent variables:

> analysis of speech units (AS-units)
> clauses
> mean length of unit (MLU)

The AS-units and clauses divide the data into complete and dependent syntactic units and enable a syntactic complexity measure to be calculated as a ratio of clauses to AS-units (see Foster et al., 2000, for a full account). The MLU was calculated as words per AS-unit and used as a triangulating measure of complexity.

> reformulations
> false starts
> word replacement
> repetition
> mid-clause pauses greater than 0.4 s
> end-clause pauses greater than 0.4 s

The first four measure repair fluency; the other two measure breakdown fluency.

> error-free clauses

This enables accuracy to be expressed as error-free clauses as a percentage of total clauses.

D

This is a measure of lexical diversity developed by Malvern and Richards (2002) and determined by using their VocD analysis program on CHAT-formatted transcripts. This analysis of diversity is based on a mathematical formula that corrects for sample size (in the way that simple type-token ratios do not) and is well suited to dealing with data such as ours, which is made up of relatively short transcripts.

A sample of 10% of the total transcripts was checked after coding and an interrater reliability score of greater than 95% was obtained on each measure. A number of quantitative analyses were conducted. Factor analyses were initially run to make sure that the measures of fluency, accuracy, and complexity represented distinct factors; performing repeated-measures MANOVA and Univariate F-tests confirmed the overall effect of task variables on different aspects of performance. The η^2 value for narrative structure was .30, and for complexity of storyline, it was .27. This allowed us to proceed with independent and paired t-tests. In preparation for the t-tests, normality of the distribution of scores for different measures of the two groups was assessed. The nonsignificant results obtained for Kolmogorov-Smirnov scores confirmed the normality of the distribution in the majority of the measures.[5]

Results

For clarity, the results are examined following Hypotheses 1 to 4 in turn, presenting scores obtained in Teheran and in London separately in order to consider Hypothesis 5.

Hypothesis 1 stated that compared to narratives with only foreground events, those in which both foreground and background information need to be described will be associated with learners producing more complex language. Complexity was calculated as a ratio of syntactic clauses to AS-units, with the lowest possible score being 1.0 (i.e., a mean of only one clause per syntactic unit). *T*-Tests were performed to compare the two tasks with background information to the two without background information. This was a between-subjects comparison.

The *t*-test results presented in Tables 1 and 2 strongly support Hypothesis 1. The narrative tasks for which the storyline contained background as well as

Table 1 *T*-Test results for complexity: Learners in Teheran

Tightly structured narratives	*M*	*SD*
Picnic (+ background)	1.59	0.38
Football (− background)	1.28	0.16
		$F = 4.13; p = .001$
Loosely structured narratives	*M*	*SD*
Walkman (+ background)	1.36	0.27
Journey (− background)	1.24	0.17
		$F = 2.02; p = .04$

Note. Figures are for mean clauses per AS-unit.

Table 2 *T*-Test results for complexity: Learners in London

Lightly structured narratives	*M*	*SD*
Picnic (+ background)	1.71	0.28
Football (− background)	1.41	0.13
		$F = 4.30; p = .001$
Loosely structured narratives	*M*	*SD*
Walkman (+ background)	1.51	0.21
Journey (− background)	1.34	0.15
		$F = 2.85; p = .007$

Note. Figures are for mean clauses per AS-unit.

foreground information resulted in learners attempting significantly more complex language to describe them, both in London (*Picnic* vs. *Football*: $F = 4.13$; $p = .001$; *Walkman* vs. *Journey*: $F = 2.02$; $p = .04$) and in Teheran (*Picnic* vs. *Football*: $F = 4.30$; $p = .001$; *Walkman* vs. *Journey*: $F = 2.85$; $p = .007$). This lends support for Hypothesis 5, which predicted that there would be a similar pattern of results for learners in both environments. However, a much higher level of significance was found in the London data for the association of syntactic complexity with background events in the loosely structured *Walkman* narrative ($p = .007$ compared to $p = .04$). *T*-Tests comparing the performance of the learners in London and Teheran (shown in Table 3) reveal that the learners in London consistently produced English that was more complex and that the difference was significant on all tasks but *Picnic* (*Football*: $p = .007$; *Journey*: $p = .04$; *Picnic*: $p = .24$ ns; *Walkman*: $p = .04$). Therefore, although Hypothesis 5 is upheld in that the variable of storyline complexity affects both groups in the same way, the groups differ significantly on the degree of this complexity.

Another measure of complexity taken was MLU (i.e., mean words per AS-unit). Tables 4 and 5 show results very similar to the measures reported earlier and offer further support for Hypotheses 1 and 5. In both the Teheran data

Table 3 *T*-Test results for complexity on all tasks: Learners in Teheran and London

	Teheran	London	p
Football	1.28	1.41	.007*
Journey	1.24	1.34	.04*
Picnic	1.59	1.71	.24 ns
Walkman	1.36	1.51	.04*

Note. Figures are for mean clauses per AS-unit.

Table 4 *T*-Test results for MLU: Learners in Teheran

Tightly structured narratives	M	SD
Picnic (+ background)	9.27	1.68
Football (− background)	7.55	1.14
		$F = 4.63$; $p = .001$
Loosely structured narratives	M	SD
Walkman (+ background)	8.43	2.19
Journey (− background)	7.15	1.08
		$F = 2.87$; $p = .006$

Note. Figures are for mean clauses per AS-unit.

Table 5 T-Test results for MLU: Learners in London

Tightly structured narratives	M	SD
Picnic (+ background)	10.86	2.50
Football (− background)	8.27	1.37
		$F = 3.78; p = .001$
Loosely structured narratives	M	SD
Walkman (+ background)	9.19	1.10
Journey (− background)	7.72	0.79
		$F = 4.82; p = .001$

Note. Figures are for mean clauses per AS-unit.

Table 6 T-Test results for MLU on all tasks: Learners in Teheran and London

	Teheran	London	p
Football	7.55	8.27	.05
Journey	7.15	7.72	.05
Picnic	9.27	10.68	.02
Walkman	8.43	9.19	.16 ns

Note. Figures are for mean clauses per AS-unit.

and the London data there is an effect for storyline complexity; in tasks with background events, learners produced significantly longer MLUs (London: *Picnic* vs. *Football*: $F = 4.63; p = .001$; *Walkman* vs. *Journey*: $F = 2.87; p = .006$. Teheran: *Picnic* vs. *Football*: $F = 3.78; p = .001$; *Walkman* vs. *Journey*: $F = 4.82; p = .001$).

Again, t-tests comparing the performance of the learners in London and Teheran show, in Table 6, that the learners in London consistently produced longer MLUs than their counterparts in Teheran and that the difference was significant on all tasks but *Walkman* (*Football*: $p = .05$; *Journey*: $p = .05$; *Picnic*: $p = .02$; *Walkman*: $p = .16$ ns). Therefore, although Hypothesis 5 is upheld in that the variable of storyline complexity affects both groups in the same way, Table 6 repeats the result of Table 3: The groups differ significantly on the degree of this complexity.

Pearson product-moment correlations were run between complexity as measured through clauses per AS-unit and complexity measured as MLU. All reached significance (*Walkman*: .759**; *Picnic*: .803**; *Journey*: .670**; *Football*: .605**).

Hypothesis 2 predicted that, compared to narratives with a loose structure, those with a tight structure will be associated with learners producing more

Table 7 *T*-Test results for accuracy: Learners in Teheran

Narratives with background	M	SD
Picnic (tight structure)	41	21
Walkman (loose structure)	30	16
		$F = 3.19; p = .003$
Narratives without background	M	SD
Football (tight structure)	42	16
Journey (loose structure)	31	17
		$F = 2.86; p = .008$

Note. Figures are for mean % error-free clauses.

accurate language. Accuracy was calculated as error-free clauses expressed as a percentage of total clauses. This was a within-subjects comparison.

Table 7 shows that Hypothesis 2 is upheld for the learners in Teheran, for whom a significant difference is seen in the mean accuracy scores from tightly structured and loosely structured narratives *(Picnic* vs. *Walkman:* $F = 3.19$; $p = .003$. *Football* vs. *Journey:* $F = 2.86$; $p = .008$). This is true regardless of whether the narrative involved background events. The picture is a little less clear-cut for the learners in London. Table 8 shows that the difference is significant for narratives with background information *(Picnic* vs. *Walkman:* $F = 4.13$; $p = .001$), but for the tasks without background information, the comparison fails to reach significance *(Football* vs. *Journey:* $F = 1.77$ ns) although the trend (38% vs. 43%) is very clear and in the predicted direction. Hypothesis 5, that a similar accuracy effect would be seen in both learning

Table 8 *T*-Test results for accuracy: Learners in London

Narratives with background	M	SD
Picnic (tight structure)	47	09
Walkman (loose structure)	36	11
		$F = 4.13; p = .001$
Narratives without background	M	SD
Football (tight structure)	43	12
Journey (loose structure)	38	12
		$F = 1.77; p = .09$ ns

Note. Figures are for mean % error-free clauses.

Table 9 *T*-Test results for accuracy on all tasks: Learners in London and Teheran

	Teheran	London	*p*
Football	42	43	.68 ns
Journey	31	38	.13 ns
Picnic	41	47	.22 ns
Walkman	30	36	.136 ns

Note. Figures are for mean % error-free clauses.

environments, receives good support. Table 9 shows *t*-tests comparing the accuracy scores of both groups across all tasks. Although the London accuracy scores are always a bit higher than the Teheran scores, there is no statistically significant difference (*Football*: $p = .68$; *Journey*: $p = .13$; *Picnic*: $p = .22$; *Walkman*: $p = .136$ ns).

Hypothesis 3 stated that, compared to narratives with a loose structure, narratives with a tight structure will be associated with learners producing more fluent language. This is a within-subjects comparison. A great many measures were taken of fluency, and ideally one would use a MANOVA to test them. However, as these dependent variables pattern consistently, we use multiple *t*-tests with Bonferroni adjustments to reduce the likelihood of a Type 1 error. For clarity, these will be presented separately as repair fluency (reformulations, repetitions, false starts, replacements) and breakdown fluency (mid- and end-clause pausing). Tables 10 and 11 show that using a Bonferroni-adjusted alpha level of .013, the only measure of repair fluency to reach statistical significance

Table 10 *T*-Test results for repair fluency measures: Learners in Teheran

	Football	Journey	*p*
Reformulations	0.63 (*SD* .61)	1.0 (*SD* 1.17)	.141 ns
False starts	2.66 (*SD* 2.05)	3.56 (*SD* 2.89)	.07 ns
Replacements	1.26 (*SD* 1.28)	1.13 (*SD* 1.15)	.601 ns
Repetitions	2.7 (*SD* 3.08)	2.56 (*SD* 2.67)	.763 ns
	Picnic	Walkman	*p*
Reformulations	0.83 (*SD* .79)	1.33 (*SD* 1.72)	.122 ns
False starts	3.63 (*SD* 2.73)	6.23 (*SD* 4.90)	.002*
Replacements	1.9 (*SD* 1.66)	2.86 (*SD* 2.31)	.02 ns
Repetitions	4.64 (*SD* 4.16)	5.46 (*SD* 5.56)	.257 ns

Note. Figures are for mean totals.

Table 11 *T*-Test results for repair fluency measures: Learners in London

	Football	Journey	*p*
Reformulations	1.40 (*SD* 1.31)	1.85 (*SD* 2.30)	.384 ns
False starts	3.6 (*SD* 2.83)	4.40 (*SD* 3.63)	.409 ns
Replacements	1.30 (*SD* 1.03)	1.55 (*SD* 1.63)	.549 ns
Repetitions	5.50 (*SD* 4.18)	6.10 (*SD* 5.14)	.374 ns
	Picnic	Walkman	*p*
Reformulations	2.35 (*SD* 1.6)	2.25 (*SD* 1.65)	.856 ns
False starts	5.40 (*SD* 3.51)	5.25 (*SD* 4.39)	.898 ns
Replacements	1.85 (*SD* 1.49)	1.55 (*SD* 1.73)	.60 ns
Repetitions	4.0 (*SD* 3.50)	4.90 (*SD* 3.22)	.186 ns

in the Teheran data was false starts ($F = 3.49; p = .002$). This is in the direction predicted by the hypothesis but in the absence of any other significant results for repair fluency this can lend little support to it.

There is a similar picture for measures of breakdown fluency. By setting a Bonferroni-adjusted level of .013 for *t*-tests, only one significant difference in breakdown fluency scores was achieved for the learners in Teheran. For narratives without background events, this was mean number of mid-clause pauses per minute ($F = 3.38; p = .002$). For the narratives with background events, none of the four measures reached significance. For the learners in London, no measure of breakdown fluency reached significance. For the narratives with background events, the measure of total silence in seconds just fell short of the Bonferroni-adjusted level of .013 ($F = 2.67; p = .02$). For both sets of data, the most consistent measure of breakdown fluency seems to be mid-clause pausing, expressed as either a mean number of such pauses or as a total number of seconds of silence; these results are presented in Tables 12 and 13.

There is thus only very limited support for Hypothesis 3. For learners in Teheran, a significant effect of narrative structure on fluency is captured by only two measures of breakdown and repair fluency. For learners in London, although a few differences came close, none achieved significance. This means that Hypothesis 5 can receive little support. There is an effect of narrative structure in fluency for learners in Teheran, but it seems to rest on mid-clause pausing only. Table 14 presents *t*-tests results comparing mid-clause pausing per minute across both groups, with a difference only in the task, for which learners in Teheran pause significantly longer (*Football*: $p = .5$ ns; *Journey*: $p = .018$; *Picnic*: $p = .579$ ns; *Walkman*: $p = .9$ ns).

Hypothesis 4 predicted that, compared to narratives with only foreground events, narratives with both foreground and background events will be associated with greater lexical diversity. This was measured using VocD (Malvern & Richards, 2002).

The mean scores for D reported in Tables 15 and 16 show no stable pattern for the variable of narrative complexity. In fact, they point in opposite directions

Table 12 T-Test results for breakdown fluency: Learners in Teheran

Narratives with background	M	SD
Picnic (tight structure)	8.02	3.93
Walkman (loose structure)	9.51	3.99
		$F = 2.36; p = .03$ ns

Narratives without background	M	SD
Football (tight structure)	9.05	4.04
Journey (loose structure)	11.46	4.56
		$F = 3.38; p = .002$

Note. Figures are for mean number of mid-clause pauses, per minute.

Table 13 T-Test results for breakdown fluency: Learners in London

Narratives with background	M	SD
Picnic (tight structure)	8.13	3.81
Walkman (loose structure)	9.89	4.97
		$F = 2.67; p = .02$ ns

Narratives without background	M	SD
Football (tight structure)	9.67	5.24
Journey (loose structure)	10.55	5.58
		$F = .93; p = .365$ ns

Note. Figures are for mean number of mid-clause pauses, per minute.

Table 14 T-Test results for breakdown fluency: Learners in London and Teheran

	Teheran	London	p
Football	9.05	8.30	.53 ns
Journey	11.46	8.38	.018
Picnic	8.02	8.30	.579 ns
Walkman	9.51	9.42	.93 ns

Note. Figures are for mean seconds of mid-clause pauses per minute.

Table 15 *T*-Test results for lexical diversity: Learners in Teheran

Tightly structured narratives	M	SD
Picnic (+ background)	27.76	5.89
Football (− background)	28.75	11.26
		$F = .43; p = 67$ ns

Loosely structured narratives	M	SD
Walkman (+ background)	33.62	6.40
Journey (− background)	25.82	9.49
		$F = 3.73; p = .001$

Note. Figures are mean values for D.

Table 16 *T*-Test results for lexical diversity: Learners in London

Tightly structured narratives	M	SD
Picnic (+ background)	36.59	9.46
Football (− background)	38.37	11.18
		$F = .53; p = .59$ ns

Loosely structured narratives	M	SD
Walkman (+ background)	43.37	12.43
Journey (− background)	36.11	11.0
		$F = 1.95; p = .06$ ns

Note. Figures are mean values for D.

(London: *Picnic* vs. *Football*: $F = .43$ ns; London: *Walkman* vs. *Journey*: $F = 3.7; p = .001$. Teheran: *Picnic* vs. *Football*: $F = .53$ ns; Teheran: *Walkman* vs. *Journey*: $F = 1.95$ ns). In the London and Teheran data, the *Picnic* task, which does have background events, gives rise to less lexical diversity than the *Football* task, which does not. However, *Walkman*, the other task with background events, gives rise to greater lexical diversity than *Journey*, which has none. Again, this is observed in both the London and Teheran data. Indeed, if the mean scores for D are placed in order from the most to the least, the ranking is the same for both London and Teheran: *Walkman, Football, Picnic,* and *Journey.* The *t*-tests comparing *Walkman* with *Journey* show a significant difference ($F = 3.73; p = .001$) for background events in the London data and a nearly significant difference ($F = 1.95; p = .06$) in the Teheran data, but there is no such significance for the *t*-test comparisons of *Picnic* with *Football* ($F = .43$ ns and .59 ns). Thus, the hypothesis has support from the results of one

Table 17 *T*-Tests for effect of Learning environment on lexical diversity

	Teheran	London	*p*
Football	28.75 (*SD* 11.26)	38.37 (*SD* 11.18)	.01
Journey	25.82 (*SD* 9.49)	36.11 (*SD* 11.0)	.02
Picnic	27.76 (*SD* 5.89)	36.59 (*SD* 9.46)	.003
Walkman	33.62 (*SD* 6.40)	43.37 (*SD* 12.43)	.006

Note. Figures are mean values for D.

of the tasks with background events but not from the other. This inconsistent effect suggests either that this independent variable is not reliably connected to lexical diversity, or the tasks do not operationalize it as well as hoped, or that comparing lexical diversity values for different tasks is not warranted.[6]

Interestingly, Tables 15 and 16 reveal that the D values for learners in London are higher on all tasks than those for learners in Iran, and in some cases much higher. *T*-Tests comparing D values for London and Teheran for each of the four tasks are presented in Table 17 and clearly indicate that greater lexical diversity is connected to the learning environment.[7] The learners in London consistently and significantly use more diverse language than their counterparts in Teheran on all four tasks (*Football*: *p* = .01; *Journey*: *p* = .02; *Picnic*: *p* = .003; *Walkman*: *p* = .006).

In sum, our results show the following: strong support for syntactic complexity being affected by narrative storyline complexity; good support for grammatical accuracy being affected by tight narrative structure; some limited support for breakdown fluency being affected by tight narrative structure; ambiguous results for lexical diversity being affected by storyline complexity; and, finally, the learning environment is shown to have little discernible effect on accuracy or fluency but a clear effect on syntactic complexity and lexical diversity.

Discussion

Our research study was designed to investigate features of narrative task design rather than to explore the relative merits of the limited-resource or multiple-pool models of attention, so it is perhaps not surprising that the results do not shed much light on this debate. Skehan's (1998) limited-resource model means that if a task demands a great amount of attention in terms of its content (as it might if two storylines were going on at the same time), then attention to language form is diminished and this is manifest in, say, reduced performance scores all around or a trade-off between different aspects of performance. This is not borne out by our results, in which, for example, *Picnic* (two storylines, tight structure) showed the highest mean scores for complexity, accuracy, *and* fluency. This could be seen as support for Robinson's (2001) multiple-pool model because such a performance profile suggests that attention to one aspect has not diminished attention to any other. Equally though, it is possible to suggest that a tight storyline structure somehow relieves the narrative processing load and frees up attentional space to be devoted to accuracy, setting us back inside Skehan's limited-attention model. Moreover, *Walkman* (two storylines, loose structure) produced a different performance profile, which could be seen as further support for Skehan's model. The lowest mean scores for accuracy appear here to trade-off with the second highest scores for fluency and complexity (see Tables 1, 2, 4, 5, 7, 8, 10, and 13). Robinson's model proposes that the more demanding a task is in terms of its content, the more complex and accurate its linguistic performance will be. Our two-storyline variable (*Picnic, Walkman*) is shown by our results to be connected with high syntactic complexity scores, but we are not convinced that this is because the presence of two storylines in a narrative necessarily makes the task more cognitively demanding and hence the language more complex. A more sustainable explanation is, we think, simply that the presence of background events in a narrative necessitates, in English, using particular structures such as subordinated clauses to connect the background information to the events that are happening in the foreground. Skehan's model would predict that because two storylines require more attention than one, attention to content will be at the expense of attention to form, and this appears to be the case in *Walkman*, for which complexity and fluency are high and accuracy is low. This does not work with our tightly structured narrative *Picnic,* in which all aspects of performance have high scores, although, again, this can be explained by the tightly structure narrative demanding less attentional capacity.

The broad conclusion we can draw from our research could fit both (or neither) of these models of attention: *L2 performance is affected in predictable ways by design features of narrative tasks.* A tight narrative structure enhances accuracy, whereas the presence of two storylines involves greater syntactic complexity. As a result, a narrative of loose structure and only foreground events (*Journey*) elicits a performance of relatively low accuracy and low syntactic complexity, whereas performance in a narrative of tight structure and both foreground and background events (*Picnic*) elicits relatively higher accuracy and complexity.

This indeed is what the research reported here was designed to illuminate. Storyline complexity was suggested as promoting syntactic complexity in Tavakoli and Skehan (2005), and this effect is replicated here. *Walkman* and *Picnic* draw the storyteller into using syntactic subordination because the two narrative lines need to be woven together. The effect is strong for both tasks in both the London and Teheran data. This is clear evidence for the way the nature of a task can manipulate the learner's performance. The *Football* and *Journey* cartoon strips show one foregrounded event per frame, inviting the speaker to describe just this before moving on. The *Picnic* story, on the other hand, carries through the idea of the dog hidden in the basket while the children leave the house, walk through the countryside, and choose their picnic spot, inviting the story teller to remind us at several points that the children still do not know about the dog. The *Walkman* story explicitly shows background events occurring in four of the six frames, with the sixth frame recapitulating that the man had been oblivious to them all. The repeated necessity in these tasks to link foreground with background means that the learner, in English at least, is drawn to formulate subordinated clauses introduced, for example, by *while, although, at the same time as, they didn't know that, he didn't notice that, he wasn't paying attention to,* in order to express conditions, reasons, or purposes in the story (Harris & Bates, 2002; Matthiessen & Thompson, 1988).

It is, however, one thing to show that performance is variable and open to manipulation through task design and another to link this feature of task design to L2 development. A cross-sectional study such as this (and the others we have referred to in this regard) cannot prove long-term benefits, or indeed any benefits, to SLA. A longitudinal study might illuminate this and would be a very welcome addition to the literature. However, in the terms of the potential usefulness of task investigations set out in the first paragraph of this article, storyline complexity has the predictable outcome of increasing syntactic complexity in performance, and a teacher might exploit this for pedagogic reasons, such as guiding learners' attention to the use of subordinating structures in English or giving learners practice in handling complex clause sequences involved by *although* and *despite* and indirect speech. If practice in something is a step toward getting better at it, then such practice is arguably (but not yet demonstrably) implicated in promoting L2 proficiency.

Regarding L2 accuracy, the results reported here are consistent with Foster and Skehan (1996) and Skehan and Foster (1997) that a tight narrative structure supports accuracy in L2 performance. Both of the tasks with a clear ordering of narrative elements were performed significantly more accurately than the tasks without this tight order. Furthermore, this was a within-subject comparison, meaning that participants telling two narratives in the same 20-min period were measurably more accurate in their English with the *Picnic* and *Football* stories, regardless of whether they did these first or second. There is no need to look for a further explanation than the one given by previous studies with this result. The orderly nature of the narrative events, as operationalized in the *Football* and *Picnic* stories, where there is an obvious progression from one picture to the next, releases attentional resources that would otherwise have to be expended on finding narrative connections. In Levelt's (1989) terms, this results in a lighter processing load for the Conceptualizer and more "space" for the Formulator to work within. The Formulator can give more attention to grammatical accuracy, and performance is subsequently more accurate.

This effect has now been shown (Foster & Skehan, 1999; Tavakoli & Skehan, 2005) in several studies using a variety of tasks, reinforcing the claim that structure is a task dimension with a clear and predictable influence on L2 performance. Again, a snapshot cross-sectional observation of performance does not demonstrate anything about progress in language learning. It does, however, allow us to argue that a tight task structure is a catalyst that enables L2 performance to be more accurate than it might otherwise be, and from there to argue that the more often an L2 form is performed accurately, the more likely its incorporation into the range of L2 forms that the learner can manage with ease. Whether accuracy during task performance has a long-term impact on learning is something for other research to demonstrate. The results of this study can only show that a learner given the *Picnic* task in a test is likely to achieve higher levels of accuracy than if she were given the *Walkman* task. Whether such a difference is noticeable to a language tester is another matter, but given the size of the difference measured in this study (30% vs. 41% in the Teheran data and 36% vs. 47% in the London data), it is certainly possible. If true, there are clear implications for anyone designing an oral language test.

Regarding fluency, the study we report here does not replicate a reliable effect for loose or tight narrative structure shown in other studies. The results for repair fluency measures such as false starts, repetitions, word replacements, and reformulations failed to show a significant effect for tight structure in either London and Teheran, apart for the measure of false starts ($p = .002$) in the Teheran data comparing *Walkman* with *Picnic*. This result is in the expected direction—that tight structure supports fluency—but as it is mostly at odds with the other results for breakdown fluency, it has to be treated with some circumspection or even discarded. The measures of breakdown fluency that point to some effect for tight structure on mid-clause pausing are also somewhat inconsistent. On the whole, Hypothesis 3 is feeble and at odds with previous research findings (Tavakoli & Skehan, 2005). These accounted for their observed effects of tight structure on fluency in the same way as they accounted for its observed effect on accuracy— that a tightly structured narrative demands less attentional capacity and therefore there is additional attention for grammar and for fluent performance. In Levelt's (1989) terms, the Formulator (and possibly the Articulator) had more space to work in because the processing burden for the Conceptualizer was diminished by the tightly structured nature of the narrative. The general failure of our data to reproduce this effect can be accounted for by suggesting that a monologic task (such as we use here) makes greater demands on attentional resources than an interactive task (such as were used in Foster & Skehan, 1996 and Skehan & Foster, 1997). This at first seems counterintuitive; after all, having to listen to, process, and respond to an interlocutor's contributions should be more demanding of attention than merely processing one's own output. However, equally it might be that a very long turn, such as a monologue, gives no breathing space for online planning, as can be snatched while listening to an interlocutor, and therefore planning has to be done while speaking or at moments of not speaking (i.e., pausing). If the attentional load gets too great, pausing has to increase in order to allow, for example, the Formulator to catch up with what the Conceptualizer has been feeding in. The only way to know if this post hoc explanation is valid is to try a within-subjects comparison of task performance on a monologue and dialogue. It is unlikely that both task types are equally demanding of attentional resources, and it would be useful to know how they compare.

Nevertheless, we have noted that the closest our results get to capturing a fluency effect is on the measure of mid-clause pausing. This is entirely consistent with Pawley and Syder's (2000) hypothesis by which language is encoded a clause at a time and pausing within clause boundaries is a sign of processing problems. The general inconsistency found with the other measures could indicate that they are not tapping into any dimension of L2 performance. After all, native speakers are not seamlessly fluent, and it is common to find dysfluencies such as reformulations, false starts, repetitions, and end-clause pausing in their speech. Measuring the fluency of a person's L2 performance ideally needs a baseline measure of their L1 performance so that it becomes possible to see the extent to which dysfluencies are idiosyncratic. It is entirely possible that many of the repair and breakdown fluencies we identified in our data were caused not by an L2 processing hiccup but by a participant's natural inclination to abandon units, replace words or lapse into silence.

In the absence of other research exploring task type and lexical diversity, hypothesis 4 predicted an effect for task type on lexical diversity by reasoning that linking background to foreground events would mean the learners would have to draw on a wider vocabulary. This was not borne out by the results. One task with background events (*Walkman*) did provoke a more diverse vocabulary than the without-background events (*Journey*), but there was no effect in the comparison of *Picnic* with *Football*. We have already noted the caveat of Tidball and Treffers-Daller (personal communication, 2005) that *t*-test comparisons of D values across-task can be suspect, and we do not need to pursue this result any further. However, just looking at the mean values of D in Tables 15 and 16 we see that the *Walkman* task has a much greater lexical variety than *Picnic* in both the London and Teheran data and this suggests that something other than background events is causing this. It is more likely to ascribe the greater lexical variety to the simple fact that the *Walkman* task just has many events, background *and* foreground. Furthermore, there is as much going on in the foreground-only *Football* task as in the foreground and background *Picnic* task; hence, the D values are about the same. More events, wherever located, mean more diversity of vocabulary.

However, although this between-task comparison was fruitless, the within-task comparison of the London and Teheran data was not. Table 17 shows the London D values to be significantly higher than those in the Teheran data. This is somewhat unexpected, as, apart from syntactic complexity, other comparisons of London and Teheran supported null Hypothesis 5 and showed little or no difference between the two groups of learners. Table 9 shows no difference in the accuracy of performance on any task. Table 12 shows no difference on breakdown fluency apart from the scores on the task for which the Teheran learners are significantly more prone to hesitate in mid-clause.[8] The syntactic complexity difference, shown in Table 3, reveals that the learners in Teheran use consistently fewer subordinate clauses on all tasks.

Both groups had broadly equivalent placement tests and were reliably matched for proficiency, as we see confirmed by their similar accuracy and fluency scores. However, they are not performing at the same level in complexity and lexical diversity, suggesting that their different learning environments have had an effect. The learners in London seem to have benefited from being in the target language environment by developing not a better command of grammar but a much more diverse vocabulary. We can see syntactic complexity as closely related to this. Vocabulary is not, after all, individual words; it is words and their collocates, and often it is entire phrases. The additional complexity of the language used by the London learners (shown in both clauses per AS-unit and MLU) could be accounted for because they picked up more lexicalized phrases and sentence frames (Boers, Eyckmans, Kapprel, Stengers,

& Demecheleer, 2006; Foster, 2001; Pawley & Syder, 1983) from their greater exposure to spoken and written English outside of the classroom. If this explanation is valid, it is surprising that the London learners are not more fluent, as phrases or frames learned as wholes should be easier to articulate fluently. It is impossible to tell from the data we have, but the explanation we used earlier (for why our fluency results do not match previous research findings) might be useful here; it is harder to be fluent in a monologue.

A proper perspective on task performance by learners of a second language needs a baseline native speaker performance (Foster, 2001). Knowing how task design can influence a native speaker's fluency, complexity and lexical choices is an important triangulation for understanding the measures we take of non-native performance. For the tasks investigated here, a native speaker baseline has already been measured and the results are reported in Foster and Tavakoli (2009). Two lines of future research suggested by the results presented here have already been mentioned earlier: It will be very useful to compare task performance fluency for L1 and L2 performance in order to determine how much dysfluency is idiosyncratic and how much is caused by L2 processing difficulty; and it will be very useful to add longitudinal research studies to the abundant cross-sectional studies, as these would be able to illuminate the relationship between L2 *performance* and long-term L2 *progress*. What our results have confirmed is that L2 performance is very sensitive to task design and, therefore, the most immediate relevance of our study is probably for testers. The four tasks we use are not equivalent to each other; they make different demands on the performer and are likely to result in different performances in terms of accuracy and complexity. If testers need language tasks to provide a level playing field for language display, then narrative task features such as structure and complexity of storyline are variables that deserve consideration. As for L2 development, the relevance of our study is less clear. We have not investigated whether a great amount of L2 task performance affects language learning in the long term, so we do not suggest what place tasks such as *Picnic* or *Football* might have in classrooms. However, the grouping variable we used (inside or outside the target language environment) produced very intriguing results. For learners in London, experience in English was not restricted to the classroom as it was (one suspects) for the learners in Teheran. Indeed, life outside their London classroom might well have consisted of multiple L2 task performances, what we have already noted that Long (1985) calls "the hundred and one things that people do in everyday life" and Bachman and Palmer (1996) describe as "using language for the purpose of achieving a particular goal or objective in a particular situation." Our data (Tables 9 and 17) suggest that this multiple-task engagement had, for the learners in London, resulted in a significantly more diverse vocabulary than their counterparts in Teheran, but not a proportional advance in grammatical accuracy. Their progress in SLA being thus "unbalanced," the learners in London perhaps need particular classroom work to bring their grammatical competence into line.

Revised version accepted 5 September 2007

Notes

1 Research results on the effect of pretask planning time have shown some effects inconsistent with this (e.g., Iwashita, McNamara, & Elder, 2001; Wigglesworth, 2001).

2 We are careful throughout to avoid confusion in terminology. Hence, *narrative type* distinguishes one design of narrative task from another. For our particular focus, we are interested in two types: *storyline complexity* and *inherent narrative structure*. *Storyline complexity* refers to whether a narrative has background as well as foreground events, with a narrative consisting of only foreground events classified as less complex than one with both. *Narrative structure* refers to how the narrative episodes lead from one to the next. Thus, a narrative with an *inherently loose* structure can have its episodes reordered without loss of coherence. A narrative with an *inherently tight* structure cannot.

3 Similarly, in the Robinson (2001) model, a loose narrative structure might be classed as "resource-dispersing," leading to an overall reduction in available attention.

4 A Pearson product-moment correlation was run to compare the local test with the Oxford Placement test. The coefficient correlation ($r = .56$, correlation is significant at the .01 level) was considered large enough to equate the two tests reliably, although some caution is still warranted in this. All learners in both venues were given oral interviews to confirm their proficiency and correct class placement.

5 For few measures of fluency, namely number of pauses at mid and end clause, slightly skewed curves were observed for some of the tasks. However, this does not necessarily indicate a problem with the comparisons (see Pallent, 2001; Tabachnick & Fidell, 1996) but might reflect the underlying nature of the construct being measured, in this case fluency of performance, which is acknowledged to be influenced by personal speaking characteristics of individuals.

6 We thank Tidball and Treffers-Daller (personal communication, 2005) for this observation. Cross-task comparisons for lexical diversity can be suspect because of the entirely different stimuli that give rise to vocabulary choices. However, our within-task comparisons of the London and Teheran data (Table 17) are safe from this criticism.

7 It could possibly be, as one reviewer has suggested, that the reasons for the London participants using more diverse vocabulary is not their location within the L2

environment but their curriculum, the pedagogical approach of their teachers, their general educational background, and/or their L1s. However, it is not obvious to us why any of these factors would impact significantly on diversity of vocabulary alone. We think it more plausible that contact with the L2 outside the classroom, which the London participants had and the Teheran participants did not, has contributed to an enriched vocabulary.

8 Close analyses of the transcripts indicate this was probably due to the learners in Teheran having particular trouble interpreting some of the pictures in this story; see Foster (2009).

References

Bachman, L. F., & Palmer, A. S. (1996). *Language testing in practice: Designing and developing useful language tests.* Oxford: Oxford University Press.

Bardovi-Harlig, K. (1992). The telling of a tale: Discourse structure and tense use in learners' narratives. *Pragmatics and Language Learning, 3,* 144–161.

Bardovi-Harlig, K. (1998). Narrative structure and lexical aspect: Conspiring factors in second language acquisition of tense-aspect morphology. *Studies in Second Language Acquisition, 20*(4), 471–508.

Boers, F., Eyckmans, J., Kapperl, J., Stengers, H., & Demecheleer, M. (2006). Formulaic sequences and perceived oral proficiency: Putting a lexical approach to the test. *Language Teaching Research, 10*(3), 245–261.

Brown, J. D., Hudson, T. D., Norris, J. M., & Bonk, W. (2002). *An investigation of second language task-based performance assessment.* Honolulu: University of Hawaii Press.

Bygate, M. (1996). Effects of task repetition: Appraising the developing language of learners. In J. Willis & D. Willis (Eds.), *Challenge and change in language teaching* (pp. 134–146). London: Heineman.

Bygate, M. (1999). Quality of language and purpose of task: Patterns of learners' language on two oral communication tasks. *Language Teaching Research, 3*(3), 185–214.

Bygate, M. (2001). Effects of task repetition on the structure and control of oral language. In M. Bygate, P. Skehan, & M. Swain (Eds.), *Researching pedagogic tasks: Second language learning, teaching and testing* (pp. 23–49). London: Longman.

Bygate, M., Skehan, P., & Swain, M. (2001). *Researching pedagogic tasks: Second language learning, teaching and testing.* London: Longman.

Candlin, C. (1987). Towards task-based language learning. In C. Candlin & D. Murphy (Eds.), *Language learning tasks* (pp. 5–22). London: Prentice Hall.

Carroll, J. B. (1993). *Human cognitive abilities.* New York: Cambridge University Press.

Cheng, P. W. (1985). Restructuring versus automaticity: Alternative accounts of skill acquisition. *Psychological Review, 92*(3), 414–423.

Doughty, C., & Williams, J. (1998). Issues and terminology. In C. Doughty & J. Williams (Eds.), *Focus on form in classroom second language acquisition* (pp. 197–262). New York: Cambridge University Press.

Dry, H. (1983). The movement of narrative time. *Journal of Literary Semantics, 12*, 19–53.

Duff, P. (1986). Another look at interlanguage talk: Talking task to task. In R. Day (Ed.), *Talking to learn* (pp. 147–181). Rowley, MA: Newbury House.

Ellis, R. (1987). Interlanguage variability in narrative discourse: Style shifting in the use of the past tense. *Studies in Second Language Acquisition, 9*, 12–20.

Ellis, R. (2001). Non-reciprocal tasks, comprehension and second language acquisition. In M. Bygate, P. Skehan, & M. Swain (Eds.), *Researching pedagogic tasks: Second language learning, teaching and testing* (pp. 49–75). London: Longman.

Foster, P. (2001). Rules and routines: A consideration of their role in the task-based language production of native and non-native speakers. In M. Bygate, P. Skehan, & M. Swain (Eds.), *Researching pedagogic tasks: Second language learning, teaching and testing* (pp. 75–95). London: Longman.

Foster, P. (2009). Lexical diversity and native-like selection: The bonus of studying abroad. In H. Daller, D. Malvern, P. Meara, J. Milton, B. Richards, & J. Treffers-Daller (Eds.), *Vocabulary studies in first and second language acquisition: The interface between theory and application* (pp. 91–106). Houndsmill, UK: Palgrave-Macmillan.

Foster, P., & Skehan, P. (1996). The influence of planning and task type on second language performances. *Studies in Second Language Acquisition, 18*, 299–323.

Foster, P., & Skehan, P. (1999). The influence of source of planning and focus of planning on task-based performance. *Language Teaching Research, 3*(3), 215–247.

Foster, P., & Tavakoli, P. (2009). Lexical diversity and lexical selection: A comparison of native and non-native speaker performance. *Language Learning, 59*(4), 866–896.

Foster, P., Tonkyn, A., & Wigglesworth, G. (2000). Measuring spoken language. *Applied Linguistics, 21*(3), 354–375.

Givón, T. (1989). *Mind, code and context: Essays in pragmatics*. Hillsdale, NJ: Erlbaum.

Givón, T. (1985). Function, structure and language acquisition. In D. Slobin (Ed.), *The crosslinguistic study of language acquisition* (Vol. 1, pp. 1008–1025). Hillsdale, NJ: Erlbaum.

Harris, C., & Bates, E. (2002). Clausal background and pronominal reference: A functionalist approach to c-command. *Language and Cognitive Processes, 17*(3), 237–269.

Heaton, J. B. (1966). *Composition through pictures*. Essex: Longman.

Hooper, P. J., & Thompson, S. (1980). Transitivity in grammar and discourse. *Language, 56*, 251–299.

Iwashita, N., McNamara, T., & Elder, C. (2001). Can we predict task difficulty in an oral proficiency test? Exploring the potential of an information-processing approach to task design. *Language Learning, 51*(3), 401–436.

Jones, L. (1980). *Notions in English*. Cambridge: University Press.

Levelt, W. (1989). *Speaking: From intention to articulation*. Cambridge, MA: MIT Press.

Levelt, W. (1993). Language use in normal speakers and its order. In G. Blanken, H. Dittman, H. Grimm, J. Marshal, & C. Wallesch (Eds.), *Linguistic disorders and pathologies* (pp. 1–15). Berlin: de Gruyter.

Long, M. H. (1983). Does second language instruction make a difference? A review of the research. *TESOL Quarterly, 17*, 359–382.

Long, M. H. (1985). A role for instruction in second language acquisition: Task-based language teaching. In K. Hyltenstam & M. Pienemann (Eds.), *Modelling and assessing second language acquisition* (pp. 77–99). Clevedon, UK: Multilingual Matters.

Long, M. H., & Robinson, P. (1998). Focus on form: Theory, research, and practice. In C. Doughty & J. Williams (Eds.), *Focus on form in classroom second language acquisition* (pp. 14–41). New York: Cambridge University Press.

Lynch, T., & Maclean, J. (2001). "A case of exercising": Effects of immediate task repetition on learners' performance. In M. Bygate, P. Skehan, & M. Swain (Eds.), *Researching pedagogic tasks: Second language learning, teaching and testing* (pp. 141–63). London: Longman.

Malvern, D., & Richards, B. (2002). Investigating accommodation in language proficiency interviews using a new measure of lexical diversity. *Language Testing, 19*(1), 85–104.

Matthiessen, C., & Thompson, S. (1988). The structure of discourse and subordination. In J. Haiman & S. Thompson (Eds.), *Clause combining in grammar and discourse* (pp. 95–120). Philadelphia: Benjamins.

Mehnert, U. (1998). The effects of different length of time for planning on second language performance. *Studies in Second Language Acquisition, 20*(1), 83–108.

Navon, D. (1989). The importance of being visible: On the role of attention in a mind viewed as an anarchic intelligence system. *European Journal of Cognitive Psychology, 1*, 191–238.

Neumann, O. (1996). Theories of attention. In O. Neumann & A. Sanders (Eds.), *Handbook of perception and action: Vol. 3. Attention* (pp. 389–446). San Diego: Academic Press.

Nunan, D. (1989). *Designing tasks for the communicative classroom*. Cambridge: Cambridge University Press.

Pallant, J. (2001). *SPSS survival manual*. Buckingham, UK: Open University Press.

Pawley, A., & Syder, F. (1983). Two puzzles for linguistic theory: Nativelike selection and nativelike fluency. In J. Richards & R. Schmidt (Eds.), *Language and cmmunication.* London: Longman.

Pawley, A., & Syder, F. (2000). The one clause at a time hypothesis. In H. Riggenbach (Ed.), *Perspectives on fluency* (pp. 163–191). Ann Arbor: University of Michigan Press.

Pica, T. (1994). Research on negotiation: What does it reveal about second language learning conditions, processes, and outcomes? *Language Learning, 44*, 493–527.

Pica, T. (1996). The essential role of negotiation in the communicative classroom. *JALT Journal, 78*, 241–268.

Plough, I., & Gass, S. (1993). Interlocutor and task familiarity: Effects on interactional structure. In G. Crookes & S. Gass (Eds.), *Tasks and language learning* (pp. 35–56). Clevedon, UK: Multilingual Matters.

Polanyi-Bowditch, L. (1976). Why the whats are when: Mutually contextualizing realms of narrative. *Berkeley Linguistics Society, 2*, 59–77.

Reinhart, T. (1984). Principles of gestalt perception in the temporal organization of narrative texts. *Linguistics, 22*, 779–809.

Robinson, P. (2000). Task complexity, task difficulty, and task production: Exploring interactions in a componential framework. *Applied Linguistics, 22*(1), 27–55.

Robinson, P. (2001). Task complexity, cognitive resources, and syllabus design: A triadic framework for examining task influences on SLA. In P. Robinson (Ed.), *Cognition and second language instruction* (pp. 287–318). Cambridge: Cambridge University Press.

Robinson, P. (2003). The cognitive hypothesis, task design and adult task-based language learning. *Second Language Studies, 21*(2), 45–107.

Robinson, P. (2005). Cognitive complexity and task sequencing: Studies in a componential framework for second language task design. *International Review of Applied Linguistics in Language Teaching (IRAL), 43*(1), 45–107.

Samuda, V. (2001). Guiding relationships between form and meaning during task performance: The role of the teacher. In M. Bygate, P. Skehan, & M. Swain (Eds.), *Researching pedagogic tasks: Second language learning, teaching and testing* (pp. 119–141). London: Longman.

Schneider, W., & Shiffrin, R. (1977). Controlled and automatic human information processing. I: Detection, search and attention. *Psychological Review, 84*, 1–66.

Sheen, R. (2003). Focus on form: A myth in the making. *ELT, 57*(3), 225–233.

Shiffrin, R., & Schneider, W. (1977). Controlled and automatic human information processing II: Perceptual learning, automatic attending, and a general theory. *Psychological Review, 84*(2), 127–190.

Skehan, P. (1998). *A cognitive approach to language learning.* Oxford: Oxford University Press.

Skehan, P., & Foster, P. (1997). Task type and task processing conditions as influences on foreign language performance. *Language Teaching Research, 1*(3), 185–212.

Skehan, P., & Foster, P. (1999). The influence of task structure and processing conditions on narrative retellings. *Language Learning, 49*(1), 93–120.

Swain, M. (1991). French immersion and its offshoots: Getting two for one. In B. Freed (Ed.), *Foreign language acquisition: Research and the classroom* (pp. 91–103). Lexington, MA: Heath.

Swain, M. (1995). Three functions of output in second language learning. In G. Cook & B. Seidlhofer (Eds.), *Principle and practice in applied linguistics* (pp. 245–256). Oxford: Oxford University Press.

Swan, M. (2005). Legislation by hypothesis: The case of task-based instruction. *Applied Linguistics, 26*(2), 376–401.

Swan, M., & Walter, C. (1990). *New Cambridge English course: Workbook level 1.* Cambridge: Cambridge University Press.

Tabachnick, B., & Fidell, L. (1996). *Using multivariate statistics.* New York: Harper Collins.

Tavakoli, P., & Skehan, P. (2005). Strategic planning, task structure and performance testing. In R. Ellis (Ed.), *Planning and task performance in a second language* (pp. 239–277). Amsterdam: Benjamins.

Tomlin, R. (1984). The treatment of foreground-background information in the on-line descriptive discourse of second language learner. *Studies in Second Language Acquisition, 6*, 115–142.

VanPatten, B. (1990). Attending to content and form in the input: An experiment in consciousness. *Studies in Second Language Acquisition, 12*, 287–301.

von Stutterheim, C. (1991). Narrative and description: Temporal reference in second language acquisition. In C. A. Ferguson & T. Huebner (Eds.), *Crosscurrents in second language acquisition and linguistic theories* (pp. 385–403). Amsterdam: Benjamins.

Wigglesworth, G. (2001). Influences on performance in task-based oral assessments. In M. Bygate, P. Skehan, & M. Swain (Eds.), *Researching pedagogic tasks: Second language teaching, learning and testing* (pp. 186–210). London: Longman.

Willis, J., & Willis, D. (1996). *Challenge and change in language teaching.* London: Heinemann.

Yuan, F., & Ellis, R. (2003). The effect of pre-task planning and on-line planning on fluency, complexity, accuracy in L2 monologic oral production. *Applied Linguistics, 23*(1), 1–27.

Appendix

Tasks

Figure A1 Journey Task, Jones, 1980.

Figure A2 Picnic Task, Heaton, 1966.

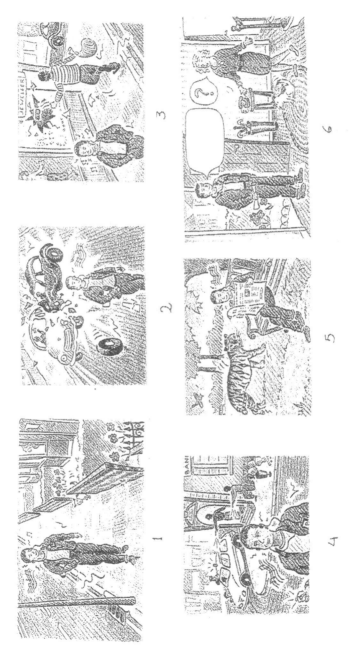

Figure A3 Walkman Task. Swain & Walter, 1990.

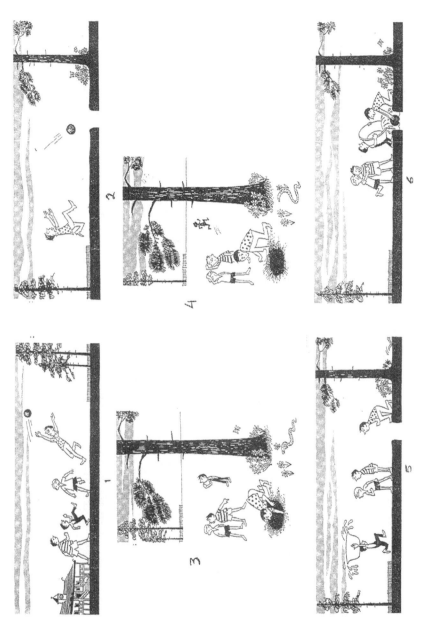

Figure A4 Football Task, Heaton, 1966.

Language Learning   ISSN 0023-8333

Creativity and Narrative Task Performance: An Exploratory Study

Ágnes Albert

Eötvös Loránd University, Budapest

Judit Kormos

Lancaster University

Methods of communicative and task-based language teaching often employ tasks that require students to use their imagination and to generate new ideas. These tasks might provide creative learners with more chance to practice and to produce more comprehensible output, which could lead to greater success in second language acquisition (SLA) (Swain, 1985). Therefore, creativity, which involves imagination, unconventionality, risk-taking, flexibility, and creating new classifications and systematizations of knowledge (Sternberg, 1985a), might be a potential factor that affects language learning outcomes. Despite its potential relevance, creativity has been a neglected individual difference variable in the field of SLA. Our study is the first attempt to examine the role of creativity in second-language oral task performance. Participants in the study were Hungarian secondary school learners of English whose creativity was measured with a standardized creativity test and who performed two versions of a narrative task. We examined the relationships among three aspects of creativity—originality, flexibility, and creative fluency—and different measures of task performance, which included the number of words and narrative clauses, subordination ratio, lexical variety, and accuracy. The findings suggest that creativity is best hypothesized as a multifaceted trait, as students scoring high on various components of creativity seemed to complete the same task in different ways. Students who invented a high number of solutions on a creativity test were found to engage in more talk; thus, in a foreign language setting, they might create more opportunities for themselves to use the language. The learners characterized by a higher level of originality tended to speak less and created more complex stories in terms of the narrative structure, but at the same time, they might deprive themselves of

We are grateful to Scott Jarvis for his advice concerning lexical diversity. Thanks are also due to the anonymous reviewers for their particularly thorough and thoughtful comments.

Correspondence concerning this article should be addressed to Judit Kormos, Department of Linguistics and English Language, Lancaster University, LA1 4YL, United Kingdom. Internet: j.kormos@lancaster.ac.uk

the beneficial effects of more output. No significant relationship among creativity and accuracy, complexity, and lexical variety was found. The magnitude of the correlations, however, indicates that creativity affects participants' output in narrative tasks only moderately. The results of the study reveal that in addition to investigating the effects of individual variables on global measures of foreign language performance, it is also possible to study their influence on specific tasks. Based on our study, we conclude that different aspects of creativity might have an effect on the amount of output students produce but not on the quality of narrative performance. Nevertheless, further research involving more participants and using different types of tasks would be necessary to be able to generalize these findings to other contexts.

Keywords oral narrative tasks; originality; flexibility; creative fluency; second language output; English

Many of the individual differences that exist among learners have been studied in an attempt to account for differential success in second language acquisition (SLA). The relevance of several cognitive, motivational, personality, and social factors has been revealed, but there is one complex phenomenon the importance of which has not been thoroughly explored to this day, and this is learner creativity. If the creative process is regarded as a rare phenomenon observable only in the exceptionally talented, its relevance for the millions of average people learning foreign languages is obviously negligible. If, however, creativity is hypothesized to be a special arrangement of those cognitive, motivational, personality, or social characteristics that are present in everyone, its effects on SLA cannot be disregarded. A number of researchers (Barkóczi & Zétényi, 1981; Cropley, 1972; Guilford, 1950; Harrington, Block, & Block, 1983; Mednick, 1962) believe that the underlying components of creativity are normally distributed in the population. Therefore creativity, which implicitly involves imagination, unconventionality, risk taking, flexibility, and creating new classifications and systematizations of knowledge (Sternberg, 1985a), might be a factor that affects SLA.

The changing methods of second language (L2) instruction, particularly the prominence of methods of communicative and task-based language teaching, which in many cases employ tasks that require students to use their imagination, provide another reason why researching this variable should become a priority. Tasks that involve the use of imagination and the generation of new ideas might provide creative learners with more chance to practice, that is, to produce more comprehensible output, which could lead to greater success in SLA (Swain, 1985). This might be even more so in a foreign language environment, in which output is mainly produced in the classroom. Support for this line of argumentation was provided by Ottó (1998), who, in a small-scale study involving Hungarian secondary school learners instructed using communicative methods, found significant positive correlations between different measures of learner creativity and students' end-of year English grades.

It is not obvious, however, whether the effects of an individual variable like creativity can be observed only in general outcomes of second or foreign language learning, such as achievement as reflected by English grades (Ottó, 1998) and presumably proficiency test results, or whether these effects can also be detected in much smaller and more specific units of learner performance, such as tasks (see Dewaele & Furnham, 1999, on the relationship between extraversion and oral task performance). The research presented in this article aimed to investigate the effects of learner creativity on several output variables of one particular task type, the oral narrative task, while controlling for the differences in the participants' level of proficiency. Since oral narrative tasks generally involve storytelling based on some cue, this task type seems to provide an opportunity for learners to use their imagination; therefore, it was found particularly well suited for demonstrating the effects of creativity. The exploratory study presented in this article involved 35 Hungarian learners of English and used a correlational design. The initial assumption of the research was that creativity enhances participants' performance on the oral narrative task, resulting in both quantitatively and qualitatively superior performance on the output variables examined.

Creativity

When we are trying to define the construct of creativity, the first difficulty we encounter is that this concept covers a wide range of distinct but related phenomena: the creative performance or product, the creative person, the creative situation, the creative process, and creative potential (Brown, 1989; Lubart, 1994). Therefore, when we attempt to define this concept, one of our first tasks should be restricting the scope of our investigation and specifying the area or aspect of creativity that is to be examined. This means that for lack of space, neither theories of the creative process (see Finke, Ward, & Smith, 1992; Hayes, 1989; Wallas, 1970), nor theories for evaluating creative products (see Finke et al., 1992), will be discussed here. Similarly, although theories of personality also address the issue of creativity and evidence suggests that it might be strongly related to the Openness to Experience factor of the Big Five model of personality (McCrae, 1987), attributes of the creative personality will not be discussed here either. The present investigation will focus on creative potential, that is, the cognitive underpinnings of the creative working of the mind.

Theories of *creativity*, similarly to the wide range of issues covered by the term creativity, are numerous. Authors working within the psychodynamic (Freud, 1908/1959; Kris, 1952) and the humanistic (Csikszentmihalyi, 1988; Maslow, 1968; Rogers, 1954), as well as the sociopsychological (Amabile, 1983, 1996), approaches have put forward theories in an attempt to account for the phenomenon of creativity. Although as proponents of recent models of creativity (Amabile, 1983, 1996; Sternberg & Lubart, 1991, 1996) rightly point out, creativity is probably best hypothesized as a complex interplay of several cognitive, personality, motivational, and social factors, those proponents also state that intellectual abilities are arguably among the most important components of creativity (Lubart, 1994). Therefore, the approach chosen in this article, which concentrates purely on the cognitive factors underlying creativity, seems to be justifiable.

Guilford (1950) was among the first to put forward a list of cognitive processes involved in creativity. He believed that these processes include sensitivity to problems, creative fluency of production, ability to come up with novel ideas, flexibility of mind, synthesizing ability, analyzing ability, reorganization or redefinition of organized wholes, a high degree of complexity of the conceptual structure, and evaluation. However, as Guilford (1959) subsequently developed a comprehensive model of human intellect, he started to focus on divergent thinking, the ability to produce many different ideas in response to a problem, as the prime cognitive component of creativity. He suggested that divergent thinking was an operation complementary to convergent thinking, the ability to find the correct solution to a problem (the cognitive process that he believed is tapped by the majority of intelligence tests). Divergent thinking is hypothesized to have four relatively independent facets: creative fluency, the ability to produce a large number of ideas; flexibility, the ability to produce a wide variety of ideas; originality, the ability to produce unusual ideas; and elaboration, the ability to develop or embellish ideas and to produce many details (Baer, 1993).

Today intellectual abilities considered to be relevant for creativity are usually grouped into two large categories: basic-level and high-level creativity-relevant abilities (Lubart, 1994). Basic-level creative abilities consist of two types: the above-described divergent thinking and different insight abilities comprising the capacities to notice relevant new information, to compare disparate information, to find relevant connections, and to combine information in a problem-relevant fashion. High-level abilities include problem finding, problem definition or redefinition, choosing a useful problem presentation, selecting an appropriate problem-solving strategy, and evaluating the generated possibilities effectively. It is interesting to note that some of these processes are hypothesized to be related to language aptitude within the Cognitive Ability for Novelty in Language Acquisition–Foreign (CANAL-F) theory, a framework of language aptitude recently developed by Grigorenko, Sternberg, and Ehrman (2000).

The two lists of creativity-relevant intellectual abilities have a number of common factors, which draws attention to the fact that over the course of almost 50 years, one thing certainly has not changed: Researchers believe that creativity rests on the same cognitive foundations as other intellectual abilities, such as intelligence. As a result, the cognitive abilities that form the basis of creativity are usually integrated into comprehensive theories of intellect (Carroll, 1993; Guilford, 1967; Sternberg, 1985b). Although theories of intellect have relevance for theories of creativity and provide a general frame of interpretation of the phenomenon, the drawback of this approach is that creativity becomes difficult to distinguish from other intellectual abilities in terms of purely cognitive factors.

Current factor-analytic research suggests, however, that factors of creativity-relevant intellectual abilities tend to load on one common higher-order factor called idea production, which provides empirical evidence of the autonomous existence of this ability. Carroll (1993), having reviewed and rean-alyzed 121 data sets, found nine basic factors to be relevant for idea production, which he believes is a basic human characteristic: ideational fluency, naming facility, associational fluency, expressional fluency, word fluency, sensitivity to problems, originality/creativity, figural fluency, and figural flexibility. In the term *idea production*, the notion of *idea* is to be taken in the broadest possible sense: It can be any verbal proposition, but it may also be a gesture, a drawing, or a musical phrase. *Production* is meant as a process distinct from recogni-tion, identification, selection, or comparison. Out of the nine factors, eight are primarily concerned with the speed of idea production and are differentiated on the basis of the type of the idea produced, whereas originality/creativity seems to determine the quality or level of idea production. Based on Carroll's findings, idea production is usually measured by tasks that prompt examinees to quickly think of a series of responses. Although this is true for all the tasks used to measure the nine factors, there is a special requirement when our aim is to measure originality/creativity. In that case the task itself needs to be diffi-cult or challenging in order to urge respondents to go beyond the obvious and common-place answers.

This factor-analytic investigation led to the formulation of Carroll's (1993) three-stratum theory of cognitive abilities, in which the concept of idea pro-duction is labeled *general retrieval ability*, the ability which is "involved in any task or performance that requires the ready retrieval of concepts or items from long-term memory" (p. 625). Since it is a fundamental characteristic of factor analysis that the input data determine the output, that is, the tests and tasks analyzed and the scoring procedures employed necessarily influence and possibly constrain the outcome, further research is needed to clarify the structure of the domain of general retrieval ability. This could probably be accomplished by devising more appropriate and highly reliable measurement procedures. It is also interesting that although Guilford's (1959) structure of intellect model is not compatible with the results of the exploratory factor analysis on which the three-stratum theory is founded, still the domain of general retrieval ability "is chiefly (but not entirely) concerned with Guilford's divergent production operation" (Carroll, 1993, p. 638).

When one is trying to assess a person's creative potentials, usually two different approaches are taken. One option is measuring several noncognitive aspects of creativity, such as personality and motivation, in addition to intellectual processes and intellectual style, as was done by Sternberg and Lubart (1991), who tried to establish individual creativity in this way. Although this approach is more in line with current constructs of creativity, it is not feasible in research designs in which creativity needs to be operationalized as one single variable. The other option, therefore, is to try to assess divergent thinking, the intellectual ability that is thought to be most characteristic of the creative process (Guilford, 1967; Torrance, 1962). Although tests of divergent thinking have been criticized on many counts (Jordan, 1975; Kogan & Pankove, 1974), because of their reported validity and reliability (Cropley, 1972; Harrington et al., 1983) and their relative ease of use, they are still widely applied as indicators of individual creativity in research on individual variables (Ghadirian, Gregoire, & Kosmidis, 2000–2001; Jung, 2000–2001; Russ & Seja-Kaugars, 2000–2001). As McCrae (1987) pointed out, "although tests like Word Fluency certainly have limited face validity as measures of creativity, their ability to identify creative individuals is an empirical matter, and in fact they are reasonably successful in this" (p. 1258).

The above-described difficulties might partly be held accountable for the fact that SLA research on individual learner variables has failed to investigate the effects of creativity, even though the influence of other cognitive variables such as intelligence, language aptitude, and different learning and thinking styles has been researched widely (for reviews see Gardner & MacIntyre, 1992, 1993; Oxford & Ehrman, 1993; Skehan, 1989, 1991). We have made an attempt at bridging this gap by carrying out research on the effects of learner creativity on the performance of oral narrative tasks. For our purposes, creativity has been defined as a person's ability to come up with a large number of novel and statistically rare solutions on a given task and has been operationalized as the total score achieved on a standardized creativity test (Barkóczi & Zétényi, 1981).

Tasks in SLA Research

During the past 2 decades foreign language teaching has become more and more characterized by the communicative approach to language teaching, whose main objective is "to develop the learner's ability to take part in spontaneous and meaningful communication in different contexts, with different people, on different topics, for different purposes" (Celce-Murcia, Dörnyei, & Thurrell, 1997, p. 149). A relatively new approach within this framework is task-based instruction, which calls for language teaching to be organized around different tasks (Long & Crookes, 1993; Pica, Kanagy, & Falodun, 1993; Plough & Gass, 1993; Skehan, 1998; Willis & Willis, 1996). Consequently, tasks—more specifically their components, characteristics, different types, and implementation conditions—have been the focus of much recent research. Although by placing emphasis on different aspects of tasks, various authors (e.g., Bygate, 1999; Candlin, 1987; Long, 1985; Nunan, 1989) suggest slightly different definitions, in this article Skehan's (1996) comprehensive definition is adopted; it states that a task is "an activity in which: meaning is primary; there is some relationship to the real world; task completion has some priority; and the assessment of task performance is in terms of task outcome" (p. 38).

The ordering of different tasks has prime importance in task-based instruction, as authors working within this framework argue that language learning and teaching should be sequenced by means of tasks; therefore, tasks form the basis of the curriculum. Several criteria have been suggested for the sequencing of tasks. It is often argued that tasks should be arranged in order of complexity (Long, 1985) or difficulty (Brown, Anderson, Shilcock, & Yule, 1984; Candlin, 1987; Skehan, 1996, 1998), although the precise meaning of these terms varies from one author to the next. In a recent article Robinson (2001) attempted to establish "theoretically motivated, empirically substantiable, and pedagogically feasible sequencing criteria" (p. 27). He distinguished three independent facets of tasks: task complexity, task difficulty, and task conditions. Task complexity, in his interpretation, is the result of various information-processing demands that the structure of the task imposes on the learners; task difficulty covers learner factors—differences between learners in their cognitive and affective resources that makes certain tasks personally difficult for them; and task conditions include participation and participant factors and the context of task performance.

Robinson (2001) argues that sequencing decisions should be solely based on task complexity, as this is a fixed and invariant feature of the task; consequently, a simple task will be less demanding than a more complex one for any given learner. Task difficulty, on the other hand, explains individual differences among learners, showing why one particular task should be more or less difficult for different learners. As differences between learners in affective variables, such as motivation, and social factors, such as group cohesion, that have been shown to contribute to differences in task performance (Dörnyei & Kormos, 2000) are variable and temporal, they should form the basis of on-line methodological decisions, according to Robinson. The effects of more stable cognitive abilities such as intelligence, aptitude, or even creativity could be taken into consideration as well, if conclusive results were available about the way they affect performance on tasks. Although Robinson's framework is primarily motivated by the aim to offer guidance regarding sequencing decisions, it also draws attention to the importance of individual variables when implementing tasks. It is quite plausible that individual differences will exert their influence on performance not only in the case of less or more complex tasks, but in the case of different task types as well.

Narrative tasks are a well-established and frequently researched task type (Bygate, 1999; Foster & Skehan, 1996; Robinson, 1995; Skehan & Foster, 1997, 1999). They usually involve the creation of a story in response to some kind of stimulus: a picture strip or a short film. As in most of the cases the stimuli given are purely visual and their verbal representations depend on the storyteller to a great extent, this task type seems ideal as far as the manifestation of creativity is concerned. The language output generated on oral narrative tasks is usually examined in terms of its complexity, accuracy, and fluency (Crookes, 1989; Foster & Skehan, 1996; Skehan & Foster, 1997, 1999). Complexity in this sense is related to the syntactic structure of language; accuracy reflects how well-controlled and target-like the forms are; and fluency gives an indication of the learner's ability to cope with real-time communication. When comparing performance on oral narrative tasks to personal-information exchange and decision-making tasks, Foster and Skehan (1996) found that language output was the most complex and least accurate in narratives. In a more recent study Skehan and Foster (1999) reported more fluent performance on tasks having clear inherent structure. Bygate (1999) argued that different task types urge learners to use a set of specific linguistic features and described oral narrative tasks as more complex both syntactically and lexically in comparison with argumentative tasks. Robinson (1995), who studied oral narrative tasks of varying cognitive complexity, found that lexical variety (measured by the type-token ratio) and accuracy (measured by the number of error-free communication units) increase in cognitively more complex tasks.

The Effect of Individual Variables on Task Performance

Only a few studies have examined the effect of individual variables on the performance of communicative tasks. MacIntyre and Gardner (1994) studied the influence of anxiety on the quality of self-descriptions in L2. Their results indicated that anxious L2 learners produced shorter self-descriptions, which were also judged to be less fluent and less complex. Dewaele and Furnham (2000) investigated how fluency, accuracy, and formality of vocabulary use were affected by extraversion. In their study extraverts were found to be more fluent and to use a greater number of colloquial words than introverts. Dörnyei and Kormos (2000) analyzed how various components of motivation affected the quantity of talk students produced in an oral argumentation task. Students with a positive attitude toward the course and toward the task to be performed spoke considerably more than those who had negative attitudes. Self-confidence and willingness to communicate in L2 were also positively related to the quantity of talk. In a recent study Kormos and Dörnyei (in press) found that students with positive attitude toward the task to be performed produced more accurate language than those whose attitude was negative. They also established a negative relationship between anxiety and lexical richness.

The Relevance of Creativity for Learner Performance on Tasks

Having reviewed the literature on creativity and tasks separately, we should now turn our attention to possible points of interaction between the two. The relevance of creativity to learner performance on tasks can be examined on two levels. One of them is the level of specific cognitive mechanisms that are believed to contribute to creativity. Since the instrument used as a test of creativity in the study presented in this article aimed at identifying divergent thinkers, why we feel that divergent thinking might be advantageous for foreign language learners when tackling language tasks should be pointed out. The other level is the wider context of language-teaching methodology, more specifically, the use of communicative methods and more recently task-based instruction; in these approaches the use of drills is discouraged, and emphasis is placed on conveying meaning. Despite the fact that these two levels can be considered separate theoretically, we are aware that they interact to a great extent in practice: In most cases language learning is mediated by some kind of methodology.

On the basis of our literature review, we hypothesized that since creativity is usually manifested in production, that is, in creative products, its effects would probably be more easily detectable in output as opposed to comprehension. We believe that there are a number of reasons that language tasks, especially open-ended ones like narrative tasks, for which there is no correct solution, but a large number of solutions are possible, could be better suited than, for example, drills for creative foreign language learners. Since creative learners are characterized by greater fluency—that is, they provide a larger number of solutions in a given amount of time (Baer, 1993)—they might be able to talk more during the tasks. As has been suggested by Swain (1985), producing a greater amount of comprehensible output has a beneficial effect on language acquisition. Flexibility, the second facet of creativity measured by divergent-thinking tests, which reflects the ability to produce a wide variety of ideas (Baer, 1993), might be manifested directly in the way language is used by the learners: If their language competence is sufficient, they might in fact use a wider range of vocabulary items in order to express their wide range of ideas. Similarly, originality, the ability to produce unusual ideas (Baer, 1993), might also prompt learners to employ a wide range of vocabulary in an attempt to give an account of the interesting ideas they have in mind. Although the above-mentioned qualities of creative people might be advantageous in any language task, we feel that narrative tasks, which obviously rely on learners' imagination, might intensify the effect of creativity on language performance. Therefore, despite the fact that the imaginativeness or creativity of the stories themselves cannot be measured, we believed that narrative tasks would be suitable for conducting exploratory research on the effects of creativity on output.

Method

The study reported in this article constitutes part of a larger longitudinal research project the primary aim of which was to investigate task-based learning in five Hungarian secondary school groups (see also Bygate, 1999; Dörnyei, 2002; Dörnyei & Kormos, 2000; Németh & Kormos, 2001). The data collection phase of the project was conducted jointly with staff members from the University of Leeds and Eötvös Loránd University.

Research Questions and Hypotheses

The aim of our study was to investigate the effect of creativity on task performance in oral narrative tasks. Our hypotheses were the following:

1. All the components of creativity have an effect on narrative task performance.
2. Among the measures of task performance, the quantity of talk produced, lexical variety, and narrative structure are influenced by creativity.
3. Grammatical complexity and accuracy are not affected by measures of creativity.

Participants

A total of 67 students from five classes in two different secondary schools participated in the project. Since the data collection took place on four different occasions, we have full data for only 35 participants (because of illnesses and other reasons for absences). The students were 15–16 years old; 20 of them were female and 15 male. The two schools that the students attended were of the same type (secondary grammar school); they provided general instruction and prepared students for further studies in higher education. The participants were all judged to be intermediate speakers of English by their classroom teachers.

Procedure

At the beginning of the project a C-test was administered to all the participants to measure their global language proficiency. The C-test used was validated for Hungarian learners of English (Dörnyei & Katona, 1992). Students completed two alternative versions of an oral narrative task with an interval of 2 months between the tasks (see the Appendix for an example of the tasks). After the completion of the second of the two tasks, students were asked to fill in a creativity test in Hungarian, which was developed by Barkóczi and Klein (cited in Barkóczi & Zétényi, 1981) and was standardized for the Hungarian adult population.

Creativity Test

The standardized creativity test (Barkóczi & Zétényi, 1981) used in the study consisted of five parts, but as the first task was meant to serve as a warm-up, only the remaining four tasks were scored. There was a time limit set for each task, and the participants were not allowed to go back to previous tasks once they had moved on to subsequent tasks. In order to ensure that this rule was strictly followed, one of the researchers was always present while students filled in the test. The warm-up task was a sentence completion exercise, in which respondents were given 3 min to finish a number of sentences. The first two scored tasks required verbal responses from the participants. In the task called *unusual uses*, respondents had to invent unusual uses for everyday objects such as a brick. In the *distant associations* task (in a similar fashion to Mednick's [1962] Remote Associates Test), students had to create associations on the basis of the common characteristics of two unrelated words (e.g., given the words *cannon* and *sky*, think of a word related to both of them but in different ways: for example, *thunder*). The last two scored tasks were drawing tasks (based on the Torrance Tests of Creative Thinking; Torrance, 1966). Respondents were asked to draw as many pictures as they could, starting out from the shape of a circle, and to finish abstract shapes in a creative manner. The four tasks lasted 5, 6, 8, and 10 min, respectively.

Tasks

Two very similar versions of an oral narrative task were used in this research and involved inventing a story on the basis of a picture. The task was designed by a group of experienced teachers and researchers for the purposes of this research. In order to ensure the feasibility and the appropriate level of difficulty of the task, the comments of the teachers who taught the students participating in the study were also taken into consideration. Students performed the task in the framework of their regular English classes. The task was presented to the students by their teachers. Students worked in pairs while performing the task; one played the role of the speaker and the other the role of the audience. In each case the members of the pair received different pictures. The students' task was to invent a short story based on the picture and tell it to their partner after 5 min of individual planning time. The 5-min planning time was meant to give students an opportunity to plan the content of their narratives. The planning time was standardized for all the groups. Although the instructions for the task said that students could tell a true story as well, all the participants invented their own stories, and none chose this option. While one of the students was planning the story, the other was trying to guess what his or her partner was going to say and predict what words he or she would use. Once the student told the story, the two students discussed the guesses. Then they reversed roles. This procedure was repeated with a 2-month interval using the same task with different pictures.

Analysis

Measures of Creativity

The standardized creativity test was scored in accordance with the process specified by Barkóczi and Zétényi (1981). Each task of the test was scored for three of the four measures of creativity as defined by Baer (1993; this creativity test does not measure elaboration), and the subscores for the different tasks on each of the three measures of creativity were added together. Each of the four subsections of the test was given three scores independently: a *fluency* score, a *flexibility* score, and an *originality* score. The fluency score, which in this study will be called *creative fluency* in order to differentiate it from the temporal variable also called fluency, equaled the number of responses given, while the flexibility score reflected the number of categories the participants selected their answers from (the categories were set up in the course of the standardization procedure by Barkóczi and Zétényi [1981]). The originality score was assigned on the basis of a list containing an index calculated from the statistical frequency of the given response (set up in the course of the standardization procedure by Barkóczi and Zétényi [1981]). Originality scores on different items varied from 0.01 to 0.99 points, whereas flexibility and creative fluency scores for each response were worth 1 point. The *total creativity* score was calculated by adding up all the creative fluency, flexibility, and originality scores of the various subtasks. Apart from this total score, different subscores were also calculated: *total creative fluency*, the sum of the four creative fluency subscores; total flexibility, the sum of the four flexibility subscores; and *total originality*, the sum of the four originality subscores. It is easy to demonstrate that in this scoring system, the creative fluency score (more precisely, the number of responses the participant produces) influences both the total originality and the total flexibility scores significantly. The high correlations between the fluency, originality, and flexibility subscores are the reason that some authors (e.g., Hargreaves & Bolton, 1972) have argued for dropping the originality and flexibility scores altogether, since in this form they provide little information in addition to the fluency score. We also believe that this scoring system is biased, since, for example, if a participant produces two highly original ideas worth the maximum score 0.99 points each, his total originality score will be 1.98 points for the given task. If, however, another student produces five statistically more common responses worth 0.50 point each, his or her originality score will be higher (2.5 points) than that of his or her less fluent peer, and in this way a misleading picture is presented about the two students' true originality. Since a similar scoring method is applied for calculating the flexibility scores (each new category is rewarded with 1 point without considering the total number of responses), they can be said to be affected by creative fluency to a great extent as well. For this reason, the establishment of creative fluency–free scores was very important, as these could provide information about other facets of the participants' creativity, regardless of the number of responses they produced. In order to accomplish this, *relative flexibility* (the ratio of total flexibility to total creative fluency) and average originality (the ratio of total originality to total creative fluency) were also calculated, in line with the procedure specified in the test (Barkóczi & Zétényi, 1981). In this way, the total creative fluency score can be used to measure creative fluency, the relative flexibility score to measure flexibility, and the average originality score to measure originality, as defined above.

Measures of Task Performance
Students' performance on the narrative tasks was transcribed by trained research assistants, and the transcripts were checked by the researchers. The two texts generated by the students were examined separately, but their measures were added up. The reason for using two texts was to reduce elements of chance, such as the lack of motivation or dislike for a certain topic. Table 1 summarizes the variables used in the study.

The quantity of talk students produced was measured by the total number of words (see also Dewaele, 2000; Dewaele & Pavlenko, 2003; Dörnyei & Kormos, 2000). In order to assess lexical diversity, we used Malvern and Richards's (1997) D-formula. This formula is based on a widely used measure of lexical variety (see, e.g., Robinson, 1995, 2001, in task-based research), the type-token ratio (TTR), which is the total number of different words (types) divided by the total number of words (tokens) produced. The problem with the TTR, however, is that it depends on the sample size, that is, on the number of words spoken by the participants. Richards (1987) found that the "type-token ratio falls rapidly as the number of tokens increases" (p. 205). In a recent study Jarvis (2002) argued that two formulas based on the TTR—Dugast's (1980) Uber U formula and Malvern and Richards's (1997) D-formula—can be used to measure lexical richness in L2 texts in a reliable way. Both measures should, however, be used with a curve-fitting approach. Because software (Vocabulary Diversity [VOCD]; McKee, Malvern, & Richards, 2000) is available only for the D-formula, we applied this formula to establish a measure of lexical diversity, the D-index. The calculation of the D-index is based on a mathematical probabilistic model, and the software uses random sampling of tokens in plotting the curve of the TTR against increasing token size for the text to be investigated. Malvern and Richards (1997) argue that the D-index is a valid measure of diversity because it does not depend on the length of the sample, and it uses all the words produced by the participants.

Accuracy was measured by the proportion of error-free clauses relative to the total number of clauses, and grammatical complexity with the ratio of total number of clauses to the total number of analysis of speech (AS)–units.

Table 1 Variables used in study

Measures	Description
Measures of creativity	
Average originality	Ratio of total originality score to total fluency score
Relative flexibility	Ratio of total flexibility score to total fluency score
Total creative fluency	Sum of responses given by respondent on four subtasks
Total creativity score	Sum of total originality, total flexibility, and total fluency scores
Quantitity of talk	
Number of words	Total number of words produced in English
Complexity	
Number of clauses per AS-unit	Ratio of total number of clauses to total number of AS-units
Accuracy	
Correct clauses per clauses	Ratio of grammatically correct clauses divided by the total number of clauses
Lexical variety	
D-index	Value calculated with the help of a mathematical probabilistic model that plots the curve of type-token ratio against increasing token size
Narrative structure	
Number of narrative clauses per AS-unit	Total number of temporally ordered independent clauses connected by temporal junctures (Labov, 1972) divided by total number of AS-units

These measures have been widely used in task-based research and have proven to reflect the accuracy and grammatical complexity of students' output in a reliable manner (see Bygate, 1999; Foster & Skehan, 1996; Skehan & Foster, 1997). Our variables only differed from those of Bygate (1999), Foster and Skehan (1996), and Skehan and Foster (1997) in that instead of communication (c)– and minimally terminable (T)–units as the unit of measurement, we used AS-units, which seem to be better measures in the case of spoken data produced by L2 speakers (Foster, Tonkyn, & Wigglesworth, 2000). Foster et al. (2000) defined an AS-unit as a "single speaker's utterance consisting of an independent clause or sub-clausal unit, together with any subordinate clause(s) associated with either" (p. 365). Foster et al. distinguish three levels of application for the use of AS-units in analyzing L2 speech. Level 1 analysis is applied for the full analysis of the data, when everything except untranscribable fragments of speech are included in the transcript. Level 2 analysis is used for highly interactional data, and at this level, one-word minor utterances are excluded from the analysis. Level 3 analysis is applied when only nonfragmented (i.e., complete) AS-units are analyzed. In this study Level 2 analysis was used, and one-word utterances such as "Yes," "No," "Okay," "Uh-huh," and "Right," as well as echo responses (responses that repeat certain parts or the whole of the interlocutor's previous utterance), were not included in the analysis. In the following example, the boundaries between AS-units are indicated with diagonals (/):

A woman who lived in Europe decided to go to Africa to to to uhm observe how the monkeys live there/uhm as as she arrived er there she had to to travel through the jungle/and she had a possibility to to observe the other animals how they live in in the jungle and how what they they make there/uhm and er she arrived to the farm where er she found a a lot of animal animals/and she saw the monkeys erm who live together in a in a small house uhm/—er the people who lived around this jungle er told that the monkeys er had had a had an illness. . ./

Our analysis of the narrative structure of the students' texts was based on Labov's (1972) classification of the elements of a narrative. According to Labov, the skeleton of any narrative consists of narrative clauses, which are temporally ordered independent clauses connected by temporal junctures. Therefore, the texts elicited by the tasks were analyzed for the number of narrative clauses per AS-unit. Narrative clauses reflect the events of the story; therefore, a high percentage of such clauses can be assumed to signal complex stories as far as their event structure is concerned. In the following example, narrative clauses are underlined and numbered:

In the picture we can see two old men and they are really best friends and they had a dream for 20 30 years. They they wanted to go to the Alps but they had no money. (1) But one day er one of them had a chance on gambling (2) and he won a travel to the Alps for two person. (3) So they decided to to go there (4) and they arrived they were happy + but eer they were very very old and and by climbing a mountain (5) one of them fall fall down and (6) then he died + and so the other was so sad that he liked to + so na the they dreaming their dreams for ever and the Alps.

In the case of the analysis of narrative structure and accuracy, the texts were coded by the two researchers separately, and interrater reliability was found to be high ($r = 0.93$ for narrative structure; $r = 0.95$ for accuracy). For the statistical analysis, the Statistical Package for the Social Sciences (SPSS) was used. The level of significance for this study was set at $p < 0.05$. The statistical analyses performed were Pearson correlations, in which we correlated the measures of task performance and creativity. Because, as will be shown in Table 2, there was considerable between-participants variation in the learners' language performance measures, for the correlational analyses we computed standard scores for both the independent and the dependent variables. Standardized z-scores express how many standard deviations above or below the mean a particular score is located. These standardized scores are widely used in testing research (Hatch & Lazaraton, 1991) and also in studies on individual differences (Dörnyei, 2002; Dörnyei & Kormos, 2000; Gardner, 1985). In order to control for the effect of proficiency, partial correlations using students' C-test scores were computed.

Table 2 Descriptive statistics for language performance measures

Variable	N	Minimum	Maximum	Mean	SD
Quantity of talk					
Number of words	35	46.00	1210.00	255.82	214.40
Complexity					
Number of clauses per AS-unit	35	1.06	2.25	1.32	0.25
Accuracy					
Number of correct clauses/clauses	35	0.07	0.91	0.50	0.21
Lexical variety					
D-index	35	9.52	53.06	31.40	14.19
Narrative structure					
Number of narrative clauses per AS-unit	35	0.08	0.73	0.34	0.16

Results

Table 2 provides descriptive statistics for the language performance measures. As can be seen in the table, there is considerable difference among the participants, especially in the case of the quantity of talk produced. Students also differed greatly as regards the number of narrative clauses produced and lexical variety. Nevertheless, none of the variables showed a skewed distribution, which allowed for the use of parametric statistical procedures. The considerable between-participants variation in the case of a number of variables was the reason for using standard scores in the subsequent correlational analyses. Table 3 presents the average originality, flexibility, and total fluency scores as well as the total creativity scores for the participants. The table also indicates the values of these variables for a larger Hungarian population investigated by Barkóczi and Zétényi (1981). It can be seen that the average scores were somewhat higher for all of the variables in our high school population than in the national sample. This tendency is especially striking for the total fluency and total creativity scores, where the national average was near the minimum value in our sample. This can probably be explained by the fact that our participants attended grammar school, whereas the national population also includes students from vocational and vocational secondary schools.

The results of the correlational analyses are summarized in Table 4. The analyses indicate that two components of creativity are associated with some measures of task performance: (a) originality, that is, the average number of original solutions students produced on the creativity test, and (b) creative fluency, that is, the total number of solutions participants gave on the creativity test. No significant correlations were found between task-related variables and flexibility and the total creativity score.

Table 3 Descriptive statistics for the creativity measures

Variable	N	Minimum	Maximum	Mean	SD	Hungarian population mean (N-1,089) (Barkóczi &) (Zétényi, 1981)
Relative flexibility	35	0.46	0.93	0.77	0.09	0.73
Average originality	35	0.27	0.63	0.50	0.07	0.44
Total creative fluency	35	34	75	50.25	11.13	36.80
Total creativity	35	81.46	157.34	113.27	21.99	80.36

Table 4 Correlational analysis of the relationship between task performance and creativity

Measures of task performance	Relative flexibility	Average originality	Total creative fluency	Total creativity
Quantity of talk				
Number of words	−0.31	−0.34*	0.33*	0.22
Complexity				
Number of clauses per AS-unit	−0.08	−0.11	−0.07	−0.11
Accuracy				
Correct clauses/clauses	−0.21	−0.22	−0.01	−0.11
Lexical variety				
D-index	−0.19	−0.25	0.04	−0.05
Narrative structure				
Number of narrative clauses per AS-unit	0.29	0.34*	0.02	0.15

Note. C-test scores were partialed out of the correlations. $^*p < 0.05$.

A modest effect of originality can be seen in the case of measures of quantity of talk. The number of words ($r = -.34$; $p < 0.03$) is negatively correlated with the average originality score of students. In other words, students who produced a high number of original ideas on the creativity test produced short stretches of talk. A weak, but significant, positive correlation was also found between creative fluency and the number of words ($r = .33$; $p < 0.03$). Lexical variety, accuracy, and complexity did not correlate with any of the measures of creativity. The discourse complexity of the narrative produced was also found to be affected by originality, as the number of narrative clauses per AS-unit correlated positively with the average originality score ($r = .34$; $p < 0.04$).

Discussion

These findings indicate that Hypothesis 1, namely, that all the components of creativity have an effect on narrative task performance, is only partially supported, as flexibility was not found to influence students' output. The results also lend only partial support to Hypothesis 2, that quantity of talk produced, lexical variety, and narrative structure are affected by originality and creative fluency. Hypothesis 3, that grammatical complexity and accuracy are not influenced by creativity, was confirmed.

In general, we can conclude that the correlations between measures of creativity and narrative task performance are not very high; approximately 10–15% of the variance in linguistic measures is related to creative fluency and originality. This shows that these components of creativity have a moderate effect on the quantity of talk and narrative structure. It is also possible that most of the variance in task performance among students is caused by motivation (Dörnyei, 2002), personality variables such as extraversion (Dewaele & Furnham, 2000), anxiety (MacIntyre & Gardner, 1994), and situational factors such as the interlocutor (Dörnyei, 2002), and that among these many factors, creativity contributes to the quality of task performance only to a limited extent.

The results support theories of creativity that argue that creativity is not a unitary trait but consists of several independent components. Among these components, creative fluency, that is, the ability to invent a high number of solutions in a task, seems to be related only to the quantity of talk. The sum of the various components (total creativity) did not influence linguistic measures in this study. It seems that from the point of view of L2 speech production, it is rather originality, in other words, the quality of creative ideas, that matters. The finding that students who produce a high number of original solutions talk less is probably related to the fact that coming up with unusual solutions requires a long period of thinking time and results in a low number of solutions in general. In the narrative task used in this study, this manifested itself in that "original" students produced less speech, but what they said had a complex discourse structure. In other words, the results also indicate that the complexity of narrative structure is influenced by originality, as the participants in the project who invented a high number of solutions in a cognitive task produced a high number of narrative clauses per AS-unit. Narrative clauses are assumed to reflect the events of the story (Labov, 1972); therefore, it can be stated that students who were more original produced stories with a higher number of events than their less original counterparts.

The accuracy of task performance was not expected to be influenced by creativity, as other individual variables such as extraversion have been found not to be related to this measure (Dewaele, 2000). We did not expect a relationship between complexity and creativity either, as we hypothesized that grammatical complexity is mainly determined by proficiency, even though in certain conditions some individual characteristics such as extra-version were found to affect the mean length of utterance (Dewaele, 2000).

The unexpected result of the study was that creativity did not correlate with the D-index, which is one of the most reliable measures of lexical diversity (see, e.g., Jarvis, 2002; Malvern & Richards, 1997). It seems that in our sample, participants' ability to come up with a wide variety of ideas in their native language was not influenced by their ability to use a large array of words in a narrative task in a foreign language. Lexical variety might also be a function of language proficiency (for a review, see Reid, 2000) and might rather be related to some other individual variables such as motivation (Kormos & Dörnyei, in press) and extraversion (Dewaele & Furnham, 1999).

These findings complement those of the series of studies conducted by Ehrman and her colleagues (Ehrman, 1996; Ehrman & Oxford, 1995; Grigorenko et al., 2000), who claim that the ability to cope with novelty is an important characteristic that affects the success of language learning. Their line of argumentation can be extended, and on the basis of our results, we can argue that the ability to produce original, that is, novel, ideas in general does moderately affect how students perform in a particular language learning task. The moderate size of the effect found in our study can be attributed to the small sample size and to the fact that only one very specific task was used for the purposes of our study.

Conclusion

The findings of our research show that differences in creativity can account for certain differences in learners' performance on oral narrative tasks. The most important effect of creativity manifests itself in productivity. The study also suggests that creativity is best hypothesized as a multifaceted trait, as students scoring high on various components of creativity seemed to complete the same task in different ways. Students who invented a high number of solutions on a creativity test were found to engage in more talk; thus, in a foreign language setting, they might create more opportunities for themselves to use the language. The learners characterized by a higher level of originality tended to speak less and created more complex stories in terms of the narrative structure, but at the same time, they might deprive themselves of the beneficial effects of more output. These results clearly indicate that besides investigating the effects of individual variables on global measures of foreign language performance, it is also possible to study their influence on specific tasks. Gathering data at this level would be desirable, because information gained about the interplay of individual differences and various aspects of task performance could contribute to pedagogical decisions during task implementation and could help the selection of language teaching and testing tasks.

It has to be pointed out, however, that in the present study, aspects of creativity were found to account only for 10–15% of the variance in the students' performance. The weak correlations might be due to the small number of participants or to the more important effect of other situational, social, and individual factors; therefore, a follow-up study with a higher number of participants would be necessary to establish with more certainty how important the role of creativity is in task performance. In addition, as one of the reviewers of this article pointed out, the relatively long planning time given to the participants (5 min) might have also caused creativity not to significantly influence task performance. Thus, in future research the effect of creativity could be investigated under different planning conditions. Moreover, further studies could also explore issues that seem particularly interesting in light of the present findings. Since it is intuitively appealing that communicative and task-based methods, books, and tasks require creativity, it might be worthwhile to analyze the relationship between creativity and achievement in language learning. Another possible research direction could involve examining possible interactions of the cognitive complexity of tasks and creativity as an individual variable that contributes to task difficulty. Although in Robinson's (2001) view, task complexity and difficulty are independent dimensions, it is also possible that for certain individual variables, the two might interact. In the case of such an interaction, the effects of task complexity and task difficulty could no longer be simply summed up, but they would vary depending on the level of the individual variable, such as creativity.

Revised version accepted 25 November 2003

References

Amabile, T. M. (1983). *The social psychology of creativity*. New York: Springer Verlag.

Amabile, T. M. (1996). *Creativity in context*. Boulder, CO: Westview Press.

Baer, J. (1993). *Creativity and divergent thinking: A task specific approach*. Hillsdale, NJ: Erlbaum.

Barkóczi, I., & Zétényi, T. (1981). *A kreativitás vizsgálata* [The examination of creativity]. Budapest: Országos Pedagógiai Intézet.

Brown, G., Anderson, A., Shilcock, R., & Yule, G. (1984). *Teaching talk: Strategies for production and assessment*. Cambridge, England: Cambridge University Press.

Brown, R. T. (1989). Creativity: What are we to measure? In J. A. Glover, R. R. Ronning, & C. R. Reynolds (Eds.), *Handbook of creativity* (pp. 1–32). New York: Plenum Press.

Bygate, M. (1999). Quality of language and purpose of task: Patterns of learners' language on two oral communication tasks. *Language Teaching Research, 3*, 185–214.

Candlin, C. (1987). Towards task based language teaching. In C. Candlin & D. Murphy (Eds.), *Language learning tasks* (pp. 5–22). Englewood Cliffs, NJ: Prentice Hall.

Carroll, J. B. (1993). *Human cognitive abilities: A survey of factor analytic studies.* Cambridge, England: Cambridge University Press.

Celce-Murcia, M., Dörnyei, Z., & Thurrell, S. (1997). Direct approaches in L2 instruction: A turning point in communicative language teaching? *TESOL Quarterly, 31,* 141–152.

Crookes, G. (1989). Planning and interlanguage variation. *Studies in Second Language Acquisition, 11,* 367–383.

Cropley, A. J. (1972). A five-year longitudinal study of the validity of creativity tests. *Developmental Psychology, 6,* 119–124.

Csikszentmihalyi, M. (1988). Society, culture, and person: A systems view of creativity. In R. J. Sternberg (Ed.), *The nature of creativity: Contemporary psychological perspectives* (pp. 325–339). New York: Cambridge University Press.

Dewaele, J.-M. (2000). Saisir l'insaisissable? Les mesures de longueur d'énoncés en linguistique appliquée. *International Review of Applied Linguistics, 38,* 31–47.

Dewaele, J.-M., & Furnham, A. (1999). Extraversion: The unloved variable in applied linguistic research. *Language Learning, 49,* 509–544.

Dewaele, J.-M., & Furnham, A. (2000). Personality and speech production: A pilot study of second language learners. *Personality and Individual Differences, 28,* 355–365.

Dewaele, J.-M., & Pavlenko, A. (2003). Productivity and lexical diversity in native and non-native speech: A study of cross-cultural effects. In V. Cook (Ed.), *The effects of the second language on the first* (pp. 120–141). Clevedon, England: Multilingual Matters.

Dörnyei, Z. (2002). The motivational basis of language learning tasks. In P. Robinson & P. Skehan (Eds.), *Individual differences in second language acquisition* (pp. 137–158). Amsterdam: John Benjamins.

Dörnyei, Z., & Katona, L. (1992). Validation of the C-test amongst Hungarian EFL learners. *Language Testing, 9,* 187–206.

Dörnyei, Z., & Kormos, J. (2000). The role of individual and social variables in oral task performance. *Language Teaching Research, 4,* 275–300.

Dugast, D. (1980). *La statistique lexicale.* Geneva, Switzerland: Slatkine.

Ehrman, M. E. (1996). *Understanding second language learning difficulties.* Thousand Oaks, CA: Sage.

Ehrman, M. E., & Oxford, R. L. (1995). Cognition plus: Correlates of language learning success. *Modern Language Journal, 79,* 67–89.

Finke, R. A., Ward, T. B., & Smith, S. M. (1992). *Creative cognition: Theory, research and applications.* Cambridge, MA: MIT Press.

Foster, P., & Skehan, P. (1996). The influence of planning and task type on second language performance. *Studies in Second Language Acquisition, 18,* 299–323.

Foster, P., Tonkyn, A., & Wigglesworth, G. (2000). Measuring spoken language: A unit for all reasons. *Applied Linguistics, 21,* 354–375.

Freud, S. (1959). Creative writers and daydreaming. In J. Strachey (Ed.), *Standard edition of the complete psychological works of Sigmund Freud* (Vol. 9, pp. 143–153). London: Hogarth Press. (Original work published 1908)

Gardner, R. C. (1985). *Social psychology and second language learning: The role of attitudes and motivation.* London: Edward Arnold.

Gardner, R. C., & MacIntyre, P. D. (1992). A student's contributions to second language learning: Part 1. Cognitive variables. *Language Teaching, 25,* 211–220.

Gardner, R. C., & MacIntyre, P. D. (1993). A student's contributions to second language learning: Part 2. Affective variables. *Language Teaching, 26,* 1–11.

Ghadirian, A. M., Gregoire, P., & Kosmidis, H. (2000–2001). Creativity and the evolution of psychopathologies. *Creativity Research Journal, 13,* 145–148.

Grigorenko, E. L., Sternberg, R. J., & Ehrman, M. E. (2000). A theory based approach to the measurement of foreign language learning ability: The Canal F theory and test. *Modern Language Journal, 84,* 390–405.

Guilford, J. P. (1950). Creativity. *American Psychologist, 5,* 444–454.

Guilford, J. P. (1959). Three faces of intellect. *American Psychologist, 14,* 469–479.

Guilford, J. P. (1967). *The nature of human intelligence.* New York: McGraw Hill.

Hargreaves, D. J., & Bolton, H. (1972). Selecting creativity tests for use in research. *British Journal of Psychology, 63,* 451–462.

Harrington, D. M., Block, J., & Block, J. H. (1983). Predicting creativity in preadolescence from divergent thinking in early childhood. *Journal of Personality and Social Psychology, 45,* 609–623.

Hayes, J. R. (1989). Cognitive processes in creativity. In J. A. Glover, R. R. Ronning, & C. R. Reynolds (Eds.), *Handbook of creativity* (pp. 135–145). New York: Plenum Press.

Hatch, A., & Lazaraton, E. (1991). *The research manual: Design and statistics for applied linguistics.* Boston: Heinle and Heinle.

Jarvis, S. (2002). Short texts, best-fitting curves, and new measures of lexical diversity. *Language Testing, 19,* 57–84.

Jordan, L. A. (1975). Use of canonical analysis in Cropley's "A Five Year Longitudinal Study of the Validity of Creativity Tests." *Developmental Psychology, 11,* 1–3.

Jung, D. I. (2000–2001). Transformational and transactional leadership and their effects on creativity in groups. *Creativity Research Journal, 13,* 185–195.

Kogan, N., & Pankove, E. (1974). Long term predictive validity of divergent thinking tests: Some negative evidence. *Journal of Educational Psychology, 66,* 802–810.

Kormos, J., & Dörnyei, Z. (2004). The interaction of linguistic and psychological variables in second language task performance. *Zeitschrift für Interkulturellen Fremdsprachunterricht, 9*(2), 1–19.

Kris, E. (1952). *Psychoanalytic exploration in art.* New York: International Universities Press.

Labov, W. (1972). *Language in the inner city*. Oxford: Basil Blackwell.

Long, M. (1985). A role for instruction for second language acquisition: Task based language training. In K. Hyltenstam & M. Pienemann (Eds.), *Modelling and assessing second language acquisition* (pp. 77–99). Clevedon, England: Multilingual Matters.

Long, M. H., & Crookes, G. (1993). Units of analysis in syllabus design: The case for task. In G. Crookes & S. Gass (Eds.), *Tasks in a pedagogical context: Integrating theory and practice* (pp. 9–54). Clevedon, England: Multilingual Matters.

Lubart, T. I. (1994). Creativity. In J. R. Sternberg (Ed.), *Thinking and problem solving* (pp. 289–332). San Diego, CA: Academic Press.

MacIntyre, P. D., & Gardner, R. C. (1994). The subtle effects of language anxiety on cognitive processing in the second language. *Language Learning, 44,* 283–305.

Malvern, D. D., & Richards, B. J. (1997). A new measure of lexical diversity. In A. Ryan & A. Wray (Eds.), *Evolving models of language* (pp. 58–71). Clevedon, England: Multilingual Matters.

Maslow, A. (1968). *Toward a psychology of being*. New York: Van Nostrand.

McCrae, R. R. (1987). Creativity, divergent thinking, and openness to experience. *Journal of Personality and Social Psychology, 52,* 1258–1265.

McKee, G. T., Malvern, D. E., & Richards, B. J. (2000). Measuring vocabulary diversity using dedicated software. *Journal of Literary and Linguistic Computing, 15,* 323–337.

Mednick, S. A. (1962). The associative basis of the creative process. *Psychological Review, 69,* 220–232.

Németh, N., & Kormos, J. (2001). Pragmatic aspects of task performance: The case of argumentation. *Language Teaching Research, 4,* 213–240.

Nunan, D. (1989). *Designing tasks for the communicative classroom*. Cambridge, England: Cambridge University Press.

Ottó, I. (1998). The relationship between individual differences in learner creativity and language learning success. *TESOL Quarterly, 32,* 763–773.

Oxford, R. L., & Ehrman, M. (1993). Second language research on individual differences. *Annual Review of Applied Linguistics, 13,* 188–205.

Pica, T., Kanagy, R., & Falodun, J. (1993). Choosing and using communication tasks for second language instruction and research. In G. Crookes & S. Gass (Eds.), *Tasks and language learning: Integrating theory and practice* (pp. 9–34). Clevedon, England: Multilingual Matters.

Plough, I., & Gass, S. M. (1993). Interlocutor and task familiarity: Effects on interactional structure. In G. Crookes & S. Gass (Eds.), *Tasks and language learning: Integrating theory and practice* (pp. 35–56). Clevedon, England: Multilingual Matters.

Reid, J. (2000). *Assessing vocabulary*. Cambridge, England: Cambridge University Press.

Richards, B. (1987). Type/token ratios: What do they really tell us? *Journal of Child Language, 14,* 201–209.

Robinson, P. (1995). Task complexity and second language narrative discourse. *Language Learning, 45,* 99–140.

Robinson, P. (2001). Task complexity, task difficulty, and task production: Exploring interaction in a componential framework. *Applied Linguistics, 22,* 27–57.

Rogers, C. R. (1954). Toward a theory of creativity. *ETC: A Review of General Semantics, 11,* 249–260.

Russ, S. W., & Seja-Kaugars, A. (2000–2001). Emotion in children's play and creative problem solving. *Creativity Research Journal, 13,* 211–219.

Skehan, P. (1989). *Individual differences in second language learning.* London: Edward Arnold.

Skehan, P. (1991). Individual differences in second language learning. *Studies in Second Language Acquisition, 13,* 275–298.

Skehan, P. (1996). A framework for the implementation of task based instruction. *Applied Linguistics, 17,* 38–62.

Skehan, P. (1998). *A cognitive approach to language learning.* Oxford, England: Oxford University Press.

Skehan, P., & Foster, P. (1997). Task type and task processing conditions as influences on foreign language performance. *Language Teaching Research, 1,* 185–211.

Skehan, P., & Foster, P. (1999). The influence of task structure and processing conditions on narrative retellings. *Language Learning, 49,* 93–120.

Sternberg, R. J. (1985a). Implicit theories of intelligence, creativity, and wisdom. *Journal of Personality and Social Psychology, 49,* 607–627.

Sternberg, R. J. (1985b). *Beyond IQ: A triarchic theory of human intelligence.* Cambridge, England: Cambridge University Press.

Sternberg, R. J., & Lubart, T. I. (1991). An investment theory of creativity and its development. *Human Development, 34,* 1–31.

Sternberg, R. J., & Lubart, T. I. (1996). Investing in creativity. *American Psychologist, 51,* 677–688.

Swain, M. (1985). Communicative competence: Some roles of comprehensible input and comprehensible output in its development. In S. Gass & C. Madden (Eds.), *Input in second language acquisition* (pp. 235–253). Rowley, MA: Newbury House.

Torrance, E. P. (1962). *Guiding creative talent.* Englewood Cliffs, NJ: Prentice Hall.

Torrance, E. P. (1966). *Torrance tests of creative thinking* (Research ed.). Princeton, NJ: Personnel Press.

Wallas, G. (1970). The art of thought. In P. E. Vernon (Ed.), *Creativity* (pp. 91–97). Middlesex, England: Penguin Books.

Willis, D., & Willis, J. (1996). Consciousness raising activities in the language classroom. In J. Willis & D. Willis (Eds.), *Challenge and change in language teaching* (pp. 63–76). London: Heinemann.

Appendix

The Task Used in the Study

Student A
Your task is to tell your partner a story about this picture. The picture can be the beginning, middle, or the end of your story. This can be a true story or an imaginary one. You have 5 min to think before you start.

Student B
Please have a look at your partner's picture and try to guess what kind of story he/she will tell you. Write down 4 adjectives or adverbs and 4 nouns that you think your partner will use. Please remember that you should not interrupt your partner while he/she is telling the story. After he/she has finished the story, discuss your guesses with your partner.

Adjectives/adverbs	Nouns
1.	
2.	
3.	
4.	

Language Learning   ISSN 0023-8333

The Role of Task-Induced Involvement and Learner Proficiency in L2 Vocabulary Acquisition

YouJin Kim

Georgia State University

Designing effective pedagogical tasks has been of critical interest among second-language (L2) researchers and teachers. Accordingly, several claims about how to classify pedagogic task characteristics in terms of their effectiveness in L2 learning have been made. One such example is the involvement load hypothesis (Hulstijn & Laufer, 2001), which claims that learning new words during vocabulary-focused tasks is dependent on the degree of cognitive processing required of an L2 learner by a given task. Building upon Hulstijn and Laufer's (2001) original research, which partially supported the hypothesis, the present study examined the hypothesis by exploring the interaction between task-induced involvement and learners' L2 proficiency on the initial learning and retention of target words. The study consisted of two experiments that were carried out with English-as-a-second-language learners at two different proficiency levels (i.e., matriculated undergraduate students vs. students in an Intensive English Program). Experiment 1 tested the hypothesis with three tasks imposing different levels of task-induced involvement ($n = 64$), whereas Experiment 2 included two tasks hypothesized to represent the same task-induced involvement ($n = 20$). In line with the predictions of the involvement load hypothesis, the findings of Experiment 1 indicated that a higher level of learner involvement during task performance promoted more effective initial learning and retention of target words. Additionally, Experiment 2 showed that different tasks with the same involvement load resulted in a similar amount of vocabulary

I am deeply indebted to Dr. Joan Jamieson, Dr. Bill Grabe, and Dr. Kim McDonough for their guidance and advice throughout developing this article. Special thanks go to Casey Keck for her insightful comments and suggestions during the revision process and to Diana Trebing, Xiangying Jiang, Brad Horn, and Camilla Vásquez for their helpful comments at different stages of the article. I am grateful to all the learners who participated in the study and would like to thank the teachers for their enthusiastic support during data collection. Finally, my sincere appreciation goes to three anonymous reviewers and Dr. Robert DeKeyser for their great support and valuable suggestions on earlier drafts. I am solely responsible for all the errors that might remain.

Correspondence concerning this article should be addressed to YouJin Kim, Department of Applied Linguistics & ESL, Georgia State University, P. O. Box 4099, Atlanta, GA 30302-4099. Internet: eslyjk@langate.gsu.edu

100

learning. These results were generally consistent across different proficiency levels, suggesting no interaction effect between task-induced involvement and L2 proficiency on vocabulary learning. The findings of the present study further the involvement load hypothesis by providing insights into how some individual differences—in this case L2 proficiency and cognitive involvement—might be more/less important to consider when implementing pedagogic tasks. Interestingly, the results indicated that as long as L2 learners' cognitive and language abilities allow them to complete vocabulary tasks in a given time, a deeper level of processing of the new words, especially the evaluation component of task-induced involvement during tasks, facilitates L2 vocabulary learning. Furthermore, the findings of Experiment 2 also provide insightful pedagogical implications demonstrating that it is possible to design different types of vocabulary tasks inducing similar amounts of involvement loads and that they can be equally beneficial for vocabulary learning. In task-based language teaching, designing tasks involves a complex series of considerations such as understanding who the target learners are and what cognitive processes each task requires. The experiments presented in this article reexamined the involvement load hypothesis and utilized tasks designed with such considerations in mind in order to explore the effectiveness of various vocabulary learning tasks.

Keywords involvement load hypothesis; processing depth theory; task-induced involvement; second language vocabulary acquisition; English as a second language; learner proficiency

Vocabulary is one of the essential components of a language, and second language (L2) vocabulary acquisition has been the focus of an increasing number of studies in second language acquisition (SLA). L2 learners are typically conscious of the extent to which limitations in their vocabulary knowledge affect their communication skills because lexical items carry the basic information they wish to comprehend and express (Nation, 2001). As a result, one of the main difficulties facing L2 learners is the vast number of words they need to acquire in order to become fluent in their L2. Teachers might well understand this need but might not know how best to support their students in this endeavor. Therefore, from a pedagogical point of view, there is clearly a need for research that helps to identify the types of learning task that provide optimal opportunities for L2 vocabulary learning.

To begin addressing this issue, a number of researchers have offered explanations of why certain tasks are more effective than other tasks in promoting L2 vocabulary acquisition (de la Fuente, 2002; Ellis & He, 1999; Ellis, Tanaka, & Yamazaki, 1994; Joe, 1995, 1998; Paribakht & Wesche, 1997; Rott, 2004; Rott, Williams, & Cameron, 2002). For instance, based on her analysis of different communicative tasks, de la Fuente concluded that learners' receptive and productive vocabulary acquisition was greater when they had the opportunity to negotiate and produce the target vocabulary (i.e., negotiation plus output) than when they were simply exposed to target words (i.e., premodified input). Joe (1995, 1998) reached a similar conclusion, finding that tasks requiring a high degree of generative process (e.g., learner-generated original context) facilitated more efficient incidental vocabulary acquisition than tasks requiring a low degree of generative process (e.g., contexts memorized from text) or no generation at all. She claimed that such generative tasks require learners to process information at semantic levels and to integrate new information with acquired knowledge. Thus, Joe hypothesized that cognitive processing enhances vocabulary learning with greater levels of generative processing, leading to greater vocabulary gains for unknown words. Paribakht and Wesche found that tasks that required students to practice new words in postreading vocabulary-focused exercises ("reading plus" group) led to significantly better retention of vocabulary than when students participated in a reading-only treatment that provided exposure to target words in texts ("reading only" group). Overall, even though these researchers analyzed different types of task in their respective attempts to identify effective task characteristics, their claims regarding what made particular tasks more effective than others seem to support Hulstijn and Laufer's claim that "the more effective task required a deeper level of processing of the new words than the other task" (2001, p. 542).

According to Laufer (2001), this claim is motivated by Craik and Lockhart's (1972) processing depth theory, which states that the chance of a new word being stored in long-term memory is determined by the depth at which that word is processed. A greater depth implies a greater degree of semantic or cognitive analysis of the new word. Thus, Craik and Lockhart (1972) argued that retention of unfamiliar words is conditional upon the amount of learner involvement while processing the meaning of those new words. This theory has been applied to several vocabulary studies to explain how the relative demands of a given task produce different levels of cognitive processing (e.g., Brown & Perry, 1991; Stahl & Clark, 1987). However, Craik and Lockhart's theory has been criticized due to the difficulty associated with operationalizing different levels of processing (Baddeley, 1978; Craik & Tulving, 1975; Hustijn & Laufer, 2001). In order to provide a more observable and measurable definition of "depth of processing" as well as to relate these general cognitive notions specifically to L2 vocabulary acquisition, Hulstijn and Laufer formulated the *involvement load hypothesis*, which is described in the next section.

Table 1 Three components of involvement

Components	Need	Search	Evaluation
Feature	Motivational, noncognitive dimension of involvement	Cognitive dimension of involvement	Cognitive dimension of involvement
Operationalization	Need for knowing words for the task	Attempt to find the meaning of unknown words	Comparison of a given word with other words (in order to assess whether a word does or does not fit its context)
		Attempt to identify the appropriate L2 form for a particular concept	Comparison of a specific meaning of a word with its other meanings
Categories[a]	Absent (0) vs. Present: Moderate (1) or Strong (2)	Absent (0) vs. Present (1)	Absent (0) vs. Present: Moderate (1) or Strong (2)

[a]The involvement index for each category is indicated in parentheses. For instance, the absence of a factor is marked as 0, a moderate presence of a factor as 1, and a strong presence as 2.

Involvement Load Hypothesis

Hulstijn and Laufer (2001) proposed a motivational-cognitive construct of *involvement* to capture the degree of cognitive processing required of an L2 learner by a given task. The construct of involvement is composed of three components: *need, search,* and *evaluation* (see Table 1). Each of the three components can be absent or present when processing a word during tasks. They contend that the degree to which an L2 learner is engaged in cognitive processing does not depend on whether the given task is input- or output-based, but on the combination of motivational and cognitive dimensions of the task, which they term *involvement load*.

As Table 1 illustrates, the *need* component is the motivational, noncognitive dimension of involvement, which exists depending on whether the word is required for completion of the given task. According to Hulstijn and Laufer (2001), *need* can occur in two degrees of prominence: moderate (1) or strong (2). *Need* is hypothesized to be moderate when it is externally necessitated (e.g., when the teacher asks students to fill in a word in a sentence) and strong when it is self-imposed by the learners (e.g., when learners decide to look up a word in a dictionary during a composition to fulfill their own needs).

Search and *evaluation* comprise the cognitive (i.e., information process-ing) dimension of involvement, and both involve attention to word form and word meaning. Although *need* can occur in two degrees of prominence (i.e., either moderate or strong), *search* is not conceptualized as the relative de-gree of cognitive processing; instead, it is either present (1) or absent (0). *Search* happens when the learner tries to find the meaning of an unknown L2 word in a dictionary or from other sources, such as teachers and peers. Furthermore, *search* can occur when the direction of translation is from the first language (L1) into the L2 or vice versa. *Evaluation* requires making a decision during tasks, such as "a comparison of a given word with other words, a specific meaning of a word with its other meanings, or comparing the word with other words in order to assess whether a word. . .does or does not fit its context" (Laufer & Hulstijn, 2001, p. 14). *Evaluation* can happen without *search* if the meaning of the tar-get word is explicitly provided by the text or a teacher. As shown in Table 1, Hulstijn and Laufer (2001) saw the presence of *evaluation* as comprising two potential degrees of cognitive processing: moderate (1) or strong (2). Moder-ate *evaluation* requires recognizing differences between words, whereas strong *evaluation* involves making a decision as to how additional words will work in combination with the new word in an original sentence or text.

Hulstijn and Laufer (2001) proposed that the involvement load of a given task is determined by the sum of the scores for *need*, *search*, and *evaluation*, and this value is called the task's *involvement index* (see Appendix A for examples). Therefore, the total possible range of an involvement index for any task is 0 (minimum) to 5 (maximum). The *involvement load hypothesis* claims that the higher the level of the involvement load (i.e., higher value of involvement index), the more effective the task is in promoting vocabulary acquisition.

Support for the Involvement Load Hypothesis

Laufer and Hulstijn (2001) revisited several studies of L2 vocabulary acqui-sition to explore how the components of *need*, *search*, and *evaluation* could account for the differential effectiveness of the tasks used in these studies. In their view, these previous studies, which did not set out to test the involvement load hypothesis, do suggest that involvement load and its relationship to task effectiveness deserve more attention in L2 vocabulary research. To illustrate how previous vocabulary studies might be reinterpreted from an involvement load perspective, Table 2 displays seven previous studies of vocabulary acquisition. Following Laufer and Hulstijn, Table 2 divides the tasks used in these studies into "more effective" and "less effective," based on the findings discussed in the original study reports. Using Laufer and Hulstijn's task-induced involvement load (pp. 16–18; and Appendix A), a score for the three involvement load components of each task (*need*, *search*, and *evaluation*) is provided in parentheses (i.e., 0 for absence of each component, 1 for moderate presence of each component, 2 for strong presence of each component). The total involvement load index (the sum of the component scores) is indicated in brackets.

As shown in Table 2, several studies have investigated the effectiveness of consulting dictionaries during reading for promoting vocabulary learning (Cho & Krashen, 1994; Knight, 1994; Luppescu & Day, 1993). When learners decide to look up a word in a dictionary of their own volition (i.e., not as an assigned requirement of the reading task), the choice of using the dictionary implies strong *need* (2), *search* (1), and moderate *evaluation* (1). In comparison, when learners do not use a dictionary, two possible involvement loads can result: moderate *need* (1) and *search* (1) when they guess the meaning of the words or no involvement load exists at all if they skip the unknown words. These studies showed that when dictionary use was self-imposed (i.e., involvement index = 4), participants achieved higher posttest scores than those who did not use a dictionary (i.e., involvement index = 0 or 2). For instance, Cho and Krashen conducted a small case study that demonstrated the benefit of using dictionaries for vocabulary learning. Among four learners who participated in a reading program for several months, two dictionary users acquired 17 and 34 words per book, respectively. In contrast, the other two learners who did not use the dictionary learned seven and eight words per book, respectively. Similarly, studies comparing the effects of marginal glosses (involvement index = 1) and dictionary use (involvement index = 4) on vocabulary learning showed that students who used dictionaries performed better in terms of vocabulary acquisition (e.g., Hulstijn, Hollander, & Greidanus, 1996; Laufer, 2000).

Although research investigating the usefulness of providing dictionaries or marginal glosses during reading appears to lend support to the involvement load hypothesis, further consideration of the fidelity of the various treatments reported in these studies seems to be warranted. For example, Hulstijn et al. (1996) originally found that their dictionary group gained much less vocabulary

Table 2 Comparison of the involvement load of different vocabulary-learning tasks

Study report[a]	More effective task	Less effective task
Cho and Krashen (1994); Knight (1994); Luppescu and Day (1993)	Using dictionary during reading [4]: *need* (2), *search* (1), *evaluation* (1)	Not using dictionary during reading [2/0][b]: *need* (1/0), *search* (1/0), *evaluation* (0)
Ellis & He (1999)	Interactionally modified output [5]: *need* (2), *search* (1), *evaluation* (2)	Interactionally modified input [3]: *need* (2), *search* (1), *evaluation* (0)
	Interactionally modified input [3]: *need* (2), *search* (1), *evaluation* (0)	Premodified input [1]: *need* (1), *search* (0), *evaluation* (0)
Hulstijn et al. (1996); Laufer (2000)	Dictionary use [4]: *need* (2), *search* (1), *evaluation* (1)	Marginal glosses [1]: *need* (1), *search* (0), *evaluation* (0)
Laufer (2003) Experiment 1	Writing original sentences [3]: *need* (1) *search* (0), *evaluation* (2)	Reading comprehension with marginal glosses [1]: *need* (1), *search* (0), *evaluation* (0)
Laufer (2003) Experiment 2	Writing a two-paragraph composition [3]: *need* (1), *search* (0), *evaluation* (2)	Reading comprehension with marginal glosses [1]: *need* (1), *search* (0), *evaluation* (0)

Task-Induced Involvement and Learner Proficiency

Table 2 *Continued*

Study report[a]	More effective task	Less effective task
Laufer (2003) Experiment 3	Writing sentences with the target words [3]: *need* (1), *search* (0), *evaluation* (2)	Reading comprehension and looking up unknown words in the dictionary [3]: *need* (1), *search* (1), *evaluation* (1)
	Completing sentences with the target words after looking up their meaning [3]: *need* (1), *search* (1), *evaluation* (1)	Reading comprehension and looking up unknown words in the dictionary [3]: *need* (1), *search* (1), *evaluation* (1)

Note. If the studies (Cho & Krashen, 1994; Ellis & He, 1999; Knight, 1994; Luppescu & Day, 1993) were introduced in Laufer and Hulstijn (2001), the involvement index given for each task in the studies would be from Laufer and Hulstijn. However, the researcher assigned involvement index for tasks from the studies that were not included in Laufer and Hulstijn (Hulstijn et al., 1996; Laufer, 2000, 2003) based on the descriptions of three components provided in relevant studies (Hulstijn & Laufer, 2001; Laufer, 2001; Laufer & Hulstijn, 2001). Each task is followed by a total involvement index in brackets. Each component of the involvement load score is also included in parentheses.
[a]Four studies that are also discussed in Laufer and Hulstijn (2001, pp. 18–20) are indicated in italics.
[b]When a student guesses the meaning of words while reading, the involvement index is (2); however, when a student simply skips unknown words, the involvement index is (0).

than the marginal gloss group because the dictionary group seldom used the dictionary provided. However, further analysis showed that when participants in the dictionary group looked up a word, their chances of remembering the word's meaning were greater than in the marginal gloss group, as measured by average retention rate. Therefore, studies that did not report whether learners engaged in the treatment as expected (i.e., actually using the dictionary rather than simply having one available) might not be as directly interpretable as their authors intend (or, in extreme cases, might contain wholly incorrect interpretations of results). Additionally, as noted in Knight (1994), different time on task raises a question about superior vocabulary learning by students who spent more time completing the tasks. For instance, Knight mentioned that the dictionary group who performed better on posttests spent more time on the passages than those in the no-dictionary group. This significant increase in vocabulary learning by the dictionary group could have been attributed to the longer exposure to the text.

In addition to studies of glossary and dictionary use during reading, research has been conducted to compare the vocabulary learning effects of reading supplemented with word-focused activities and word-focused activities alone. For example, Laufer (2003) conducted three experiments exploring different types of vocabulary tasks. As shown in Table 2, the first ($N = 60$) and second ($N = 82$) experiments compared reading comprehension with marginal glosses (involvement index = 1) with two different writing tasks that induced the same amount of involvement load (involvement index = 3): writing original sentences and writing a composition. In Experiment 3, Laufer asked 90 high school Arabic speakers to complete three tasks and tested them with regard to the number of words retained after each task: (a) reading comprehension and looking up unknown words in the dictionary (involvement index = 3), (b) writing sentences with the target words (involvement index = 3), and (c) completing sentences provided by the researcher with the target words after looking up their meaning (involvement index = 3).

Whereas the results of Experiments 1 and 2 supported the involvement load hypothesis, the outcome of Experiment 3 provided only partial support of the hypothesis. Although all three tasks were hypothesized to have the same involvement index (3), the three groups differed in their posttest scores. For instance, the results of Experiment 3 indicated that on the immediate posttest, the scores of the reading group were significantly lower than the other two groups, although there was no significant difference between the sentence completion group and the sentence writing group. On the delayed posttest, the scores of all three groups were significantly different from each other, with the sentence completion group acquiring the highest scores. Thus, in Laufer's (2003) Experiment 3, the differences observed between groups did not corroborate predictions made based on the involvement load hypothesis.

According to Laufer (2001), face-to-face oral interaction studies targeting L2 vocabulary acquisition can also be interpreted from an involvement load perspective. Laufer and Hulstijn (2001) explained that there are similarities between students' behaviors during a reading or writing task (e.g., using dictionaries, writing a composition) and their behaviors during oral interaction tasks. For example, they mention that negotiating the meaning of unknown words with interlocutors is similar to looking up words in a dictionary, in that it entails both strong *need* and *search*. From an involvement load perspective, studies that illustrate that words negotiated for meaning are retained better than nonnegotiated words (e.g., de la Fuente, 2002; Ellis et al., 1994; Newton, 1995) also demonstrate that tasks with a higher involvement load (i.e., those tasks that engage learners in negotiation of word meaning) are more effective than tasks with no involvement load (i.e., tasks with no opportunities to negotiate word meaning). Similarly, producing target words verbally as a form of modified output during communicative tasks might induce the same amount of involvement load as writing original sentences using target words (Laufer & Hulstijn, 2001). Laufer and Hulstijn also described that modified output, from an involvement load perspective, would be more effective than interactionally modified input (i.e., input that included clarifications), because whereas modified output involves strong *evaluation*, *evaluation* is absent in premodified input tasks (involvement index = 1).

For instance, as described in Table 2, Ellis and He (1999) conducted an experimental study that investigated the effect of premodified input, interactionally modified input, and modified output on comprehension, recognition, and production of new words. During the treatment, the premodified input group (*n* = 18) listened to a teacher's directions and followed the directions without negotiating meaning with the teacher or other participants. This task had an involvement index of 1 (moderate *need*) because the task conditions, rather than the learners themselves, determined which vocabulary items were to be processed. The interactionally modified group (*n* = 16) completed the same task as the modified input group, but they were allowed to interact with the teacher using a number of formulaic requests. The interactionally modified task had an involvement index of 3 (strong *need* and *search*) because learners had opportunities to ask about the meaning of the target words. The modified output group (*n* = 16) wrote 10 directions for locating the target words on a picture. When they were ready, the teacher put the students into pairs and asked them to exchange the directions orally. The learners were allowed to negotiate meaning if they did not understand a direction, which indicated an involvement index of 5 (strong *need*, *search*, and *evaluation*). The results of the study supported the involvement load hypothesis in that the modified output group significantly outscored the other two groups and the interactionally modified group scored significantly higher than the premodified group.

Although the studies listed in Table 2 provide indirect support for the involvement load hypothesis, it is important to remember that these studies have been *interpreted* from an involvement load perspective; they were not designed to directly test the hypothesis. Therefore, the descriptions of tasks reported in the studies might not be sufficient to determine the involvement load index. For instance, if the study did not report whether learners actually guessed the meaning of the words or used the available glossaries during reading, it is rather difficult to identify the accurate involvement index. Additionally, several intervening variables other than involvement load could potentially explain the observed between-group differences (e.g., topic differences, time on task, frequency of words' occurrence in the input). This shows that a purely post hoc analysis of previous research is not enough to provide definitive support for the hypothesis. As Laufer and Hulstijn (2001) strongly recommended, direct empirical investigation of the hypothesis is needed if we are to understand the role that involvement load plays in task effectiveness.

Testing the Involvement Load Hypothesis

To date, only one empirical study (Hulstijn & Laufer, 2001) has directly investigated the involvement load hypothesis. Hulstijn and Laufer examined the effect of task-induced involvement on the initial learning and subsequent retention of 10 new vocabulary words by young adult English as a foreign language (EFL) learners in Israel ($N = 128$) and the Netherlands ($N = 97$). Three tasks, which represented three different levels of involvement, were compared: reading comprehension with marginal glosses (moderate *need*, no *search*, and no *evaluation*), reading comprehension plus gap-fill (moderate *need*, no *search*, and moderate *evaluation*), and writing a composition with incorporating the target words (moderate *need*, no *search*, and strong *evaluation*). To measure short-term retention of the words, Hulstijn and Laufer asked students to provide the L1 translation or English explanations for 10 target words immediately after the completion of the task. Additionally, to measure students' long-term retention, they administered the same test again 1 week later in the Netherlands and 2 weeks later in Israel.

The results of Hulstijn and Laufer's (2001) two experiments (the Hebrew-English Experiment and the Dutch-English Experiment) were somewhat different. The findings of the Hebrew-English Experiment were in line with the predictions of the involvement load hypothesis: The composition group scored significantly higher than the gap-fill group on both posttests, and the gap-fill group scored significantly higher than the reading group. However, the results of the Dutch-English Experiment lent only partial support to the involvement load hypothesis. In this experiment, scores obtained for the composition group and the gap-fill group were consistent with what was predicted by the hypothesis. However, contrary to the hypothesis, the gap-fill group did not achieve significantly higher scores than the reading group on either posttest.

One question related to interpreting the results of Hulstijn and Laufer's (2001) study lies in time on task. The three groups of students participating in the study were given different amounts of time to complete their respective tasks: 40–45 min (reading), 50–55 min (gap-fill), and 70–80 min (composition). Therefore, the superior results attributed to the composition condition might have been due to time on task rather than the involvement load associated with the tasks.

Additional studies are also needed to explore the extent to which the assumptions underlying the involvement load hypothesis are warranted. For example, when determining the involvement index of each task, Laufer and Hulstijn (2001) focused on cognitive processing only, as it related to the processing of individual words not to completing the task in general; that is, they claimed that two tasks—writing original sentences and writing a composition with glossed words—induced the same amount of involvement load: a moderate *need*, no *search*, and strong *evaluation* (as shown in Appendix A). Laufer contended that the task of writing a composition is more difficult as a whole, but that this greater overall difficulty cannot be attributed solely to processing the new words that are to be included in the essay (personal communication, March 14, 2005). Other factors, such as the need to maintain coherence, also contribute to the overall difficulty of the composition task. She maintained that, as far as the individual new words are concerned, the two tasks require a similar level of cognitive processing because the vocabulary items must be used in an original context in both tasks. However, because there has been no empirical evidence to substantiate this claim, it is unclear whether these two tasks induce the same amount of involvement and thus promise a similar amount of vocabulary learning, or whether vocabulary-specific involvement can somehow be separated from something like "overall task involvement."

Overall then, there is thus far only limited evidence for the involvement load hypothesis. As Laufer and Hulstijn (2001) argued, more empirical studies designed to test predictions made by the involvement load hypothesis are greatly needed. For instance, it will be important to investigate the involvement load hypothesis in a variety of educational contexts. In addition, Hulstijn and Laufer (2001) have called for studies that examine whether both advanced learners and less proficient learners can benefit from tasks that require high involvement loads. The first step in addressing these issues is to replicate Hulstijn and Laufer's original study in different English language learning settings across a wider variety of proficiency levels and task types, ideally with time on task controlled.

Purpose of the Study

In order to enrich our understanding of the role that involvement load might play in vocabulary task effectiveness, the present study was designed to test particular predictions of the involvement load hypothesis in an English as a second language (ESL) setting, across different proficiency levels and task types. The study was composed of two experiments. The first, Experiment 1, was a partial replication study of Hulstijn and Laufer's (2001) Dutch/Hebrew experiments, which involved two proficiency levels of ESL learners in the United States and controlled for time on task. The purpose of Experiment 1 was to examine how different levels of task-induced involvement affect the initial learning and retention[1] of target words by L2 learners with two different levels of proficiency. Experiment 2 explored whether initial learning and retention of target words varied across two different tasks with the same hypothesized level of task-induced involvement. Experiment 2 was also carried out in an ESL setting with learners of two different proficiency levels and controlled for time on task. The purpose of Experiment 2 was to investigate Laufer's (2005) claim that writing sentences and composing an essay represent the same level of task-induced involvement.

Experiment 1

Experiment 1 was guided by the following two research questions:

1. Does the level of task-induced involvement affect the *initial* vocabulary learning of ESL learners from different proficiency levels when three tasks with different levels of involvement are administered?

2. Does the level of task-induced involvement affect the *retention* of new vocabulary words of ESL learners from different proficiency levels when three tasks with different levels of involvement are administered?

Method
Participants
The target population in this study was ESL students who were (a) currently enrolled in an undergraduate degree program or (b) studying English in an Intensive English Program (IEP) prior to enrolling in a degree program. The 64 participants in Experiment 1 were 34 matriculated undergraduates at a midwestern university in the United States and 30 ESL students in two different IEPs: one at a southwestern university and the other at the same midwestern university in the United States.[2] The participants were young adults with an average age of 24 who represented 27 different countries. A total of 19 different L1s were represented; of these, the languages spoken most by the participants were Korean ($n = 13$), Chinese ($n = 11$), Japanese ($n = 7$), Spanish ($n = 6$), Vietnamese ($n = 5$), Arabic ($n = 4$), and French ($n = 4$). They were grouped into two levels of proficiency (IEP and Undergraduate) based on their enrollment status and their paper-based TOEFL scores (IEP: 470–520; Undergraduate: above 520). All of the participants were from nine intact groups of classes, and the data were collected during their regularly scheduled class periods. For each proficiency level, participants were randomly assigned into one of three task-type subgroups (Reading, Gap-fill, Composition). Therefore, for Experiment 1, there were six subgroups, as shown in Table 3.

Materials
   Tasks.   Following Hulstijn and Laufer (2001), three different tasks were used to operationalize different levels of task-induced involvement (see Table 3): reading with comprehension questions including graphic organizers ("Reading"; involvement index = 1), reading with comprehension questions and gap-fill activity ("Gap-fill"; involvement index = 2), and a writing task ("Composition"; involvement index = 3).

   For Reading and Gap-fill groups, the reading text "Coping with Procrastination" and a set of accompanying comprehension questions were adapted from the textbook *Wordsmith: A Guide to College Writing* (Arlov, 2000).[3] With the help of three current teachers of the classes, the length and complexity of the original text were modified so that each task could be completed during one regular class period. The appropriateness of the revised text's difficulty level was also confirmed by two other previous and current teachers of the classes.

Table 3 Characteristics and size of the subgroups

Subgroups	Reading		Gap-fill		Composition	
	IEP	Undergraduate	IEP	Undergraduate	IEP	Undergraduate
Sample size	10	12	10	12	10	10
Treatment	Reading comprehension with marginal glosses		Reading comprehension with marginal glosses plus gap-fill		Writing a composition and incorporating the target words	
Involvement load (index)	Moderate need, no search, no evaluation (1)		Moderate need, no search, moderate evaluation (2)		Moderate need, no search, strong evaluation (3)	

The topic, procrastination, was chosen because the underlying concept was one with which all students had a similar level of familiarity and experience. Previous studies have suggested that a greater level of topic familiarity and expertise in a given subject contribute to efficiency of attentional allocation to input during reading, enabling better comprehension and, in turn, superior memory performance (Ellis, 2001; Nassaji, 2002; Pulido, 2003). This indicates that individual learners' different levels of topic familiarity might influence the comprehension of the text as well as the acquisition of vocabulary. Therefore, learners' topic familiarity was controlled in order to prevent the introduction of another variable caused by different levels of topic familiarity. The text contained 575 words, and its Flesch-Kincaid readability measure was grade level 9.6.

Students in the Reading group were required to read the text, answer the accompanying comprehension questions, and complete graphic organizers (see Appendix B). The graphic organizers, which did not explicitly focus on any of the target words, were used in the study as a part of the comprehension activity in order to control for time on task across the three groups.[4] In the text provided, the 10 target words were highlighted in bold print and a glossary of the words was provided in the right-hand margin of the text. According to Laufer and Hulstijn (2001), reading comprehension tasks with glossed words that are relevant to answering the questions induced only a moderate *need* to look at the glosses; this *need* was imposed by the task itself, rather than the students. Therefore, in terms of involvement load, the Reading group's task induced moderate *need*, but neither *search* nor *evaluation*, which indicated an involvement index of 1 (Hulstijn & Laufer, 2001).

The Gap-fill group received the same text and the same questions as the Reading group. However, the 10 target words were deleted from the original text, leaving 10 gaps numbered 1–10 (see Appendix C). These 10 words and their English explanations were provided in random order as a list on a separate page along with five distractors. The required task for this group was to complete the 10 gaps with the most appropriate words from a list of 15 words and answer the comprehension questions. According to Hulstijn and Laufer (2001), this task induced a moderate *need* to answer the comprehension questions and no *search* because the words were already explained. Additionally, moderate *evaluation* was induced because all of the words in the list had to be evaluated against each other and in the context of the gaps. Therefore, the involvement index for the gap-fill task was 2.

The Composition group wrote a one- to three-paragraph essay about procrastination (see Appendix D). A list of 10 target words with their English explanation was provided. In this short essay, students were asked to include all 10 target words. Hulstijn and Laufer (2001) argued that the involvement index of this task was 3, including a moderate *need*, no *search*, and a strong *evaluation*, because without looking up the words, new words must be evaluated against suitable collocations in a learner-generated context.

Target Vocabulary. A total of 10 target words were chosen according to the following criteria. First, two international undergraduate students at the same southwestern university were asked to choose unknown words from a list of 50 words selected from the reading material.[5] Based on their responses, 10 target words that were unfamiliar to both students were selected for the study. Second, participants' teachers confirmed that these 10 words would likely be unknown to the participants in the current study. The target words consisted of five verbs, three adjectives, and two nouns: *assiduous, apprehensive, oration, vexed, spawn, envision, caveat, stymie, divulge*, and *abate*.

Vocabulary Tests. To measure participants' initial vocabulary learning and retention, the current study included two vocabulary tests: an immediate posttest (immediately after the treatments) and a delayed posttest (2 weeks after the treatments). In Hulstijn and Laufer's (2001) study, because all of the participants shared the same L1, either Dutch or Hebrew, the researchers required the participants to produce L1 translations or English explanations to measure their vocabulary knowledge. However, because the current study

included participants with 19 different language backgrounds, it was not feasible to use the same type of testing system as the original study. Instead, the
current study adapted Paribakht and Wesche's (1993) Vocabulary Knowledge
Scale (VKS) to measure participants' initial vocabulary learning and retention
of new vocabulary knowledge.

The VKS uses a 5-point scale combining self-report and performance items
to measure both self-perceived and demonstrated knowledge of specific words
in written form. Each score indicates the following level of vocabulary knowledge: 1 (not familiar), 2 (familiar but meaning is not known), 3 (correct syn-
onym or translation is given), 4 (word is used with semantic appropriateness
in a sentence), and 5 (word is used with grammatical and semantic appropriateness in a sentence). This instrument was considered a valid measure of
participants' vocabulary knowledge for this study because it is not designed
to estimate general vocabulary knowledge but rather to track the early development of specific word knowledge (Read, 2000; Wesche & Paribakht, 1996).
Moreover, the major benefit of the VKS is that it elicits students' perceived
knowledge of vocabulary items and allows verification with demonstrated
knowledge.

Participants were presented with a list of 10 target words and asked to
indicate their level of knowledge for each item on the VKS. The possible range
of vocabulary scores for both posttests was 10–50. When scoring the VKS,
blind scoring was used, and both posttests were graded by two raters who were
native speakers of English and who had prior experience with teaching ESL
students. Pearson's r for interrater reliability was .92 for the immediate posttest
and .95 for the delayed posttest, indicating a high degree of agreement between
the two raters. Due to the high interrater reliability, one of the rater's scores was
randomly chosen for inclusion in the data analysis. The results of the internal
consistency reliability analysis for this rater's scores was .85 for scores on the
immediate posttest and .79 for scores on the delayed posttest.

Procedure

The experiment was conducted on two separate days over a 2-week period. The
treatment and immediate vocabulary test were administered by the researcher
on the same day, and the delayed posttest was carried out by teachers 2 weeks
after the treatment. The researcher visited a total of nine intact ESL classes and
followed the same administration procedure in each: The project was introduced
to the students, and they were asked to sign a consent form if they were willing
to participate in the study. Each student was given one of three randomly
distributed tasks. Before each treatment, the students were asked to complete a

questionnaire about their language and educational background. Time on task was the same for all three groups: approximately 40 min. Upon completion of the vocabulary task, the worksheets were collected and the students were given an immediate posttest designed to measure their *initial* vocabulary learning. For each vocabulary item, they were also asked to indicate whether they had known the words prior to the task in order to check for their preknowledge of the target words. If a participant checked more than two words as previously known, the data collected from that student were eliminated from the analysis. Two weeks later, the participants received the delayed posttest, which had the same format but which displayed the test items in a different order to measure their *retention* of vocabulary knowledge. All teachers informed the researcher that students did not practice the target words in class between the immediate and delayed posttests.

Analyses

As presented earlier, the two research questions asked whether the level of task-induced involvement load affected (a) the *initial* vocabulary learning and (b) the *retention* of new vocabulary words of ESL students from different proficiency levels when three tasks with different levels of involvement were administered. Each research question examined one dependent variable: scores on the immediate and delayed posttests. Both research questions had the same independent variables: level of task-induced involvement and proficiency level. In order to test the two research questions, the data were analyzed using SPSS version 13.0. The results of data screening indicated that the assumptions of using a parametric test (normality, homogeneity of variance, and the independence of observations) were met (Howell, 2002). As a result, two, two-way ANOVAs were conducted to analyze the results in order to address each of the two research questions. The alpha level was set at .05. When significant results were found, Bonferroni post hoc comparisons were used to locate significant differences among pairs of variables.

Results

The descriptive statistics for the immediate and delayed posttests of the 30 IEP students and 34 undergraduates are displayed in Table 4. Because the mean VKS scores for each subgroup do not explicitly illustrate how students performed on the individual target words, more precise information regarding the number of items receiving scores of 1, 2, or 3 or more is provided for each subgroup in Table 5. Because every participant in each subgroup was provided with 10 target words on VKS, the total number of vocabulary items tested for each

Table 4 Results of descriptive statistics for immediate and delayed posttests

		Immediate		Delayed	
	N	*M*	*SD*	*M*	*SD*
IEP					
Reading (1)	10	17.6	4.8	14.5	2.5
Gap-fill (2)	10	21.0	7.1	17.4	4.1
Composition (3)	10	26.0	5.9	19.8	2.4
Undergraduate					
Reading (1)	12	18.2	2.7	15.1	2.4
Gap-fill (2)	12	20.3	4.7	17.9	3.1
Composition (3)	10	27.4	2.7	22.3	3.4

Note. Each task is followed by the total involvement index in parentheses.

Table 5 Number of vocabulary items for each VKS score per group

	N	Total no. of voc. items[a]	No. of voc. items for VKS scores (immediate)			No. of voc. items for VKS scores (delayed)		
VKS score			1	2	3+	1	2	3+
IEP								
Reading (1)	10	100	43	41	16	44	53	3
Gap-fill (2)	10	100	43	32	25	31	61	8
Composition (3)	10	100	9	51	40	17	66	17
Undergraduate								
Reading (1)	12	120	38	72	10	61	57	2
Gap-fill (2)	12	120	26	72	22	35	82	3
Composition (3)	10	100	16	46	38	25	62	13

Note. Each task is followed by a total involvement index in parentheses.
[a]Total number of vocabulary items = number of participants in each subgroup × 10 target words.

subgroup was: the number of participants × the number of target words (10). A score of 1 indicated that a participant had no familiarity with the target word at all, and a score of 2 indicated that a participant had some level of familiarity but did not know the meaning of the target word. However, a score of 3, 4, or 5 on the VKS indicated that a participant at least knew the meaning of the target word. Therefore, in Table 5, scores of 3 or higher on the VKS were combined to indicate the participants' knowledge of word meaning.

Overall, the descriptive statistics indicated that the Composition group at both proficiency levels acquired the highest mean score on the VKS and had the highest number of vocabulary items scoring 3 or higher on the VKS (see Tables 4 and 5). For instance, Table 5 shows that the Composition groups received scores of 3 or higher on more items than the Gap-fill groups on both immediate and delayed posttests. For the immediate posttest, in particular, the IEP Composition group had a combined total of 40 words receiving 3+ scores and the undergraduate Composition group had a combined total of 38 words, whereas the number of items receiving scores of 3 or higher was no more than 25 (IEP) or 22 (Undergraduate) for the Gap-fill groups. It was also the case that the Gap-fill groups received scores of 3 or higher on more items than the Reading groups on both immediate and delayed posttests (see totals provided in Table 5).

These differences can also be seen if one considers, for each group, the mean number of items out of 10 test items that received scores of 3 or more. The Composition group at both proficiency levels had a mean of about 4 words out of 10 target words with a VKS score of 3 or higher on the immediate posttest. However, the mean number of items with scores of 3 or more for both Reading groups was less than 2 (IEP = 1.60, Undergraduate = . 83), and for both Gap-fill groups, it was less than 3 (IEP = 2.50, Undergraduate = 1.83). A similar pattern was found on the delayed posttest. The mean number of items with scores of 3 or higher for both Composition groups (IEP = 1.70, Undergraduate = 1.30) outnumbered the Gap-fill (IEP = 0.80, Undergraduate = 0.25) and Reading groups (IEP = 0.30, Undergraduate = 0.17) at both proficiency levels.

The first research question asked whether the level of task-induced involvement affects the *initial* vocabulary learning of ESL students from two different proficiency levels when three tasks with different levels of involvement are administered. The two-way ANOVA for the Level of involvement × Proficiency level interaction and the main effect for proficiency level on the immediate posttest revealed no significant results. However, a significant main effect for level of involvement was obtained on the immediate posttest, $F(2, 58) = 68.17$, $p < .05$. A strength-of-association value (η^2) was calculated for this statistic and was found to be .38.

The Bonferroni post hoc comparisons revealed that the mean score of the Composition group was significantly different than the mean scores of the Reading and Gap-fill groups on the immediate vocabulary posttest. The mean scores on the immediate posttests showed that for both IEP and Undergraduate students, performance in the Composition groups was higher than that in the

Gap-fill groups, which, in turn, was higher than that in the Reading groups. However, the means of the latter two groups did not significantly differ from each other. Therefore, the results of the two-way ANOVA showed a significant main effect for level of involvement due to a greater immediate posttest mean score for the Composition group compared to the other two groups.

The second research question asked whether the level of task-induced involvement affects the amount of *retention* of new vocabulary by ESL students from different proficiency levels when three tasks with different levels of involvement are administered. The results of the two-way ANOVA indicated that neither the main effect for proficiency level nor the Task type × Proficiency level interaction on the delayed posttest was significant. On the other hand, as with the results obtained for Research Question 1, the main effect for task type was significant, $F(2, 58) = 50.06, p < .05$. A strength-of-association value (η^2) was found to be .40. A Bonferroni post hoc comparison revealed that the mean scores for all three task types were significantly different from each other. As shown in Table 4, students in the Composition groups for both IEP ($M = 19.8$) and Undergraduate ($M = 22.3$) performed best overall, followed by the Gap-fill and Reading groups.

Experiment 2

As discussed previously, Experiment 2 examined how two tasks with the same theoretical level of task-induced involvement affected the *initial* learning and *retention* of target words by L2 students with different levels of proficiency. According to the involvement load hypothesis, two tasks that induce the same amount of involvement should promote similar results of vocabulary acquisition. Laufer claimed that although overall task difficulty of writing a composition seemed more difficult than writing individual sentences using the words as a whole, the involvement load for both tasks are the same (personal communication, March 14, 2005). In Experiment 2, the efficacy of two tasks (writing a composition vs. writing original sentences) with the same involvement index of 3 were compared. Experiment 2 was guided by the following research questions:

1. Is there an effect of task type on the amount of *initial* vocabulary learning by ESL students at two proficiency levels when two tasks with same levels of involvement are administered?
2. Is there an effect of task type on the *retention* of new vocabulary by ESL students at two proficiency levels when two tasks with same levels of involvement are administered?

Table 6 Characteristics and size of the subgroups

	Composition		Sentence Writing	
Subgroups	IEP	Undergraduate	IEP	Undergraduate
Sample size	10	10	10	10
Treatment	Writing a composition with incorporating the target words		Writing an original sentence for each of the target words	
Involvement load (index)	Moderate *need*, no *search*, strong *evaluation* (3)		Moderate *need*, no *search*, strong *evaluation* (3)	

Method

Participants

Using the same methods as in Experiment 1, the participants of Experiment 2 were divided into two different proficiency levels (see Table 6). As illustrated in Table 6, participants were also randomly assigned to two different tasks: writing a composition ("Composition") and writing original sentences ("Sentence Writing"). For the composition task, the same data from a subset of Experiment 1 were used; that is, Experiment 1's Composition group was also used in Experiment 2 to represent the Composition group. Additionally, a total of 20 students who did not participate in Experiment 1 were selected for the sentence writing task of Experiment 2: 10 undergraduate students at the midwestern university described in Experiment 1 and 10 students from the two IEPs of Experiment 1. As a group, the participants of Experiment 2 were young adult students with an average age of 25 who came from nine different countries. A total of 18 different L1s were represented; of these, the languages spoken most by the participants were Korean ($n = 12$), Chinese ($n = 7$), French ($n = 4$), and Spanish ($n = 4$).

Materials

Tasks. For the treatments, two different worksheets were used to operationalize the two different tasks: composition and sentence writing. As explained in Experiment 1, students in the first group (Composition) were asked to write a one- to three-paragraph essay about procrastination. Students in the second group (Sentence Writing) were given a worksheet that included 10 target words in a word list with glosses. They were asked to write an original sentence for each of the 10 target words (see Appendix E). According to Laufer and Hulstijn (2001) these two tasks were hypothesized as having the same level of task involvement (moderate *need*, no *search*, and a strong *evaluation*) because the L2 word forms and their meanings were already provided and the new words were evaluated against suitable collocations in a learner-generated context (see Table 6).

Target Vocabulary. The same 10 target words from Experiment 1 were also used in Experiment 2: *assiduous, apprehensive, oration, vexed, spawn, envision, caveat, stymie, divulge,* and *abate.*

Vocabulary Tests. The vocabulary knowledge measures for Experiment 2 were the same as for Experiment 1: an adaptation of the VKS (Paribakht & Wesche, 1993). Students were presented with a list of 10 target words and asked to indicate their level of knowledge for each item on the VKS. The same scoring system from the original VKS was used in Experiment 2 and the same raters from Experiment 1 scored both posttests. Pearson's *r* for interrater reliability was .97 for the immediate posttest and .94 for the delayed posttest. Due to the high interrater reliability, only one of the rater's scores were randomly selected for further analysis. The results of the internal consistency reliability analysis for this rater's scores was .75 for scores on the immediate posttest and .73 for scores on the delayed posttest.

Procedure

The procedures used to conduct the treatments and administer the immediate and delayed posttests were the same as those in Experiment 1.

Analysis

The two research questions in Experiment 2 asked whether task type affects (a) the *initial* vocabulary learning and (b) the *retention* of new vocabulary words of ESL students at different proficiency levels when two tasks with the same levels of involvement are administered.

Each of the research questions investigated one dependent variable with two independent variables. The dependent variable for each research question was the scores on the immediate and delayed posttests. Both research questions had the same two independent variables: task type and proficiency level. As Howell (2002) suggested, the data were screened and met the underlying assumptions for using a parametric test (i.e., normality, homogeneity of variance, and the independence of observations). Therefore, as in Experiment 1, two, two-way ANOVAs were conducted and Bonferroni post hoc comparisons were used to locate significant differences among the variables when significant results were found in the ANOVA.

Results

The descriptive statistics for the immediate posttest and delayed posttest of the subgroups are displayed in Table 7. For more comprehensive description regarding the acquisition of individual target words, Table 8 shows the distribution of the VKS scores per group at different proficiency levels. As in the results of Experiment 1, the total number of vocabulary items receiving scores of 1, 2, or 3 or higher is presented. As Table 8 shows, there was little difference between the Composition and Sentence Writing groups in the combined number of items receiving scores of 3 or more. For example, on the immediate posttest, IEP students from the Composition group scored a 3 or higher on a total of 40 words, and IEP students from the Sentence Writing group scored 3

Table 7 Descriptive statistics for immediate and delayed posttests

		Immediate		Delayed	
	N	*M*	*SD*	*M*	*SD*
IEP					
Composition (3)	10	26.0	5.9	19.8	2.4
Sentence Writing (3)	10	23.9	4.3	17.3	2.8
Undergraduate					
Composition (3)	10	27.4	2.7	22.3	3.4
Sentence Writing (3)	10	27.5	2.9	22.6	4.7

Note. Each task is followed by a total involvement index in parentheses.

Table 8 Number of vocabulary items for each VKS score per group

	N	Total no. of voc. items[a]	No. of voc. items for VKS scores (immediate)			No. of voc. items for VKS scores (delayed)		
VKS score			1	2	3+	1	2	3+
IEP								
Composition (3)	10	100	9	51	40	17	66	17
Sentence Writing (3)	10	100	21	57	49	37	57	6
Undergraduate								
Composition (3)	10	100	16	46	38	25	62	13
Sentence Writing (3)	10	100	24	40	33	24	57	16

Note. Each task is followed by a total involvement index in parentheses.
[a]Total number of vocabulary items = number of participants in each subgroup × 10 target words.

or higher on 49 words. Similarly, Undergraduate students in the Composition group scored 3 or higher on a total of 38 words, and Undergraduate students in the Sentence Writing group scored 3 or higher on 33 words. This was also the case for the delayed posttest (see totals provided in Table 8).

These differences can also be seen if one considers, for each group, the mean number of items out of 10 test items that received scores of 3 or more. For instance, on the immediate posttest, Undergraduate students from the Composition group and the Sentence Writing group had a mean number of 3.80 and 3.30 words, respectively, out of 10 target words with VKS scores of 3 or higher. For IEP students, the Composition group had a mean of 4.00 words receiving 3+ scores and the Sentence Writing group had a mean of 4.90 words. On the delayed posttest, the Undergraduate Composition group had a mean of 1.30 words receiving 3+ scores and the Undergraduate Sentence Writing group had a mean of 1.60 words. The IEP Composition group had a mean of 1.70 words receiving 3+ scores and the IEP Sentence Writing group had a mean of 0.60 words.

The first research question examined whether there was an effect of task type on the amount of *initial* vocabulary learning by ESL students at different proficiency levels when two tasks with the same level of involvement were administered. The result of the two-way ANOVA showed that there was no significant main effect for either task type or proficiency level and also no Task type × Proficiency level interaction in the immediate posttest.

The second research question asked whether there was an effect of task type on the amount of *retention* of new vocabulary by ESL students at two proficiency levels when two tasks with the same level of involvement were completed. As with Research Question 1 in Experiment 2, the results of the two-way ANOVA revealed no significant results. This indicated that there were no significant main or interaction effects between the independent variables for the delayed posttest scores.

To summarize, Experiment 2 found that two tasks (composition and sentence writing) with the same involvement index resulted in similar outcomes for both *initial* vocabulary learning and *retention* of new vocabulary. In addition, as in Experiment 1, the effect of learners' proficiency levels on *initial* learning and *retention* of vocabulary was not found to be significant. Furthermore, the absence of a significant interaction effect between task type and proficiency level suggests that the effect of the different tasks on vocabulary acquisition was not influenced by students' proficiency levels.

Discussion

The two experiments described attempted to provide empirical evidence for the involvement load hypothesis in L2 vocabulary acquisition. The purpose of Experiment 1 was to examine how different levels of task-induced involvement affected the *initial* learning and *retention* of target words by L2 learners and to investigate whether the impact of involvement load varied across two proficiency levels. Experiment 1 partially replicated Hulstijn and Laufer's (2001) original study while controlling for time on task. The results of the first research question in Experiment 1 regarding students' *initial* vocabulary acquisition provided partial support for the involvement load hypothesis, in that learners acquired words more effectively through tasks that required a higher level of involvement load. The Composition group yielded higher scores on the immediate posttest than the Reading and Gap-fill groups. However, the Gap-fill group did not perform significantly better than the Reading group. This finding is the same as that obtained in Hulstijn and Laufer's (2001) Dutch-English Experiment.

As a result, one possible suggestion is that the extent to which different degrees (moderate and strong) of each individual component (*need*, *search*, and *evaluation*) might contribute to an overall involvement load might not be the same, at least not for the *initial* vocabulary acquisition. Although Hulstijn and Laufer (2001) treated every component equally when determining the involvement index for vocabulary tasks, it might be the case that strong *evaluation* induces much greater involvement in processing a word than the moderate *evaluation* and the other two components. This indicated that strong *evaluation* might be the most influential factor for learner's *initial* vocabulary acquisition. Consequently, more studies are needed to examine whether it is reasonable to assign the same value (i.e., 0 or 1 depending on the existence of a component) of involvement index for the different levels of the individual three components. Future studies examining the extent to which individual components contribute to the overall involvement load will help to refine the coding and weighting of the three components of the involvement load to test the involvement load hypothesis more precisely.

In answering Research Question 2, which investigated the *retention* of new vocabulary knowledge, Experiment 1 fully supported the involvement load hypothesis. The difference among the three tasks supported the proposition that tasks that induce higher involvement loads result in greater vocabulary gains over time. Although, on the immediate posttest, the Gap-fill and Reading groups did not differ significantly from one another, all three groups were significantly different from each other in terms of their *retention* of vocabulary knowledge (i.e., their delayed posttest scores). This result suggests that the differential effects of certain low and high involvement load tasks (such as gap-fill vs. reading) might not be observable immediately. It will be important to investigate further the long-term effects of tasks with different involvement loads on the acquisition of L2 vocabulary.

Experiment 2 examined whether two tasks (i.e., writing composition and writing sentences) claiming to involve the same theoretical level of task-induced involvement would have similar effects on the *initial* learning and *retention* of target words by L2 learners with different levels of proficiency. The results suggested that the two tasks, with identical involvement loads (moderate *need*, no *search*, and strong *evaluation*), were equally effective in promoting both the *initial* learning and *retention* of new words and thus lend support to the involvement load hypothesis. These findings also lend support to Laufer's claim that even though writing a composition seems to require deeper cognitive processing than writing original sentences as a whole, the fact that the learners were processing new words in a self-generated context on both tasks suggests that these two tasks have similar involvement loads (personal communication, March 15, 2005). This equivalent involvement load for both writing tasks led to equal levels of performance for both groups in *initial* vocabulary learning and in longer-term *retention* of the target lexical items.

In both experiments, the effect of English proficiency levels on *initial* learning and *retention* of vocabulary was investigated and was not found to be significant. The nonsignificant results regarding the interaction between task type and proficiency level showed that the effect of different types of tasks on promoting vocabulary acquisition was not influenced by the learners' different proficiency levels. This finding provides some support for Hulstijn and Laufer's (2001) claim that less proficient learners can also perform an involving task: Less proficient learners (i.e., the IEP groups) experienced similar benefits learning new vocabulary as more proficient learners did by completing the same tasks. It seems that once learners have reached a level of proficiency sufficient to allow them to complete basic vocabulary-focused tasks, it is possible for them to benefit from tasks with higher involvement loads. At the same time, however, it is important to note that the "less proficient" learners in this study were students with enough English language proficiency to at least study within an IEP in a US university—by no means were they beginners. It will be important for future studies to investigate a wider range of proficiency levels in a variety of educational contexts.

Based on the results of the study, important implications for L2 pedagogy can be drawn. First, teachers need to consider involvement load when they design vocabulary tasks because tasks with a higher involvement are more beneficial for retention of new words than tasks with a lower involvement. It is also important to note that attending to involvement load does not necessarily limit teachers' choice of task types. As the results of Experiment 2 suggest, two different tasks with the same involvement load can lead to similar learning gains. Therefore, teachers have options when designing tasks with high involvement loads. It is not the case, for example, that teachers must always engage students in vocabulary-focused composition tasks if they wish to induce a high involvement load. Other tasks, such as writing individual sentences, if designed in such a way as to promote *need*, *search*, and *evaluation*, are likely to be as effective. Additionally, the current study suggests that vocabulary tasks with high involvement loads might benefit learners at different proficiency levels. Specifically, this study found that both ESL learners enrolled in credit-bearing US university courses and ESL learners enrolled in IEPs benefited from tasks with high levels of involvement.

In addition to considering the ways in which the present study supports the involvement load hypothesis, however, it is also important to keep in mind the present study's limitations. For instance, this study cannot be generalized to other educational settings, as a relatively small number of participants were sampled from only two universities. Furthermore, the participants in the current study engaged in each task only once. Multiple treatment sections for each task would allow a more definite conclusion regarding the effectiveness of each task on L2 vocabulary acquisition.

One major concern in the current study is related to the use of the VKS as a vocabulary knowledge measurement and how participants' scores on the VKS might be interpreted. Even though, in Experiment 1, the statistical tests indicated significant differences in learners' overall scores on the VKS, it seems rather difficult to determine the practical differences between groups; that is, the total score of the VKS for 10 target words does not reveal the scores of each vocabulary item, which makes it difficult to interpret the acquisition of individual words. For example, using the VKS, one participant indicated level 2 (familiar but meaning is not known) for all 10 words and received 20 points. Another participant indicated level 1 (not familiar) for five words and level 2 for two words but provided translations for three of the words (level 3) and received a score of 18 points. Based on the *total* score, the first learner, overall, appears to show better acquisition of L2 vocabulary. However, if one considers *individual* item scores, the second learner demonstrated that he clearly knew the meaning of three words, whereas the first learner did not. Thus, the total score of the VKS might not always accurately represent the extent of an individual learner's L2 vocabulary acquisition. To address this concern, the current study also reported, for each group, the total number of vocabulary items receiving scores of 1, 2, or 3 or more in order to aid readers in their interpretation of the results. It is recommended that future studies also include information about item scores, so that VKS mean scores for different learner groups can be interpreted in a more meaningful way.

As discussed in Read (2000), the VKS represents an interesting effort to measure some aspects of quality or depth of vocabulary knowledge, especially for the purpose of tracking the early development of specific words. However, it should be noted that the VKS is a recall test, which is more difficult than a recognition test such as multiple choice. A recognition test thus might be more appropriate to determine the early development of words than a recall test. Future studies might employ multiple measures, including recognition tests that are more sensitive to small increases in vocabulary knowledge, as illustrated in Waring and Takaki (2003). Overall, the inclusion of different types of vocabulary tests would enhance the credibility of the involvement load hypothesis and would offer more specific information regarding how involvement load contributes to the development of both receptive and productive vocabulary knowledge (e.g., Knight, 1994).

Furthermore, the current study and the original study by Hulstijn and Laufer (2001) focused on only one aspect of vocabulary learning: learning word meaning. Therefore, the findings from these studies do not represent the effects of task-induced involvement for all aspects of vocabulary learning. For instance, the effect of task-induced involvement on word-form learning might differ from its effect on learning word meaning. In order to verify the reliability of the involvement load hypothesis more broadly, it is important to examine different aspects of vocabulary learning. As illustrated in Barcroft (2002), future studies would benefit from investigating the effects of task-induced involvement for different aspects of vocabulary learning (form, meaning, form-meaning mapping) and different learning contexts (incidental, intentional).

Finally, the current study also suggests that Hulstijn and Laufer's (2001) methods for determining the involvement index for different tasks might need to be reexamined. Originally, Laufer and Hulstijn (2001) determined the amount of involvement load as the sum of scores for each component (see Appendix A). For instance, a task consisting of moderate *need* (1), *search* (1), and no *evaluation* (0) has the same involvement load (i.e., involvement index = 2) as a task of moderate *need* (1), no *search*, and moderate *evaluation* (1). However, as addressed previously, it is possible that all three components might not be equal in contributing to vocabulary learning. Experiment 2 supported the hypothesis that if two tasks induce the same amount of involvement index (i.e., involvement index = 3) with the same distribution of components (i.e., moderate *need*, no *search*, and strong *evaluation*), both tasks result in a similar amount of vocabulary learning. Nevertheless, there is no empirical evidence on the equivalency of the level of effectiveness of vocabulary learning when the two tasks have the same amount of involvement index but a different distribution of the components involved. For instance, Laufer (2003) could not support the involvement load hypothesis with two tasks (i.e., writing sentences with the target words and completing sentences with the target words after looking up their meaning). These two tasks have the same involvement index (3) but have a different distribution of components (i.e., moderate *need*, no *search*, and strong *evaluation* vs. moderate *need*, *search*, and moderate *evaluation*). In order to develop the involvement load hypothesis more fully, it will be necessary to examine whether tasks with the same amount of involvement index but a different distribution of the components involved also induce the same amount of vocabulary learning (Laufer & Hulstijn).

Conclusion

The results of the two experiments presented in this article generally corroborated Hulstijn and Laufer's (2001) findings. Experiment 1 indicated that higher involvement induced by the task resulted in more effective *initial* vocabulary learning and better *retention* of the new words. Experiment 2 provided some evidence that tasks were equally beneficial for vocabulary learning when their involvement loads were the same. Furthermore, the lack of differences between learners with two different proficiency levels suggested that as long as the learners were able to complete vocabulary-focused tasks, the involvement load hypothesis applied to the learners with different proficiency levels. However, for the comparison of the findings of Hulstijn and Laufer's original study and the current study, the current study should not be considered a strict replication because the two studies did not use the same test measurement. As a result, it is necessary to recognize the characteristics of different vocabulary tests used in each study when applying the test results to the *involvement load hypothesis*.

Since Laufer and Hulstijn (2001) proposed the involvement load hypothesis, it has not been investigated widely. As discussed earlier, there is only one empirical study (Hulstijn & Laufer, 2001) that was initially designed to investigate the involvement load hypothesis. Laufer and Hulstijn tried to provide additional support for the hypothesis by analyzing, post hoc, the vocabulary tasks used in previous L2 studies (i.e., post hoc analysis). However, in order to gain better insight and more pertinent data, there is an absolute need for controlled experiments that aim to test the hypothesis with a variety of tasks. Because the construct of involvement can be operationalized and investigated in a variety of ways, researchers will need to devise tasks with different involvement loads and compare them with regard to their effect on vocabulary acquisition. The current study tried to help fill this research gap, keeping in mind that more precise definitions of the involvement components and more thorough theoretical links between them should be examined further.

Revised version accepted 18 July 2007

Notes

1 Following the earlier study (Hulstijn & Laufer, 2001), the current study included both immediate and delayed posttests. Hulstijn and Laufer used short- and long-term retention for the results of both tests, respectively. However, 1 or 2 weeks do not seem long enough to be considered as long-term retention. Therefore, the current study used the terms "initial learning" and "retention of the meaning of target words." Initial learning indicated the learners' vocabulary knowledge measured immediately after completing vocabulary tasks, and the retention of the meaning of vocabulary indicated learners' vocabulary knowledge measured 2 weeks after the tasks.
2 Students from these two IEP programs were comparable because the two programs have similar institutional goals and curricula. Furthermore, the students' proficiency level was found to be similar, based on their TOEFL scores.
3 The official permission to adapt the text was obtained from Prentice Hall on June 20, 2005.
4 A pilot study with six undergraduate ESL students who had an average TOEFL score of 530 indicated that the reading task took less time than the other two tasks. Therefore, an additional task was necessary to make sure that students in the Reading group spent the same amount of time working as the students in the other two groups: Graphic organizers were designed by the researcher to offer a form of comprehension activity that the students could complete without knowing target words. For the purpose of the present study, the graphic organizers did not seem to affect the original involvement load index for the Reading group because they were simply engaged in an extended reading comprehension activity, which did not require target vocabulary knowledge (Grabe, personal communication, March 16, 2005).
5 One female Korean student who had a TOEFL score of 546 and one German student whose TOEFL score was 560 were asked to select unknown words from the list of 50 words.

References

Arlov, P. (2000). *Wordsmith: A guide to college writing*. Upper Saddler River, NJ: Prentice Hall.

Barcroft, J. (2002). Semantic and structural elaboration in L2 lexical acquisition. *Language Learning, 52*(2), 323–363.

Baddeley, A. D. (1978). The trouble with levels: A reexamination of Craik and Lockhart's framework for memory research. *Psychological Review, 85*, 139–152.

Brown, T. S., & Perry, F. L., Jr. (1991). A comparison of three learning strategies for ESL vocabulary acquisition, *TESOL Quarterly, 25*, 655–671.

Cho, K-S., & Krashen, S. (1994). Acquisition of vocabulary from the Sweet Valley Kids Series: Adult ESL acquisition. *Journal of Reading, 37*, 662–667.

Craik, F. I. M., & Lockhart, R. S. (1972). Levels of processing: A framework for memory research. *Journal of Verbal Learning and Verbal Behavior, 11*, 671–684.

Craik, F. I. M., & Tulving, E. (1975). Depth of processing and the retention of words in episodic memory. *Journal of Experimental Psychology; General, 104*, 268–294.

de la Fuente, M. J. (2002). Negotiation and oral acquisition of L2 vocabulary: The roles of input and output in the receptive and productive acquisition of words. *Studies in Second Language Acquisition, 24*, 81–112.

Ellis, N. C. (2001). Memory for language. In P. Robinson (Ed.), *Cognition and second language instruction* (pp. 33–68). Cambridge: Cambridge University Press.

Ellis, R., & He, X. (1999). The role of modified input and output in the incidental acquisition of word meaning. *Studies in Second Language Acquisition, 21*, 285–301.

Ellis, R., Tanaka, Y., & Yamazaki, A. (1994). Classroom interaction, comprehension, and L2 vocabulary acquisition. *Language Learning, 44*, 449–491.

Howell, D. C. (2002). *Statistical methods for psychology* (5th ed.). Pacific Grove, CA: Duxbury.

Hulstijn, J. H., Hollander, M., & Greidanus, T. (1996). Incidental vocabulary learning by advanced foreign language students: The influence of marginal glosses, dictionary use, and reoccurrence of unknown words. *The Modern Language Journal, 80*, 327–339.

Hulstijn, J. H., & Laufer, B. (2001). Some empirical evidence for the involvement load hypothesis in vocabulary acquisition. *Language Learning, 51*, 539–558.

Joe, A. (1995). Text-based tasks and incidental vocabulary learning. *Second Language Research, 11*, 149–158.

Joe, A. (1998). What effects do text-based tasks promoting generation have on incidental vocabulary acquisition? *Applied Linguistics, 19*, 357–377.

Knight, S. M. (1994). Dictionary use while reading: The effects on comprehension and vocabulary acquisition for students of different verbal abilities. *Modern Language Journal, 78*, 285–299.

Laufer, B. (2000). Electronic dictionaries and incidental vocabulary acquisition: Does technology make a difference? In U. Heid, S. Evert, E. Lehmann, & C. Rohrer (Eds.), *EURALEX* (pp. 849–854). Stuttgart: Stuttgart University Press.

Laufer, B. (2001). Reading, word-focused activities and incidental vocabulary acquisition in a second language. *Prospect, 16*(3), 44–54.

Laufer, B. (2003). Vocabulary acquisition in a second language: Do learners really acquire most vocabulary by reading? Some empirical evidence. *Canadian Modern Language Review, 59,* 567–587.

Laufer, B., & Hulstijn, J. H. (2001). Incidental vocabulary acquisition in a second language: The construct of task-induced involvement. *Applied Linguistics, 22,* 1–26.

Luppescu, S., & Day, R. R. (1993). Reading, dictionaries and vocabulary learning. *Language Learning, 43,* 263–287.

Nassaji, H. (2002). Schema theory and knowledge-based processes in second language reading comprehension: A need for alternative perspectives. *Language Learning, 52*(2), 439–482.

Nation, P. (2001). *Learning vocabulary in another language.* Cambridge: Cambridge University Press.

Newton, J. (1995). Task-based interaction and incidental vocabulary learning: A case study. *Second Language Research, 11,* 159–177.

Paribakht, T. S., & Wesche, M. (1993). The relationship between reading comprehension and second language development in a comprehension-based ESL program. *TESL Canada Journal, 11,* 9–29.

Paribakht, T. S., & Wesche, M. (1997). Vocabulary enhancement activities and reading for meaning in second language vocabulary acquisition. In J. Coady & T. Huckin (Eds.), *Second language vocabulary acquisition: A rationale for pedagogy* (pp.174–200). Cambridge: Cambridge University Press.

Pulido, D. (2003). Modeling the role of second language proficiency and topic familiarity in second language incidental vocabulary acquisition through reading. *Language Learning, 53*(2), 233–284.

Read, J. (2000). *Assessing vocabulary.* Cambridge: Cambridge University Press.

Rott, S. (2004). A comparison of output interventions and un-enhanced reading conditions on vocabulary acquisition and text comprehension. *The Canadian Modern Language Review, 61*(2), 169–202.

Rott, S., Williams, J., & Cameron, R. (2002). The effect of multiple-choice L1 glosses and input-output cycles on lexical acquisition and retention. *Language Teaching Research, 6,* 183–222.

Stahl, S. A., & Clark, C. H. (1987). The effects of participatory expectations in classroom discussion on the learning of science vocabulary. *American Educational Research Journal, 24*(1), 541–555.

Waring, R., & Takaki, M. (2003). At what rate do learners learn and retain new vocabulary from reading a graded reader? *Reading in a Foreign Language, 15*(2), 130–163.

Wesche, M., & Paribakht, T. S. (1996). Assessing second language vocabulary knowledge: Depth vs. breadth. *Canadian Modern Language Review, 53,* 13–39.

Appendix A

Task-Induced Involvement Load

Task	Status of target words	Need	Search	Evaluation	Involvement index
1. Reading and comprehension questions	Glossed in text but irrelevant to task	−	−	−	0
2. Reading and comprehension questions	Glossed in text and relevant to task	+	−	−	1
3. Reading and comprehension questions	Not glossed but relevant to task	+	+	−/+[a]	2 or 3
4. Reading and comprehension questions and filling gaps	Relevant to reading comprehension. Listed with glosses at the end of text	+	−	+	2
5. Writing original sentences	Listed with glosses	+	−	++	3
6. Writing a composition	Listed with glosses	+	−	++	3
7. Writing a composition	Concepts selected by the teacher (and provided in L1) The L2 learner-writer must look up the L2 form	+	+	++	4
8. Writing a composition	Concepts selected (and looked up) by L2 learner-writer	++	+	++	5

Note. The symbol + represents the presence of each component and − represents the absence of each component. In addition, the number of each symbol indicates the degree of the components (i.e. ++ for strong and + for moderate). The absence of a factor is counted as 0, a moderate presence of a factor as 1, and a strong presence of a factor as 2.
[a]The presence or absence of evaluation varies depending on the type of word and its context. If an unknown word has only one meaning and if the context allows a straightforward, literal interpretation, no evaluation is needed. On the other hand, if the word has several meanings, the reader has to decide which meaning is appropriate in the context (i.e., moderate need).
Source. Adapted from Laufer & Hulstijn (2001).

Appendix B

"Reading" task

Directions:
1. Please read the following passage.
2. Based on the reading, answer the questions that follow. Choose the best answers.

Coping with procrastination
By Roberta Moore, Barbara Baker, and Arnold H. Packer

Any discussion of time management would not be complete without an examination of the most well-intentioned person's worst enemy: procrastination. The dictionary (Dictionary.com) defines procrastination as "the act of putting off or delaying an action to a later time." Interestingly, most procrastinators do not feel that they are acting intentionally. On the contrary, they feel they fully intend to do whatever it is, but they simply cannot, will not, or—bottom line—they do not do it. Procrastinators usually have good reasons for their procrastination: "don't have time," "couldn't find what I needed,"—the list is never-ending.

Even procrastinators themselves know that the surface reasons for their procrastination are, for the most part, not valid. When procrastination becomes extreme, it is a self-destructive course. However, people feel incapable of stopping it. This perception can become reality if the underlying cause is not uncovered. Experts have identified some of the serious underlying causes of procrastination.

Often procrastination stems from a real or imagined fear or worry that is focused more on the potential consequences of that which is being avoided. For instance, you procrastinate preparing for an oral presentation because you are **apprehensive**[1] about forgetting your entire **oration**[2] despite your preparation. You are so **vexed**[3] about doing "a bad job" that you are unable to concentrate on your speech.

Being a perfectionist is one of the main traits that **spawns**[4] fear and anxiety. Often it is our own harsh judgment of ourselves that creates the problem. We elevate our standards and then critically judge ourselves. When you **envision**[5] yourself speaking before a group, are you thinking about how nervous the other students will be as well, or are you comparing your speaking abilities to the anchorperson on the six o'clock news? Concentrating on improving your own past performance, and thinking of specific ways to do so, **abates**[6] performance anxiety.

It would seem that the obvious answer to a lack of production is for the procrastinator to find a way to "get motivated." There are situations where lack of motivation is a **caveat**[7] of a poor decision. When you seriously do not want to do what is obligatory, you may need to reevaluate your situation. Did you decide to get a degree in a field with a high salary when you really knew you would be happier studying in another area? If so, when you find yourself wasting time instead of being **assiduous**[8], it may be time to reexamine your decision. Setting out to accomplish something difficult when your heart isn't in it is often the root cause of self-destructive behavior.

Often procrastination is due to an inability to concentrate or a feeling of being overwhelmed and indecisive. Many experience these feelings during a particularly stressful day or week. The persistence of these feelings, however, indicates that you are in a state of burnout. Burnout is especially likely to occur if you are pushing yourself both physically and mentally and not having time to unwind. Learning to balance your time and set realistic expectations for yourself will prevent burnout.

1. **apprehensive** *adj.*
   afraid

2. **oration** *n.*
   a formal speech, especially one given on a ceremonial occasion

3. **vexed** *adj.*
   worried; distressed

4. **spawn** *v.*
   to cause; to create

5. **envision** *v.*
   imagine

6. **abate** *v.*
   decrease; lessen

7. **caveat** *n.*
   a warning; caution

8. **assiduous** *adj.*
   diligent

Sometimes you put off doing something because you literally don't know how to do it. This may be hard to admit to yourself, so you may make other excuses. When you can't get started on something, consider the possibility that you need help. For example, if you get approval from your favorite instructor for a term paper topic that requires collecting data and creating graphics, you can be **stymied**[9] if you don't have the necessary skills and tools to do the work. Sometimes it is difficult to ask for help and sometimes it is even hard to recognize that you need help. Being able to **divulge**[10] personal limitations and seek out support and resources where needed is a skill used everyday by highly successful people.

9. stymie *v. (mostly used as passive; be+stymied)*
    to present an obstacle to

10. divulge *v.*
    to make (something secret) known

<Comprehension questions>

1. Which of the following most closely expresses the main idea of the essay?
    a. People who procrastinate need to get motivated.
    b. Procrastination is unintentional.
    c. Procrastination can be understood and controlled.
    d. Some of the world's most famous people have been procrastinators.

2. Procrastinators tend to be
    a. lazy
    b. male
    c. perfectionists
    d. low achievers

3. Which of the following is **not** mentioned as a cause of procrastination?
    a. Not being sure how to do something
    b. Expecting too much of oneself
    c. Not being sure when a project is due
    d. Not being motivated

4. According to the authors, inability to concentrate or of feeling overwhelmed and indecisive could be a sign of
    a. Procrastination
    b. Physical illness
    c. Burnout
    d. Mental instability

5. The authors imply that a tendency to procrastinate
    a. Is always a problem for college students.
    b. Can be controlled easily with several simple steps.
    c. Is something the individual can at least partly control.
    d. Is a sign of more serious problems.

6. To overcome procrastination, the authors suggest all **but** which of the following?
  a. Set realistic expectations
  b. Do things that you would enjoy
  c. Seek out support
  d. Spend more time on planning

<Graphic Organizers>

Directions: Based on the reading, fill in the following graphic organizers as precisely as possible.

1.

What is procrastination?

Procrastination is:

2. According to the authors, what are the underlying causes of procrastination?

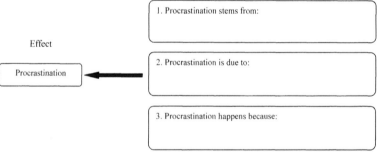

Cause

1. Procrastination stems from:

Effect

Procrastination

2. Procrastination is due to:

3. Procrastination happens because:

3. Provide the authors' suggestion for what to do in each situation.

Situation	Suggestion
When you do not want to do what is obligatory	
When you feel fear and anxiety	
When you are in a state of burnout	
When you cannot get started on something	

Appendix C

"Gap-fill" task
Directions:

1. Please read the following passage.
2. Fill in the blanks with the most appropriate words from the list.
3. Based on the reading, answer the questions that follow. Choose the best answers.

Coping with procrastination
By Roberta Moore, Barbara Baker, and Arnold H. Packer

Any discussion of time management would not be complete without an examination of the most well-intentioned person's worst enemy: procrastination. The dictionary (Dictionary.com) defines procrastination as "the act of putting off or delaying an action to a later time." Interestingly, most procrastinators do not feel that they are acting intentionally. On the contrary, they feel they fully intend to do whatever it is, but they simply cannot, will not, or—bottom line—they do not do it. Procrastinators usually have good reasons for their procrastination: "don't have time," "couldn't find what I needed,"—the list is never-ending.

Even procrastinators themselves know that the surface reasons for their procrastination are, for the most part, not valid. When procrastination becomes extreme, it is a self-destructive course. However, people feel incapable of stopping it. This perception can become reality if the underlying cause is not uncovered. Experts have identified some of the serious underlying causes of procrastination.

Often procrastination stems from a real or imagined fear or worry that is focused more on the potential consequences of that which is being avoided. For instance, you procrastinate preparing for an oral presentation because you are **(1)**_____ about forgetting your entire **(2)**_____ despite your preparation. You are so **(3)**_____ about doing "a bad job" that you are unable to concentrate on your speech.

Being a perfectionist is one of the main traits that **(4)**_____ fear and anxiety. Often it is our own harsh judgment of ourselves that creates the problem. We elevate our standards and then critically judge ourselves. When you **(5)**_____ yourself speaking before a group, are you thinking about how nervous the other students will be as well, or are you comparing your speaking abilities to the anchorperson on the six o'clock news?

Concentrating on improving your own past performance, and thinking of specific ways to do so, **(6)**_____ performance anxiety.

It would seem that the obvious answer to a lack of production is for the procrastinator to find a way to "get motivated." There are situations where lack of motivation is a **(7)**_____ of a poor decision. When you seriously do not want to do what is obligatory, you may need to reevaluate your situation. Did you decide to get a degree in a field with a high salary when you really knew you would be happier studying in another area? If so, when you find yourself wasting time instead of being **(8)**_____, it may be time to reexamine your decision. Setting out to accomplish something difficult when your heart isn't in it is often the root cause of self-destructive behavior.

Often procrastination is due to an inability to concentrate or a feeling of being overwhelmed and indecisive. Many experience these feelings during a particularly stressful day or week. The persistence of these feelings; however, indicates that you are in a state of burnout. Burnout is especially likely to occur if you are pushing yourself both physically and mentally and not having time to unwind. Learning to balance your time and set realistic expectations for yourself will prevent burnout.

Sometimes you put off doing something because you literally don't know how to do it. This may be hard to admit to yourself, so you may make other excuses. When you can't get started on something, consider the possibility that you need help. For example, if you get approval from your favorite instructor for a term paper topic that requires collecting data and creating graphics, you can be **(9)**_____ if you don't have the necessary skills and tools to do the work. Sometimes it is difficult to ask for help and sometimes it is even hard to recognize that you need help. Being able to **(10)**_____ personal limitations and seek out support and resources where needed is a skill used everyday by highly successful people.

<Vocabulary list>

(a) vexed *adj.*
    worried, irritated, or distressed
(b) abate *v.*
    decrease; relieve
(c) irrevocable *adj.*
    impossible to change

(d) compound *n.*
an area that contains a group of buildings and is surrounded by a fence or wall

(e) apprehensive *adj.*
afraid

(f) oration *n.*
a formal speech, especially one given on a ceremonial occasion

(g) stymie *v.* **(mostly used as passive; be+stymied)**
to present an obstacle to; stand in the way of

(h) assiduous *adj.*
diligent

(i) procure *v.*
to obtain something, especially after an effort

(j) prosperous *adj.*
successful, usually by earning a lot of money

(k) envision *v.*
imagine

(l) divulge *v.*
to make (something secret) known

(m) caveat *n.*
a warning or caution

(g) spawn *v.*
to cause or to create

Appendix D

"Composition" task
Directions:
The dictionary (Dictionary.com) defines **procrastination** as **"the act of putting off or delaying an action to a later time."** Choose **one** of the questions below and respond by writing a well-developed answer. In your response, YOU MUST USE THE FOLLOWING TEN WORDS.

1. Write an essay of one to three paragraphs about advice you would give to someone who has a problem with procrastination. **Be sure to include the vocabulary listed below.**
OR
2. Write an essay of one to three paragraphs about reasons why people procrastinate. **Be sure to include the vocabulary listed below.**

Words		Meaning
(a) apprehensive	*Adj.*	afraid
(b) oration	*n.*	a formal speech, especially one given on a ceremonial occasion
(c) vexed	*Adj.*	worried; distressed
(d) spawn	*v.*	to cause or create
(e) envision	*v.*	imagine
(f) abate	*v.*	decrease; lessen
(g) caveat	*n.*	a warning or caution
(h) assiduous	*Adj.*	diligent
(i) stymie	*v.*	to present an obstacle to: stand in the way of **(mostly used as passive; be+stymied)**
(j) divulge	*v.*	to make (something secret) known

Note. v: verb, adj: adjective, n: noun.

Appendix E

"Sentence Writing" task
Directions:

There are ten words listed below. Write a sentence for each word which includes the word showing its meaning. Each of your sentences should include more than **seven words**.

Word		Meaning	Sentence which uses the word
(a) apprehensive	*adj.*	afraid	
(b) oration	*n.*	a formal speech, especially one given on a ceremonial occasion	
(c) vexed	*adj.*	worried; distressed	
(d) spawn	*v.*	to cause or create	
(e) envision	*v.*	imagine	
(f) abate	*v.*	decrease; lessen	
(g) caveat	*n.*	a warning or caution	
(h) assiduous	*adj.*	diligent	
(i) stymie (mostly used as passive; be+stymied)	*v.*	to present an obstacle to: stand in the way of	
(j) divulge	*v.*	to make (something secret) known	

Note. v: verb, adj: adjective, n: noun.

Language Learning   ISSN 0023-8333

Teacher- and Learner-Led Discourse in Task-Based Grammar Instruction: Providing Procedural Assistance for Morphosyntactic Development

Paul D. Toth

Temple University

For many years, task-based second-language (L2) grammar instruction has been considered the ideal means for achieving a focus on linguistic form within meaningful, purposeful communication (Ellis, 2003; Long & Crookes, 1993; Nunan, 1989; Samuda & Bygate, 2008). Within this framework, small-group, learner-led discourse (LLD) is often believed to facilitate L2 development better than whole-class, teacher-led discourse (TLD), given the greater discursive autonomy for learners and presumed greater opportunities for negotiated interaction (Lee, 2000; Long & Porter, 1985; Pica, 1987; van Lier, 1996). Indeed, many have criticized TLD, given evidence of disfluent exchanges during which teacher turns impede rather than support learner participation (e.g., Brooks, 1993; Donato & Brooks, 2004; Hall, 1995, 2004; Leemann-Guthrie, 1984). Still, some have argued that TLD may greatly benefit learners if teacher assistance, negotiation, and feedback are well managed (Adair-Hauck & Donato, 1994; Antón, 1999; McCormick & Donato, 2000) and that witnesses to such exchanges may benefit as much as active participants (Ohta, 2001). However, only a few studies have directly compared TLD with LLD, and these have yielded conflicting results (Fotos, 1993, 1994; Pica & Doughty,

I am greatly indebted to the Spanish students at the University of Pittsburgh and the University of Akron who participated in this study, as well as the instructors who graciously volunteered much time and effort to implement the treatment conditions, including Joyce Rowan, Fernando Feliu, Jessie Carduner, and Tim Aiken. A number of individuals also gave helpful advice, comments, and feedback on the design of this study since its inception as a dissertation project, as well as in its current format as a journal article. Special thanks are due to Alan Juffs, Richard Donato, Merrill Swain, Teresa Pica, and three anonymous reviewers. Invaluable statistical advice was provided by Carol Baker at the University of Pittsburgh, Richard Steiner at the University of Akron, and Amy Atwood and Edward Taylor at the University of Wisconsin-Madison. Any remaining errors are my own.

Correspondence concerning this article should be addressed to Paul D. Toth, Department of Spanish and Portuguese, Temple University, Anderson Hall 4th Floor, West Berks Street, Philadelphia, PA 19122-6090. Internet: ptoth@temple.edu

1985; Van den Branden, 1997, 2000). This study therefore aimed to contribute to the literature by presenting quantitative and qualitative classroom data gathered under similar task conditions for both TLD and LLD. Rather than unequivocally advocating for one discourse format over the other, I evaluated the strengths and limitations of both as tools for L2 morphosyntactic development. Participants in the study included 78 English-speaking adults from six university classes of beginning L2 Spanish, with two assigned to each treatment (LLD = 25; TLD = 28) and two other classes comprising a control group ($n = 25$). Instruction involved seven lessons targeting the anticausative clitic *se*, with one recorded and transcribed in each treatment. Results on grammaticality judgment and guided production tasks administered as a pretest, posttest, and delayed posttest indicated a stronger performance for TLD learners on both tasks. Although the transcript data revealed numerous episodes of constructive L2 negotiation and support in LLD—often addressing topics that were not assessed quantitatively—the transcripts nonetheless suggest that the teachers facilitated L2 development by directing attention more consistently to target structures and providing morphosyntactic "procedural assistance" to learners during utterance formulation. Because such moves are unlikely to occur among learner peers alone, I argued that teachers may be uniquely positioned to assist L2 development through their discursive role, such that an ideal task-based L2 pedagogy would include principled sequences of both TLD and LLD.

Keywords classroom research; teacher-led discourse; learner discourse; task-based instruction; instructed SLA; L2 Spanish; anticausativity; pushed output; proceduralization; scaffolding

Much recent research on second language (L2) instruction has suggested that drawing learners' attention to connections between formal properties of the L2 and the meanings they convey facilitates L2 morphosyntactic development (Doughty & Williams, 1998b; VanPatten, 2004a). Within the interactionist model of acquisition, this is said to occur when communication difficulties between speakers lead to conversational modifications that enhance the comprehensibility of both the language that learners hear and that which they produce (Long, 1981, 1996). This negotiation of meaning is said to simultaneously cause learners to attend to, or focus on, L2 form as a means of accomplishing their desired communicative act (Doughty, 2001). Thus, where classroom instruction is concerned, meaningful interaction is held to be an essential ingredient for L2 development, especially when it entails modified, comprehensible input, opportunities for purposeful output, and feedback on formal accuracy (Ellis, 1997; Gass, 2003). Although the utility of implementing L2 grammar instruction in this way, as a "focus on form" (Doughty & Williams, 1998a; Long, 1991), has been documented both in the context of teacher-led, whole-class discourse as well as small-group interactions among learners (e.g., Ellis, 2003;

Norris & Ortega, 2000; Ohta, 2001), little work has made direct comparisons of learning outcomes for these two primary formats within which L2 grammar instruction most often takes place. This article therefore aims to contribute to the literature by considering both quantitative and qualitative data from teacher- and learner-led discourse (henceforth, TLD and LLD, respectively) during a week of beginning-level, university L2 Spanish instruction on the pronoun *se*.

Task-Based Instruction and Classroom Discourse Formats

For a number of years, L2 educators have advocated a task-based approach to grammar instruction as the ideal way to accomplish a focus on form within meaningful, purposeful communication (Breen & Candlin, 1980; Ellis, 2003; Lee, 2000; Long & Crookes, 1993; Nunan, 1989; Skehan, 1996; Van den Branden, 2006). Based in part on a view of natural communication as a series of intentioned "speech acts" (Austin, 1962; Hymes, 1972; Searle, 1969), task-based lessons are organized into discrete acts of communication such as identifying, describing, comparing, evaluating, summarizing, or narrating, often in response to images, texts, or realia from native-speaking target-language communities. Tasks might also include content designed to heighten sensitivity to cultural perspectives within the L2 speech community and/or engage learners in problem-solving related to other academic subjects (National Standards in Foreign Language Learning Project, 1999; Pica, 2005). Once a task has been chosen, teachers spend class time equipping learners for performance by highlighting necessary L2 structures and then having learners interact with varying amounts of support and feedback, ideally leading to an autonomous performance. Often, support is provided by breaking the task down into simpler subcomponent steps, with trial runs and feedback given before independent interaction, as well as materials containing relevant linguistic, contextual, and procedural cues (Samuda, 2001; Skehan, 1996, 1998). Whatever the task format or objective, however, the essential role of L2 grammar within this approach is to support task performance rather than to serve in and of itself as the organizing feature for classroom discourse (Long, 1991; Long & Crookes).

Despite a general agreement on the role of grammar instruction in task-based teaching, much recent work on L2 grammar instruction has been more focused on the relationship between learning outcomes and specific interactional features—such as the quantity and quality of positive or negative evidence—than with the contribution of the discourse format to these outcomes (cf. Leeman, 2003; Lyster, 2001; Mackey, 1999). In one example of earlier work that did make such comparisons, Pica and Doughty (Doughty & Pica, 1986; Pica, 1987; Pica & Doughty, 1985) investigated the quantity and quality of discourse features claimed to benefit L2 acquisition, but did not assess learning outcomes. All three studies were short-term investigations of intermediate L2 English classrooms in which similar tasks were performed first as TLD and then as LLD. In all three, they found that although LLD consistently provided learners with more speaking turns, beneficial conversational adjustments could be found to varying degrees in either format, depending on the task design. For example, Pica (1987) reported that when the task involved open-ended, collaborative decision-making, LLD yielded somewhat fewer adjustments (6% of learner utterances vs. TLD's 11%), given that learners in small groups could easily opt out of participation. However, when the task required an information exchange, LLD yielded many more modifications (24% of learner utterances versus vs. TLD's 15%), because each learner was required to contribute. Doughty and Pica then showed that negotiation in LLD increased further when learners were arranged in dyads rather than in small groups. In all three studies, the authors concluded that with adequate task design, LLD creates participant roles that more aptly allow for negotiation than TLD. However, Pica (1994) later argued that documenting such theoretically justified modifications ought to be followed by independent measures of learning outcomes in order to affirm that negotiation does in fact lead to morphosyntactic development. Although many recent studies have indeed provided such evidence in LLD contexts (see Ellis, 2003, for a review), few have compared results for similar tasks performed as TLD.

Two important exceptions to this lack of comparison work are Van den Branden's (1997, 2000) research in multilingual upper elementary classrooms in Belgium and Fotos's (1993, 1994) work in university-level L2 English classes in Japan. Van den Branden investigated the impact of teacher versus peer negotiation on L2 Dutch children's performance on reading comprehension (2000) and oral picture description tasks (1997). He found in both cases that negotiation occurred most frequently and learning outcomes were strongest when L2 learners interacted with a teacher/researcher rather than with native language (L1) Dutch-speaking peers. Contrary to Pica and Doughty, Van den Branden attributed his results to a "pupil-centered" yet systematic "pushing" of learner output that could only be accomplished by an interlocutor with a pedagogical purpose (1997, p. 628). Fotos's studies in adult learning contexts were less conclusive. She compared TLD to LLD in grammar-oriented communicative tasks during 9 weeks of instruction, with a third group given meaning-oriented tasks as LLD with no overt grammatical focus. Using a pretest, posttest, and delayed posttest design, she found equal gains for grammar-oriented TLD and LLD on grammaticality judgment and production tasks, with meaning-oriented LLD lagging behind. However, in the earlier study, Fotos also assessed the frequency of learners' "noticing" of three target structures, operationalized as the ability to underline any "special uses of English" appearing in a printed narrative (1993, p. 390). The results showed the two grammar groups (LLD and TLD) again outperforming the meaning-oriented LLD group, but no differences between them except that TLD learners noticed more tokens of one of the three target grammar items. In explaining the difference, Fotos (1993) speculated that her dual role as both researcher and TLD instructor might have influenced the outcome. Given equal gains on the other tasks, however, she argued that LLD was at least as effective as TLD in facilitating morphosyntactic development.

Strengths and Limitations of LLD and TLD

Despite the lack of conclusive evidence indicating superior outcomes for either LLD or TLD, some have explicitly advocated that small-group or dyadic interactions be the essential format for task-based L2 instruction. Often, it has been claimed that LLD is more essentially communicative than TLD, in that it better prepares learners for the negotiated interactions that take place outside the classroom (Jacobs, 1998; Lee, 2000; Long & Porter, 1985; Nunan, 1987, 1989). Meanwhile, others have argued that LLD confers greater linguistic autonomy, creativity, and self-regulation upon learners, all of which are necessary if they are to master the L2 as a tool for communication (Brooks, Donato, & McGlone, 1997; Donato, 1994; van Lier, 1996). Early proposals for task-based curricula furthermore viewed LLD as a logical response to research documenting gaps between direct instruction on L2 forms and learners' ability to use them in obligatory contexts (cf. Breen & Candlin, 1980; Krashen, Sferlazza, Feldman, & Fathman, 1976; Larsen-Freeman, 1975; Long, 1985). Likewise, many of the instructional benefits ascribed to the teacher talk of TLD were also documented during LLD, namely comprehensible input, modified interaction, and negotiation over L2 form (Doughty & Pica, 1986; Pica & Doughty, 1985; Pica, Holliday, Lewis, & Morgenthaler, 1989; Porter, 1986; Varonis & Gass, 1985). Furthermore, TLD in some studies was shown to be a less-than-ideal context for developing L2 grammatical and communicative competence, given the dominance of the teacher in shaping discourse and the impossibility of engaging all students in meaningful language use (Hall, 1995, 2004; Lee, 2000; Leemann-Guthrie, 1984; Musumeci, 1996; Nunan, 1987).

Even during open-ended discussions, Lee, for example, observed that too often TLD "degenerates into a conversation between the instructor and the two best learners in the class," effectively "disenfranchising" the other learners and allowing them to be "cognitively [un]engaged" (p. 33).

With regard to LLD as grammar instruction, however, similar concerns have arisen that learners might not all be fully engaged in the instructional goal (Ellis, 2003). It has been observed that learners at times produce minimal L2 utterances in order to expediently accomplish the task (Seedhouse, 1999), that they sometimes provide poor L2 models for each other (Prabhu, 1987), and that they might be more inclined to focus on lexical rather than morphosyntactic issues when negotiating over form (Buckwalter, 2001; Morris, 2002; Williams, 1999). Proponents have argued, however, that many of these concerns can be addressed by adequate task design. For example, Pica, Kanagy, and Falodun (1993) claim that because "information gap tasks" require a two-way exchange leading to only one acceptable outcome, negotiation over L2 form is more likely. Furthermore, transcripts from more open-ended, collaborative tasks requiring editing or composing in the L2 have shown that learners can indeed serve as effective assistants to peers in producing, analyzing, and correcting L2 structures (Donato, 1994; Foster & Ohta, 2005; Swain, 1998, 2000; Swain & Lapkin, 1995, 2001). It is also claimed that specific L2 structures can be effectively targeted if they are either "useful" or "essential" to the communicative act being performed (Fotos, 2002; Loschky & Bley-Vroman, 1993)[1] and that learners might employ target structures more fluently if pretask activities prime their attention to the necessary task language and posttask follow-ups hold them accountable for adequate task performance (Skehan, 1996, 1998; Skehan & Foster, 1999). Pica, Kang, and Sauro (2006) indeed found a strong relationship between negotiations that had occurred during information gap tasks and L2 English learners' immediate recall of connections between target forms and their meaning. Because LLD engages all learners simultaneously in interaction, it can be argued that as long as the task effectively focuses attention on L2 form-meaning relationships, the sheer mathematics of LLD's interactional opportunities favors this format over TLD as a tool for L2 morphosyntactic development.

Nonetheless, in actual practice, much L2 grammar instruction often occurs as whole-class TLD, and research to date has yielded disparate conclusions about its benefits and drawbacks. It has long been observed that TLD often yields a recurrent cycle of teacher "Initiation" moves (i.e., questions or prompts directed at the class), followed by learner "Responses," and subsequent teacher "Feedback" (Mehan, 1979; Sinclair & Coulthard, 1975). One disadvantage of these "IRF" sequences, in addition to yielding fewer turns per learner than LLD, is that they are often used by teachers during grammar instruction to limit learner participation to the mere recitation of vocabulary and grammatical paradigms, with little opportunity to develop a broader interactional competence (Brooks, 1993; Hall, 1995, 2004; Nunan, 1990). Still, others have argued that it is not the IRF pattern itself that makes TLD problematic but rather teacher turns within IRF that either fail to establish cohesion to a broader discourse purpose, or that too narrowly frame desirable learner responses (Cullen, 1998; Johnson, 1995; Toth, 2004; Wells, 1998). When teacher utterances more consistently adhere to communicative task goals and build upon the topical content of learner utterances, research has indicated that fewer comprehension difficulties (Toth) and greater numbers of learner-initiated turns (Johnson) result. Indeed, teacher turns occurring in the context of whole-class collaborative interactions have also been shown to "scaffold" learners through tasks that they could not have performed on their own, thus deepening their engagement with needed L2 forms (Adair-Hauck & Donato, 1994; Antón, 1999; McCormick & Donato, 2000).

Ohta's (2000, 2001) research on feedback during TLD further suggests that learners not directly participating in classroom discourse might nonetheless be cognitively engaged as the interaction unfolds. After equipping adult L2 Japanese learners with individual microphones, her recordings of their subvocal, private speech during whole-class interactions showed that many nonparticipants were actively hypothesizing about L2 form-meaning relationships while feedback was provided to others. If indeed nonparticipants might be quietly mapping out L2 form-meaning relationships during TLD, then this would mitigate its disadvantage in providing fewer turns per learner, as well as Lee's (2000) concern that nonparticipants are effectively disenfranchised. Given Swain's (1995, 1998, 2000) contention that L2 output benefits grammatical development by "pushing" learners to test hypotheses, notice gaps in their knowledge, and engage in metalinguistic reflection, Ohta's (2000, 2001) work suggests that well-implemented TLD might indeed engage learners in this mental activity, even when the teacher does not directly call on them to respond.

The Present Study

Design and Research Questions

The present study investigates the relationship between classroom discourse format and L2 morphosyntactic development by comparing Spanish classes where similar tasks were performed as either small-group LLD or whole-class TLD. The data to be considered here were gathered as part of a larger study (Toth, 1997) that investigated not only improvements with the object of instruction but also changes in L1 transfer and overgeneralization errors.[2] Although postinstruction improvements with *se* revealed differences between the treatment groups, significant decreases in L1 transfer and increases in overgeneralization were statistically similar. Thus, because group contrasts appeared to be related more to the way learners responded to object of instruction itself, rather than to its concomitant repercussions in inducing or expunging other grammatical errors, this study will, due to space limitations, focus only on the results of the larger study that pertain to improvements with *se*. A full reporting of the learners' overgeneralization and transfer errors can be found in Toth (1997, 2000, 2003).

Given that many of the strengths and weaknesses identified for either LLD or TLD have as much to do with adequate instructional design as inherent discourse features, implementation of LLD and TLD will necessarily require that each treatment reflect current proposals for maximizing meaningful language use and attention to L2 form, in order to avoid confounding factors that would render either one a straw man. Thus, following the work of Pica and her colleagues (Pica et al., 1993, 2006), LLD will be implemented strictly as two-way information exchanges, with Spanish *se* being either "useful" or "essential" to the task (Fotos, 2002; Loschky & Bley-Vroman, 1993). Furthermore, task performance will be preceded by a pretask warm-up for the planning and priming of necessary language, followed by a posttask follow-up to lend accountability to its completion (Skehan 1996, 1998). Meanwhile, TLD will be designed to avoid the noncohesive "local lexical chaining" of teacher questions observed by Hall (1995, p. 44) during attempts to elicit target forms. Instead, TLD instructors will use task topics and goals as the basis for building cohesion, with multiple responses elicited for each teacher initiation and scaffolded feedback given to facilitate form-meaning mapping, as in Adair-Hauck and Donato (1994) and Antón (1999). Although the task goal in each group will be identical (i.e., describing a picture, narrating an event, comparing two halves of an information pool), the participatory structure of TLD will necessarily involve more open-ended, collaborative turn-taking than LLD, given the difficulty of designing numerous whole-class information exchanges for 20 or more learners.[3] Thus, whereas the information gap tasks of LLD will attempt to regulate turn-taking and attention to L2 form-meaning connections via task design, responsibility for such regulation under the more collaborative structure of TLD will necessarily rest with the teacher. Therefore, a teacher's skill in discourse management will have to be more effective than that of the information-gap design in order to offset the greater number of learner turns and greater learner control over discourse that LLD entails.

The dependent variable in this study—development in knowledge of Spanish anticausative *se*—will be operationalized as performance on a timed, written test including a grammaticality judgment (GJ) task and a sentence-level picture description task. Although the validity of any GJ task ultimately hinges on the particulars of its design and implementation, the present task's validity in assessing L2 grammatical development can be inferred from the larger related study (Toth, 1997, 2000, 2003), in which group results for the GJ task revealed overgeneralizations of *se* that could only be explained by underlying linguistic knowledge, rather than explicit instruction, L1 transfer, or L2 input data. Thus, it is unlikely that learners will have simply answered blindly or relied exclusively on remembered explicit information for their answers. Hence, results for improvements with *se* on the GJ task will be assumed to represent a performance that draws at least in part on internalized L2 grammatical knowledge. The GJ task will also triangulate the production task with one that does not as closely reflect the instructional practices of the treatment groups. Furthermore, qualitative data will be provided to shed light on the interaction patterns in each group during a picture description activity implemented as whole-class interaction in TLD and as an information gap in LLD. However, note that because the study involves four course sections meeting for 7 total hours each, it will not be possible to quantify all tokens of *se* to which learners are exposed or the quantity of interaction in which each participant engages. Thus, the limited qualitative data will be used here simply to characterize the support and feedback provided to learners during task performance under either condition. The research questions are thus as follows:

Question 1: Will LLD provide an advantage in grammaticality judgments for Spanish anticausative *se* when compared to TLD?
Question 2: Will LLD provide an advantage over TLD in performance with anticausative *se* on sentence-level picture descriptions?
Question 3: Will excerpts of classroom interactions reveal differences in the way learners in each group attend to the form-meaning relationships associated with anticausative *se* and use the target form for output?

Method
Participants
Participants in the two experimental treatments included 53 native English-speaking adult learners in four intact classes of a second-semester, beginning

L2 Spanish course in a large, public university in the United States. The LLD and TLD groups each consisted of two classes taught by different instructors in order to control for variation in teaching style and class rapport (LLD: $n = 25$; TLD: $n = 28$). An additional 25 English-speaking adult learners from two classes of second-semester Spanish formed a control group (C) at a second large, public American university nearby, in which the L2 Spanish curriculum was nearly identical to that of the first. Most learners in the three groups had taken some Spanish in secondary school (LLD: $n = 20$; TLD: $n = 25$; C: $n = 19$), with the overwhelming majority having studied for 1 or 2 years. However, prior departmental placement testing at both universities had determined that none were proficient enough to take more advanced L2 Spanish courses, and participant questionnaires revealed that none had been exposed to Spanish at home. Nonetheless, to ensure the absence of false beginners prior to instruction, any participant who scored 50% or higher for anticausative *se* on the picture description portion of the pretest was eliminated from the study. Hence, the participant numbers reported here reflect the elimination of seven participants for this reason, along with a number of others who were excluded due to absenteeism. Finally, a native-speaker comparison group comprised of 30 adult Spanish native speakers from all parts of Latin America also participated. A questionnaire showed that none of them had any significant experience teaching Spanish, and so it was assumed that any awareness of pedagogical rules for *se* would not affect their test performance.

Spanish Anticausative se

Within generative syntactic theory, most linguists have argued that a primary function of Spanish *se* is to derive variations in sentence meaning by "absorbing" one of the noun phrase (NP) arguments associated with a given verb (Dobrobie-Sorin, 1998; Montrul, 2004; Raposo & Uriagereka, 1996). This derivational process can be seen in Examples 1a–1c by comparing the transitive sentences on the left side of each arrow with their "detransitivized" counterparts on the right. Thus, in Example 1a, when the patient of the sentence on the left is absorbed, leaving only an agent plus *se* on the right, a reflexive or reciprocal meaning is derived. In Example 1b, meanwhile, the same sentence on the left yields a passive or impersonal reading when the agent is absorbed and *se* appears on the right with the patient as postverbal subject. Finally, absorption of the agent with a different verb in Example 1c derives the possibility of a middle voice reading, in addition to the passive or impersonal, given that the meaning of *cocinar* "to cook" implies the possibility of a spontaneous, inchoative event when used intransitively (Levin & Rappaport-Hovav, 1995; Pustejovsky, 1995).

Thus, by detransitivizing verbs in this way, *se* derives a number of possible meanings in Spanish that depend on the subtle semantic properties of verbs and the thematic roles they assign to NPs. For English-speaking learners, acquisition is further complicated by the fact that corresponding morphology in the L1 varies considerably. Nonetheless, the distinctions made in many instructional materials among a passive, impersonal, and middle voice *se* use English-based classifications that belie a unitary Spanish phenomenon embracing both inchoative and externally caused events. Throughout this study, then, although the learners' curricular materials might make reference to a passive, impersonal, and middle voice *se*, the term "anticausative *se*" will refer collectively to all of these cases where *se* absorbs the agents of verbs and patients become subjects.

Example 1
  a. *Ellos prepararon la comida.* → *Ellos se prepararon.*
    AGENT   PATIENT   AGENT
    "They prepared the food."   "They prepared themselves/each other."

  b. *Ellos prepararon la comida.* → *Se preparó la comida.*
    AGENT   PATIENT   PATIENT
    "They prepared the food."   "The food was prepared/One prepared food."

  c. *Ellos cocinaron la comida.* → *Se cocinó la comida.*
    AGENT   PATIENT   PATIENT
    "They cooked the food."   "The food Ø cooked/was cooked/One cooked food."

Treatment Procedures
The instructional period lasted for seven consecutive, 50-min class meetings, with 25 min taken on Day 1 and Day 7 for testing. The control group likewise took a pretest and immediate posttest 1 week apart, whereas instruction offered a mix of both whole-class and small-group interaction targeting unrelated grammar items. Their classroom input thus included only incidental tokens of *se*, given that no purposeful attempt was made to either avoid or include it in the instructors' speech.

Although all learner groups had been introduced to *se* the previous semester during a lesson on reflexive pronouns (e.g., Example 1a), at the time of this study they had not yet learned of the anticausative *se* shown in Examples 1b and 1c, or its L1 equivalents, including the problematic zero derivation for the English middle voice (Example 1c). The number of class meetings dedicated to

Table 1 Lesson topics for instruction on Spanish *se*

Day	Lesson topics
Day 1 (Monday)	Administer pretest, review reflexive *se* with remaining time.
Day 2 (Tuesday)	Introduce and practice impersonal *se*.
Day 3 (Wednesday)	Introduce and practice passive *se*.
Day 4 (Thursday)	Introduce and practice middle voice *se* of "unplanned occurrences."
Day 5 (Friday)	Practice middle voice *se* with indirect object pronouns.
Day 6 (Monday)	Introduce and practice verbs of emotion with *se*.
Day 7 (Tuesday)	Review week's lesson, administer immediate posttest.

se for this study was normal for the second-semester curriculum, with the only difference being that *se* topics were grouped together into a single week rather than being dispersed throughout the semester. Table 1 indicates the sequencing of *se* topics for the treatment groups. Here, it can be seen that after first reviewing reflexive and reciprocal uses, four class meetings dealt exclusively with the anticausative. Day 6 addressed *se* with psychological changes of state, which, due to the unique semantic features of these verbs, was presented in a separate publication (Toth, 2003).

Teachers for each group underwent separate 2-hr training sessions on how to implement instruction before beginning the treatment period. The lesson plans were designed and distributed to teachers the day before each class. For both treatments, each lesson began with a 5–10 min, whole-class "warm-up" during which teachers elicited multiple answers to one or two open-ended questions requiring the previous day's use of *se*, as well as vocabulary items that had been assigned for that day's lesson. The warm-up was then followed by 5–10 min of explicit, metalinguistic information on the current day's use of *se*, which was identical for both treatments in order to confine their differences to the discourse format of subsequent activities. The grammar presentations first outlined the formation of sentences using *se* and then contrasted the form-meaning relationships signaled by its presence in detransitivized sentences versus its absence in transitive ones. English equivalents were given to identify the anticausative meaning in the examples, and learners were informed about typical errors that English speakers make.[4]

The remaining 30–35 min of each class involved either TLD or LLD activities requiring that day's use of *se*, according to each treatment. In both groups, this time was generally organized around the completion of two communication tasks, such as describing and comparing pictures, putting a series of events in order, or exchanging short personal narratives. The tasks were performed as information gap activities in groups of two or three for the LLD treatment and as whole-class collaborative activities for TLD. Some of these activities were designed specifically for this project; others came directly from the regular course textbook (Terrell, Andrade, Egasse, & Muñoz, 1994). Both treatments were then assigned the same homework, which usually included reading a grammar explanation about the next day's target item from the textbook, studying assigned vocabulary, and completing two to four accompanying written exercises, which occasionally involved short readings.

In the LLD group, implementation of each day's tasks involved brief pretask planning and posttask follow-up phases, both of which were conducted as whole-class interactions bracketing the small-group context in which the task itself was carried out. The pretask routine had teachers distributing necessary materials, informing learners of task objectives, and then asking them to brainstorm vocabulary items and interrogative expressions necessary for conducting the task in the L2. Answers to the brainstorm were often tabulated on the blackboard for reference during task performance. For the posttask activity, learners usually reported their results back to the whole class in order to receive feedback and confirm accuracy. Meanwhile, the task itself consistently required a two- or three-way exchange of information, so that each learner had to produce meaningful language and negotiate for mutual comprehension. During this time, LLD teachers circulated around the class, providing ad hoc assistance upon request. On average, LLD learners spent about 20 min total per lesson interacting in pairs or small groups to perform the two main tasks. Although one might argue that the time spent in groups could have been greater, learner peers were nonetheless the exclusive source of linguistic support during the tasks, which served as the principal points of contrast between the two groups.

Figure 1 provides an illustration of the picture description task used on Day 4 to target anticausative *se* for describing physical changes of state. Here, learners were told that a hurricane had caused considerable damage to two similar-looking houses and that they had to identify the differences between them, with one person looking only at Picture A and the other looking only at Picture B. A pretask vocabulary brainstorm and posttask answer check bookended the task. The following day, learners worked with eight numbered pictures depicting a series of "unfortunate events" that happened to characters in their textbook, all of which required anticausative *se* plus an indirect object pronoun. One learner in each pair received the odd-numbered pictures in the sequence and the other received the even-numbered ones. Together, they then had to

Figure 1 A picture comparison information exchange activity targeting middle voice *se*.

reconstruct the sequence by describing each picture and pooling their information. Answers were confirmed in the posttask follow-up. The second task then engaged learners in a structured interview, during which they told each other of any accident like those in the first task that might have recently happened to them. After first rehearsing questions and follow-ups in a pretask activity, partners had to ask for three additional details and take notes before reversing roles. The posttask activity then required them to write a short summary of their partner's accident based on the exchange. In this way, learners moved from controlled picture descriptions to more open-ended personal narratives over the course of Day 4 and Day 5.

Meanwhile, activities in the TLD group were similar to those of LLD, except that they were conducted as whole-class interactions rather than in small groups. On Day 4 and Day 5, for example, TLD learners used the same materials as LLD learners to describe the hurricane damage in Figure 1 and the "unfortunate events" of their textbook characters, except that all TLD learners could see both halves of the visual information and the tasks were implemented by having the teacher call on volunteers. Thus, at the beginning of each, teacher-initiated questions signaled the communicative goal to be accomplished (e.g., "*Díganme, ¿qué ocurrió en el dibujo?*" [Tell me, what happened in the picture?]), whereas subsequent initiation moves repeatedly referred back to the task purpose in order to elicit responses from other learners (e.g., "*¿Qué más pasó?*" [What else happened?]). Often, like the pretask activities of the LLD group, a brainstormed list of necessary vocabulary was put on the board before engaging in the task itself. Because there was no need for posttask feedback, there was often time for one or two short, additional activities. For example, on Day 5, after describing their recent accidents to the class, TLD learners had time for another activity in which they used anticausative *se* to think up unfortunate events that would make good excuses for not coming to class. Thus, whereas individual LLD learners undoubtedly had more opportunities for L2 production in their groups, TLD learners performed a greater number of tasks due to lighter time constraints.

To summarize, apart from time for additional activities in TLD, the principal points of contrast between the two treatments were found in the interactional features of the primary tasks. Both groups engaged in the same warm-up activities and received the same explicit grammar information; both engaged in pretask brainstorming; and both performed nearly identical meaning-oriented tasks requiring use of the target structure. Although LLD afforded greater opportunities for output to all learners, teachers rather than learner peers played a more prominent role in providing input and directing attention to form in TLD.

Data Gathering and Assessment
Assessment consisted of written production and grammaticality judgment tasks administered immediately prior to (pretest), immediately following (posttest),

and 24 days after instruction (delayed posttest) during testing periods that lasted 25 min total for each administration. In addition, Day 4's lesson was videotaped in both treatments and selected portions transcribed. In each of the two LLD classes, one group of learner volunteers had their small-group interactions recorded on a portable audio recorder. Afterward, during the time between the posttest and delayed posttest, *se* appeared incidentally in the teachers' input as it does in natural speech, but it was no longer the object of instruction. As mentioned previously, the control group took the tests at the same time intervals as the experimental groups, but with no intervening instruction on *se*. Native speakers took the same tests as learners, but only once.

Before being administered to learners, test items were piloted on two Spanish native speakers to ensure their validity as assessments of targetlike performance. To control for test learning effects, two separate versions of the test were designed and distributed evenly and randomly among learners for the pretest. On the posttest, the version the learners received was switched to the one they had not yet taken. For the delayed posttest, the versions were switched again so that learners took the same one they had taken as a pretest over 1 month prior. As with the learners, when the native speakers took the test, both test versions were distributed randomly and evenly. Although each version had completely different items, the tasks were identical in overall length and in the number of items targeting anticausative *se*. An equal number of distracter items also appeared on both test versions. All words chosen for the test items came from a list of vocabulary that had appeared prominently in the Spanish curriculum prior to the beginning of the study. When taking the test, learners were instructed to ask for any vocabulary help they needed, although few actually did so.

In order to prevent performance on the production task from being influenced by GJ task items, the production task was administered first. This consisted of 12 drawings accompanied by a verb and an NP, as shown in Figure 2, where the target response would have been "*El vaso se rompió* (The glass broke)." Learners were asked to write a description for each picture using the words given. Four items were meant to elicit anticausative *se*, with two consisting of verbs representing inchoative events (Example 1c) and two consisting of externally caused ones (Example 1b).[5] The other eight items on the task targeted *se* with verbs of emotion and cases where the use of *se* would have been ungrammatical, as reported in Toth (1997, 2000, 2003). For all anticausative items, the given NP represented a patient undergoing the action of the verb. A reliability analysis of all learners' posttest responses for these four items yielded Cronbach's α values of .76 for Version A of the task, and .81 for

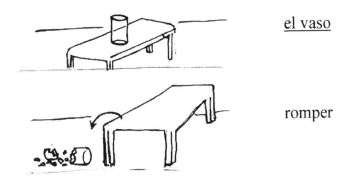

el vaso

romper

Figure 2 A sample item on the production task targeting middle voice *se*.

Version B. Meanwhile, a *t*-test checking for differences between the posttest means for the two versions found none, $t(75) = 1.48; p = .14$.

Meanwhile, the GJ task asked learners to rate the acceptability of 50 sentences on a Likert scale from -3 for "very bad," through 0 for "not sure," to $+3$ for "very good," as shown in Example 2.[6] The instructions explicitly asked learners not to analyze the sentences, to move quickly through each item, and to answer intuitively according to how correct the sentence "felt." The items to be considered here were eight sentences representing grammatical uses of anticausative *se*, including three middle-voice constructions and five impersonal or passive sentences.[7] The Cronbach's α value for all learners' posttest responses on Version A was .83 and for Version B it was .73, with no differences between the versions found on a *t*-test, $t(76) = -1.31; p = .19$. The other 30 items on the task assessed overgeneralization, L1 transfer errors, and *se*'s use with verbs of emotion. Meanwhile, 12 distracters pertained to features of Spanish grammar unrelated to *se*. Again, a full report of these results can be found in Toth (1997, 2000, 2003).

Example 2. Sample items from the grammaticality judgment task:

No se fuma aquí. -3 -2 -1 0 $+1$ $+2$ $+3$
Se descompusieron las máquinas. -3 -2 -1 0 $+1$ $+2$ $+3$
Se trae cerveza a todas las fiestas. -3 -2 -1 0 $+1$ $+2$ $+3$
(One doesn't smoke here.)
(The machines broke down.)
(Beer is brought to every party.)

Finally, upon recording the class interactions on Day 4, the spotting-differences task shown in Figure 1 was chosen for transcription as a prototypical example of an information-gap task that would best exemplify the contrasts between the two treatment groups. In accordance with Research Question 3, discourse segments were selected to shed light on the way anticausative *se*'s form-meaning relationships were attended to by the participants.

Scoring and Coding Procedures for the Production and GJ Tasks

Because items on both tasks had been randomly ordered, those pertaining to anticausative *se* were first separated from the others to determine the participants' scores. For the production task, given that the aim was to quantify use of the anticausative, answers that correctly used *se* in an intransitive sentence were awarded one point (e.g., for Figure 2, "*Se rompió el vaso*" [The glass broke]), whereas all other answer types received a zero, even if they were grammatically acceptable alternatives. Thus, although some, including the native speakers, wrote grammatical transitive sentences without *se* at times (e.g., "*Yo rompí el vaso*" [I broke the glass]), these answers received the same zero score as ungrammatical intransitives without *se* (e.g., "*El vaso rompió*" [The glass broke]) in order to facilitate assessment of the instructional object with inferential statistics. Likewise, errors pertaining to other features of Spanish morphosyntax, such as person-number or tense-aspect suffixes, were ignored unless they interfered with assessing the sentence's transitivity, in which case they too received a zero. In this way, the production task scoring isolated grammatical uses of *se* in intransitive sentences from all other possible answers.

After coding and scoring all responses, an average for each participant was determined by dividing the points earned by the four total anticausative items. Overall participant scores thus ranged from zero for no intransitive uses of *se* to a maximum of 1.00 for four uses, with intermediate scores representing the percent of intransitive *se* answers that the individual had provided. Having determined individual scores in this way, an analysis of variance (ANOVA) was performed as described in the Results section.

On the GJ task, as on the production task, scoring involved first separating out the anticausative *se* items. The numbers used by learners to indicate their judgments were entered as raw scores into calculations of individual means for the eight grammatical items. Thus, scores ranged from -3 to $+3$. If a zero was given for any item, indicating an answer of "don't know," this data point was treated as a nonresponse and removed, so that individual means of zero would only come from averaging positive and negative answers. As on the production task, individual scores were then entered in the ANOVA presented in the Results section.

Table 2 Quantitative group results for anticausative *se*

Task and statistic	Control			Learner-led			Teacher-led			Native
	Pre	Post	Delay	Pre	Post	Delay	Pre	Post	Delay	
Production task										
Group mean	0.01	0.00	0.03	0.02	0.48	0.33	0.04	0.63	0.50	0.48
Stand. deviation	0.05	0.00	0.11	0.08	0.32	0.30	0.10	0.32	0.34	0.20
GT task										
Group mean	0.71	0.61	0.80	0.91	1.74	1.27	0.86	2.17	1.93	2.24
Stand. deviation	1.18	1.31	0.85	0.94	0.64	0.99	1.01	0.66	0.71	0.75

Results

Production Task

The middle rows of Table 2 show group means and standard deviations for using anticausative *se* with intransitive syntax on the three test administrations. The means are also plotted in Figure 3, with native-speaker (NS) results included for comparison. From the graph it is clear that whereas NSs wrote intransitive *se* answers for roughly half the anticausative items ($M = 0.48$),[8] the TLD group greatly exceeded this score on the immediate posttest ($M = 0.63$) and then reached a similar score on the delayed test ($M = 0.50$), albeit with considerably greater variation, as their larger standard deviations indicate. Meanwhile, the LLD group nearly reached the NS mean on the immediate posttest ($M = 0.47$) but then decreased somewhat on the delayed test ($M = 0.33$), with standard

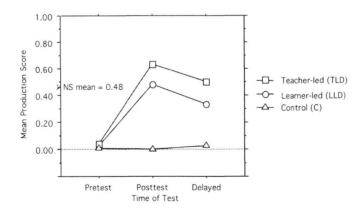

Figure 3 Production task group means for use of anticausative *se* in intransitive sentences.

deviations on both posttests similar to those of TLD. By contrast, the control (C) group means and standard deviations remained close to zero throughout.

A repeated-measures ANOVA with one between-subjects variable (treatment group) and one within-subjects variable (time of test) was performed on the three learner groups' scores using a General Linear Model. This yielded statistically significant results for the interaction of treatment group with time of test, $F(4, 148) = 15.20$, $p < .001$, $\eta_p^2 = 0.29$, as well as significant main effects for treatment, $F(2, 74) = 50.38$, $p < .001$, $\eta_p^2 = 0.58$, and time of test $F(2, 148) = 55.26$, $p < .001$, $\eta_p^2 = 0.43$. The η_p^2 figures here suggest considerable effect sizes for all three results, given that each accounted for at least 29% of the total variance (i.e., effect + error).

Because the significant interaction of group with time of test meant that the three groups changed differently over time, separate univariate ANOVAs were conducted for each test administration, with treatment group as the between-subjects variable. For the pretest, there were no significant differences between the groups, $F(2, 75) = 0.86$, $p > .05$, $\eta_p^2 = 0.02$, but on the two posttests there were: for the immediate posttest, $F(2, 74) = 40.73$, $p < .001$, $\eta_p^2 = 0.52$; for the delayed posttest, $F(2, 75) = 20.40$, $p < .001$, $\eta_p^2 = 0.35$. A Fisher's PLSD post hoc analysis of the immediate posttest found significant differences among all three groups, with the greatest gap between the C group and the two instructed groups ($p < .01$ in both cases) and a lesser one between LLD and TLD ($p < .05$). The more conservative Tukey HSD post hoc analysis also reported significant differences between the instructed groups and the C group ($p < .01$ in both cases) and a near-significant difference between LLD and TLD ($p = .09$). On the delayed posttest, the Fisher PLSD and Tukey HSD found the same differences as on the immediate posttest: The instructed groups contrasted significantly with the C group ($p < .01$ for both treatments in both analyses), whereas the gap between LLD and TLD was statistically significant for the Fisher analysis ($p < .05$) and approached significance on the Tukey analysis ($p = .09$).[9] Thus, an overall effect for instruction is evident in that both experimental groups performed similarly to the C group on the pretest while later obtaining much higher means on both posttests. Nonetheless, the differences between TLD and LLD on both posttests, although less drastic, suggest that TLD yielded overall stronger means than did LLD.

GJ Task

The lower two rows of Table 2 display group means and standard deviations for the acceptance of anticausative *se* on the GJ task over the three test

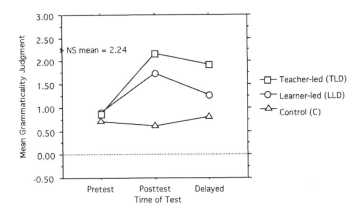

Figure 4 GJ task results for learner groups' acceptance of anticausative *se*.

administrations. Group means are also plotted in Figure 4, with the NS result given for comparison. Here, it is clear that both instructed groups improved markedly from the pretest to posttest, with some decrease on the delayed posttest, whereas the C group remained nearly unchanged. From pretest to immediate posttest, the TLD mean increased by 1.31, nearly reaching that of the NS group, whereas the LLD mean increased by 0.83 to within a half-point of the NS mean (posttest: TLD = 2.17, LLD = 1.74, NS = 2.24). Changes from the immediate to delayed posttest were greater for LLD than for TLD, with LLD decreasing by 0.47 and TLD by 0.24. From pretest to delayed posttest then, TLD gains were greatest at 1.03, followed by LLD gains at 0.36, and C group gains 0.09.

Of further interest is the change in standard deviations among the three groups over time. For the C group, standard deviations on all three tests were considerably higher than the NS group's 0.75, indicating more variation among C group individuals than among NSs. Standard deviations for the two instructed groups were also greater than NSs on the pretest (LLD = 0.94, TLD = 1.01) but became smaller on the immediate posttest (LLD = 0.64, TLD = 0.66), indicating that individual scores were closer to the group means. By the delayed posttest, however, the LLD standard deviation returned to the higher pretest value (0.99), whereas the TLD group remained lower than the NS result and closer to the immediate posttest outcome (0.71). Thus, in addition to a lower group mean for LLD on the delayed posttest, individual scores fell farther from that mean in LLD than in TLD. This greater variation in LLD scores suggests that whereas the instructional benefits evident on the immediate posttest might have persisted for some in that group, they did not do so for as many as in the TLD group.

As on the production task, a General Linear Model repeated-measures ANOVA was performed on the GJ data, with treatment group as the between-subjects variable and time of test as the within-subjects variable. Statistically significant results were found for the interaction of treatment group with time of test, $F(4, 150) = 6.45$, $p < .001$, $\eta_p^2 = 0.15$, as well as the main effects of treatment group, $F(2, 75) = 12.19$, $p < .001$, $\eta_p^2 = 0.25$, and time of test $F(2, 150) = 16.56$, $p < .001$, $\eta_p^2 = 0.18$. The η_p^2 figures again suggest nonnegligible effect sizes in all three cases, given that each accounted for at least 15% of the total variance in the result. The interaction of treatment group with time of test also indicates that group means changed differently over the test administrations. As the discussion thus far suggests, this appears to be due not only to differences between the C group and the two instructed groups but also to differences between the two instructed groups themselves. Univariate ANOVAs performed on each of the three tests, with treatment group as the between-subjects variable, confirm this conclusion. On the pretest, there were no differences between the three groups, $F(2, 75) = 0.25, p > .05, \eta_p^2 = 0.01$, but significant differences were found on both the immediate posttest, $F(2, 75) = 20.08, p < .001, \eta_p^2 = 0.35$, and the delayed posttest $F(2, 75) = 11.86, p < .001, \eta_p^2 = 0.24$. Both Fisher's PLSD and Tukey HSD post hoc analyses showed significant differences on the immediate posttest between the two instructed groups and the C group ($p < .001$ for both comparisons in both analyses) but no differences between TLD and LLD. However, on the delayed posttest, the differences shifted, such that gaps between TLD and the two other groups were significant in both post hoc analyses (for C, $p < .001$; for LLD $p < .05$), whereas the gap between LLD and C only approached significance on Fisher's PLSD ($p = .06$) and failed to do so on the Tukey HSD ($p > .10$). Thus, on the GJ task, as on guided production, a case can be made for beneficial effects attributable to both treatments. However, after instruction, the TLD group showed a stronger performance on both tasks, and where grammaticality judgments are concerned, TLD learners appeared to have retained the benefits of instruction more consistently than did their LLD counterparts.

Discourse Transcripts

Excerpts from the two instructed groups' performance of Day 4's picture description task (Figure 1) are presented here, with the transcribed segment starting roughly at the beginning of the interaction. As per Research Question 3, the discussion of each excerpt focuses on the learners' use of anticausative *se* as well as their feedback and comments on L2 form-meaning relationships. Throughout the transcriptions, English equivalents are given in parentheses and nonverbal gestures, as well as errors and relevant L2 linguistic information, are given in brackets. A zero with a slash (Ø) indicates an incorrect omission of *se*; three periods indicate extended pauses; an extended dash indicates an interrupted utterance; and all names appearing in the text have been changed to aliases.

The LLD discourse samples below come from one of the two course sections, where, after dividing an odd number of individuals into pairs, it was the one group comprised of three learners that volunteered to have their interaction recorded.[10] As a result, in Example 3, the learners began with Student 1 having picture A in Figure 1, and Students 2 and 3 sharing picture B. From their interaction, it is clear that despite instructions to the contrary, all three were holding the pictures so that their partners could see them, and Student 2 seemed to believe that the sofa stain in Student 1's picture came from the wine bottle on the floor.

Example 3

    a. Student 1: *Sí, pregúntame, Raúl, de mi foto.*
        (Yes, ask me, Raúl, about my picture.)

    b. Student 2: *Ah, en tu dibujo, ¿Qué le pasó el botalla?* [pronunciation and gender error]
        (Ah, in your picture, What happened the bottle?)

    c. Student 1: *¿Botalla?* [again, pronounced incorrectly]
        (Bottle?)

    d. Student 2: *¿de vino?*
        (of wine?)

    e. Student 1: *Oh, nadie le pasó.* [lexical error using *nadie* to mean "nothing"]
        (Oh, no one [sic] happened to it.)

    f. Student 2: *vino en—* [indicating the wet spot on the sofa]
        (wine on—)

    g. Student 1: *Oh, ok. El vino, la botella se moja la sofá.* [errors w. *se* and gender of *sofá*]
        (Oh, ok. The wine, the bottle [*se*] wets the sofa.)

    h. Student 2: *¿Moja o mojo?*
        (Wets or wet?)

    i. Student 1: *Se mojó.* Like it wet the couch. *So, la botella se mojó la sofá.*
        ([*Se*] wet. Like it wet the couch. So, the bottle [*se*] wet the couch.)

j. Student 3: *O se cayó.*
  (Or it fell down.)
k. Student 1: *¿Se cayó?*
l. Student 3: *Se cayó.*
m. Student 1: But it didn't break the couch.
n. Student 3: No, *caer*. It fell.

Here, it is clear that during the task, learners were indeed focusing on, negotiating over, and proposing hypotheses for a number of necessary L2 forms. Specifically, in line h, Student 2 questioned Student 1 about the correct past tense suffix for the verb *mojar* (to wet), and in lines j–n, Student 3's proposal to use the verb *caer* (to fall) resulted in a negotiation with Student 1 over the verb's meaning. Clearly, this provides evidence that LLD yielded facilitative L2 "metatalk" (Swain, 1998, 2000) while also supporting Pica et al.'s (1993) claim that information gap tasks are well suited to trigger negotiation. However, despite the learners' considerable attention to L2 morphosyntax and lexis, it is noteworthy that in lines g and i, Student 1's incorrect use of *se* with the transitive form of *mojar* failed to capture attention, as her peers' concerns centered on correct past tense forms. Although not shown here, preoccupation with the past tense was also evident later in the recording, where Student 2 initiated another round of negotiation over the possibility that the vowel /e/ in the verb *cerrar* (to close) might change to a diphthong when inflected in the past, as indeed it does in the present. Although Student 1 then played an important role in resolving this uncertainty, *se* often appeared to be an "unanalyzed chunk" in her spontaneous speech throughout the recording, not unlike the clitic pronouns documented by Myles, Mitchell, and Hooper (1999) among beginning L2 French learners.

Nonetheless, a few moments later, Student 1 demonstrated that with peer assistance, she could apply instruction-derived metalinguistic knowledge to reanalyze one of her *se* + verb chunks and correct the overgeneralization error, which this time involved the verb *entrar* (to enter).

Example 4

a. Student 2: *¿Cómo se dice* "wind"?
  (How do you say "wind"?)
b. Student 1: *Viento.* Ok, you could say, maybe, *"Se, se entra* [overgeneralized *se*] *viento en la casa,"* like—
  (Wind. Ok, you could say, maybe, "Wind [*se*], [*se*] enters the house," like—)
c. Student 3: *Se, uh, entró, ¿verdad?*

(It [*se*], uh, entered, right?)

d. Student 1: *Se entró viento en la casa.*

(Wind [*se*] entered the house.)

e. Student 3: *Se entró.*

(It [*se*] entered.)

f. Student 2: *Oh, se— ¿Se entró?*

(Oh, [*se*]— It [*se*] entered?)

g. Student 1: *Se entró.* Oh, but would you use *se* with that?

h. Student 2: You wouldn't.

i. Student 1: No, because that's a subject. Right. *Viento entré, entró en la casa*

(Wind enter, entered the house.)

j. Student 3: *Sí.*

(Right.)

Here again, it is evident that a major preoccupation for the learners was the past tense, as in line c, where Student 3 questioned Student 1's use of the present in line b. An overgeneralized *se* also appeared in this utterance and was repeated by Students 1 and 3 in lines d and e before Student 2 detected a possible problem in line f. This then led Student 1 to reconsider her use of *se* in line g and, with support from Student 2 in line h, apply her own explicit, metalinguistic understanding to correct the overgeneralization in line i. This dynamic is thus reminiscent of the small-group interactions in Donato (1994), in which collaboration among peers yielded linguistic outcomes that exceeded the limitations that any one of them would have faced alone. Given this evidence of facilitative interactions for L2 grammatical development, the question then arises as to how TLD interactions might have differed to yield the stronger quantitative results observed here.

Example 5 demonstrates how the picture description task in Figure 1 began in one of the two TLD classes. As previously mentioned, all learners were looking at pictures A and B, and the teacher started by asking them to describe differences between the pictures and then continued by soliciting multiple responses without changing the task focus.

Example 5

a. Teacher: *Venga, vamos a ver. ¿Qué ocurrió durante la tormenta? ¿Qué ocurrió? Sí.*

(Okay, let's see. What happened during the storm? What happened? Yes?)

b. Student 4: *Um, la ventana se, um abrió.*
   (Um, the window, [*se*] um opened)
c. Teacher: *Bien. En el dibujo B, ¿verdad? En el dibujo B la ventana se abrió. En el dibujo A, ¿qué?*
   (Good. In drawing B, right? In drawing B the window [*se*] opened. In drawing A, what?)
d. Student 4: *En el dibujo A, la ventana. . .*
   (In drawing A the window. . .)
e. Teacher: *Sí. . .¿Se abrió? No. Se. . .*
   (Yes. . .Did it [se] open? No. It [*se*]. . .)
f. Student 4: *No, se. . .ce-, ce-, cerró.*
   (No, it [*se*]. . .cl-, cl- closed.)
g. Teacher: *Perfecto. En el dibujo A se abrió la ventana, y en el dibujo B— No. En el dibujo A se cerró la ventana y en el dibujo B, se abrió. ¿Más? Jim.*
   (Perfect. In drawing A the window [*se*] opened and in drawing B—No. In drawing A the window [*se*] closed and in drawing B it [*se*] opened. What else? Jim.)
h. Student 5: *Um, en B, la luz, uh, ca-, uh, cayó.* [incorrect omission of *se*]
   (Um, in B, the light, uh, f-, uh, [Ø] fell.)
i. Teacher: *S*— [making a falling gesture with her hands, and then pointing toward another learner with his hand up.]
j. Student 6: *Se cayó.*
   (It [*se*] fell down.)
k. Teacher: *Perfecto.*
   (Perfect.)
l. Student 5: *Se cayó.*
   (It [*se*] fell down.)
m. Teacher: *Se cayó. La luz se cayó.*
   (It [*se*] fell down. The light [*se*] fell down.)

Thus, following the teacher's elicitation in line a, Student 4 successfully used *se* in line b with the verb *abrir* (to open). The teacher's feedback in line c affirmed the answer and repeated it to the class before prompting Student 4 to expand her utterance and comment on the second picture. When Student 4 hesitated in line d, the teacher's response in line e was to further model *se* in a false statement (*se abrió*) and then assist her by starting the target sentence with *se*. After the learner was able to complete the utterance in line f, the teacher then summarized what had been said so far in line g and elicited another response.

When Student 5 incorrectly omitted *se* from his answer in line h, the teacher's feedback in line i consisted simply of the sound of an "s" accompanied by a hand movement. Student 6 then volunteered a correct answer in line j, which was repeated by Student 5 in line l and the teacher in line m.

Unlike the LLD group, this example reveals that the teacher's participation produced a recognizable IRF pattern, with utterances in lines c and g consisting of feedback for the preceding learner turn, followed by subsequent initiation moves. However, a number of the lines in between, such as lines e and i, seemed to serve the additional function of assisting with utterance formulation rather than merely evaluating performance (i.e., feedback) or posing an additional question and nominating a speaker (i.e., initiation). This kind of assistance is somewhat different from typical characterizations of IRF-based instructor "scaffolding" because it is not designed to shape the topical content of discourse or engage analytic abilities, as initiation and feedback moves often do (e.g., Cazden, 2001; Tharp & Gallimore, 1988; Wells, 1993; Wood, Bruner, & Ross, 1976). Instead, lines e and i appear uniquely intended to lighten the cognitive load that mapping the target L2 form onto meaning entails during production, particularly when learners have insufficient control over necessary forms. Although there was also ample evidence of assistance in working out L2 form-meaning relationships among peers during LLD, it did not occur as direct procedural support for articulating L2 utterances, as in TLD.

As the task continued, Example 6 suggests that the teacher's ongoing assistance in formulating targetlike utterances with *se* led some learners to monitor their speech and attempt to preempt errors on their own.

Example 6

  a. Teacher: *Muy bien. ¿Qué más? Luis.*
      (Very good. What else? Luis.)
  b. Student 7: *Dibajo A* [both mispronounced] *la puerta—*
      (Drawing A the door—)
  c. Teacher: '*A*' [correcting his pronunciation of the letter A]
  d. Student 7: '*A*', *la puerta, uh, a-, ¿abrió?. . .Se, se abrió.*
      ('A' the door, uh, [Ø] o-, opened?. . .It [*se*] opened.)
  e. Teacher: *Sí, la puerta se abrió.*
      (Yes, the door [*se*] opened.)
  f. Student 7: *En dibujo B, la puerta cerró.* [incorrect omission of *se*]
      (In drawing B, the door [Ø] closed.)
  g. Teacher: *S—*

h. Student 7: [simultaneously] *Se cerró.*
    (It [*se*] opened.)
i. Teacher: *Perfecto. La puerta se cerró.*
    (Perfect. The door [*se*] closed.)

Thus, in line d, as Student 7 began monitoring his output, he was able to detect his L1-derived tendency to omit *se* with the verb and correct the error. However, when it appeared that he would omit *se* in line f, the teacher's immediate assistance in line g—again, with the sound of an "s"—led to simultaneous self-correction and a targetlike utterance in line h. Again, it appears that the teacher's support helped him not only to formulate his utterance but also to develop the procedural self-regulation necessary for overriding an L1 transfer error.

In addition to correcting omission of the object of instruction, Example 7 demonstrates how teacher feedback and assistance also led learners away from overgeneralizing *se*. It is indeed noteworthy that Student 8's error with the verb *mojar* in this example is nearly identical to that of Student 1 in the LLD group, discussed in Example 3.

Example 7

a. Teacher: *Sí. Susana.*
    (Yes, Susana.)
b. Student 8: *Um, en dibujo A, um, la lluvia...*
    (Um in drawing A, um, the rain...)
c. Teacher: ...Mm-hm...
d. Student 8: ...*¿Se?* [overgeneralization error]
    (...got?)
e. Teacher: *No sé. Venga, venga. La lluvia ¿qué?*
    (I don't know. Come on, come on. The rain what?)
f. Student 8: *mojó.*
    (wet)
g. Teacher: *¿La lluvia se mojó?*
    (The rain got wet?)
h. Student 8: Mm-hm.
i. Teacher: *¿La lluvia se mojó* [making a hand motion toward herself]*? Eso es muy metafísico. Eso es muy, como, misticismo. ¿Cómo que la lluvia—? La lluvia no se mojó* [again, motioning toward herself]. *La lluvia, a sí misma.*

(The rain got wet? That is very metaphysical. That's very, like, mysticism. How could the rain—? The rain didn't get itself wet. The rain, to itself.)

j. Student 8: *¿Mojó? Mojó.*

It wet? It wet.

k. Teacher: *La lluvia mojó* [motioning as if putting the sentence together linearly] *¿qué?*

(The rain got what wet?)

l. Student 8: *¿Cómo se dice* ≪carpet≫*?*

(How do you say "carpet"?)

m. Teacher: *¿Cómo se dice?*

(How do you say it?)

n. Student 9: *El alfombro* [incorrectly marked as masculine noun class]

(The carpet)

o. Teacher: *Alfombra. Muy bien. La alfombra. La lluvia mojó la alfombra. O ¿la alfombra...?*

(Carpet. Very good. The carpet. The rain got the carpet wet. Or the carpet...?)

p. Student 8: *Se mojó.*

(Got wet.)

q. Teacher: *Perfecto. La alfombra se mojó.*

(Perfect. The carpet got wet.)

Thus, as Student 7 began to formulate her utterance in lines b and d, the teacher provided a supportive syntactic frame in line e to indicate a missing element ("*La lluvia ¿qué?*"). When the learner completed her sentence with "*se mojó*" in line f and confirmed in line h that she indeed meant to say it, the teacher then gave metalinguistic feedback in line i to demonstrate the anomalous reflexive that had been created. When Student 7 then proposed the same verb without *se* in line j, the teacher again offered procedural support, this time for a transitive sentence, by repeating the utterance to that point and adding an interrogative "*¿qué?*" to indicate the slot that had yet to be filled. When a vocabulary problem emerged in line l, the teacher then posed the question to the whole class, with another learner responding in line n but making an error in the noun's gender. Without detracting attention from the instructional object, the teacher in line o simply recast the noun with correct gender to complete the transitive sentence. Then, to confirm knowledge of when *se* is and is not required, the teacher posed the beginning of an intransitive sentence to Student 7, who in line p then used *se* in a targetlike manner.

In Examples 5, 6, and 7, the teacher's discourse leadership appeared to have yielded a more consistent focus on the object of instruction than the LLD learners' discussion of L2 forms, which embraced a broader gamut of structures. The TLD instructor's initiation moves provided targetlike models of *se* and elicited focused learner output, whereas assisting moves lightened the procedural burden of mapping L2 form onto meaning and reminded learners of targetlike sentence patterns. Finally, feedback moves either confirmed the grammatical hypotheses underlying learners' responses or gave disconfirming evidence requiring a reformulation of their utterances. Often, they also provided elaborated input demonstrating a key grammatical contrast. In LLD however, with no one designated as an L2 expert, attention was directed to L2 forms via questions, feedback, and metatalk, without the singular focus on one linguistic issue and with greater negotiation among participants. In addition, without a manager of turn-taking and elicitation, the available participant roles did not seem to allow direct assistance to others in articulating their utterances, as the instructor role did in TLD.

This final excerpt from the three LLD learners aptly demonstrates this point, as, toward the end of the interaction, Student 3 sought assistance from Student 1 in saying that the couch in his drawing had moved. Although Student 1 had begun to emerge as a relative expert among the participants, the assistance provided nonetheless required negotiation and did not directly push Student 3 to formulate his intended utterance, as Student 8 did in Example 7 during TLD.

Example 8

a. Student 3: *¿Qué es la palabra para desde aquí a allí?*
   (What is the word for from here to there?)
b. Student 1: *"Derecha."*
   ("Right" [i.e., the opposite of "left"])
c. Student 3: *"Derecha."*
   ("Right.")
d. Student 1: Mm-hm, *verdad.*
   (Mm-hm, correct.)
e. Student 3: *Sí.*
   (Yes.)
f. Student 2: Hm. *Sí.*
   (Hm. Yes.)
g. Student 1: *Derecha a izquierda.*
   (Right to left)

h. Student 3: [simultaneously] ¿ *"Derecha" es el verbo?*
       ("Right" is the verb?)

i. Student 1: *No, no, no. Derecha es el. . .*
       (No, no, no. Right is the. . .)

j. Student 3: The direction.

k. Student 1: Yeah, right. Like *derecha a izquierda.*
       (Yeah right. Like right to left.)

l. Student 3: ¿*Qué es, ah, el, qué es el verbo?*
       (What is, ah, the, what is the verb?)

m. Student 1: [to Student 2] ¿*Tus padres hablan español?*
       (Do your parents speak Spanish?)

n. Student 2: *Sí.*
       (Yeah.)

o. Student 3: [to Student 1] ¿*Qué es el verbo?*
       (What is the verb?)

p. Student 1: *Oh, para—mojar, mojar, mojar. Er, no, no, no. Moverse.* That's
       it.
       (Oh, for—to wet, to wet, to wet. Er, no, no, no. To move. That's
       it.)

[Student 3 starts spelling *moverse* aloud, and the other assist him, letter
   by letter.]

q. Student 2: *Se movió la sofá—*
       (The sofa [*se*] moved—)

r. Student 1: *Se movió—*
       (It [*se*] moved—)

s. Student 2: *a la derecha.*
       (to the right.)

t. Student 1: *a la derecha. Muy bien, Raúl. Eres muy inteligente. . .Hoy!*
       [laughs].
       (to the right. Very good, Raúl. You're very intelligent. . .
       Today!)

Although this excerpt took up no more than 40 s in real time, the 10 turns in lines
b–k clearly occurred due to a misunderstanding of what Student 3 intended to
ask. Although such misunderstandings could obviously occur in TLD as well,
the difference between Student 1's role as relative authority and that of the
instructor in TLD is evident in that Student 1 at no point took responsibility
for making Student 3 produce his sentence. In other words, Student 1 never
sought to confirm Student 3's learning by prompting him to use the new word

in a meaningful sentence, as the teacher in Example 7 did when checking that Student 8 could use *se* intransitively. Indeed, Student 3's discovery in line h that he had the wrong word apparently occurred by accident after Student 1 in line g provided an unprompted amplification of her previous utterance. By the time Student 3 gained clarification of the meaning of "*derecha*" in line i and line k, his request for the verb he wanted had to be made twice, in line l and line o, given that Student 1's attention had momentarily shifted from the task to asking Student 2 about his family. Although in line q and line s, Student 2 ultimately assembled the parts of the sentence that had thus far emerged, and in line t, Student 1 provided teacherlike feedback to Student 3, it is clear that the linguistic work of articulating Student 3's intended sentence took place only after an extended negotiation not only for meaning but also for attention and without the online procedural assistance evident in TLD.

Summary

To review, on the quantitative assessments, the LLD and TLD groups both outperformed the C group for knowledge of Spanish *se* after a week of specialized instruction. However, regarding Research Questions 1 and 2, which asked whether LLD learners would outperform TLD learners, it appears the answer is "no" in both cases, given the TLD group's higher postinstruction means on the production task and greater retention of gains on the GJ task. For Research Question 3, which inquired about qualitative differences in the way LLD and TLD learners attended to L2 form-meaning relationships, it appears that learners' attention to form in LLD might have been more broadly focused on a number of linguistic issues than in TLD and that LLD participatory roles might not have allowed for the same procedural assistance in using the target form that was afforded to TLD learners.

Discussion

Taken together, the quantitative and qualitative data suggest that the teacher-coordinated interactions in the TLD group might have better equipped learners for performance with the instructional object than the small-group learner-led interactions in LLD. Although the larger study (Toth, 1997, 2000, 2003) showed that L1-derived errors decreased similarly in both groups after instruction, and indeed the assessments here were not sophisticated enough to demonstrate a broader grammatical restructuring along the lines of the parameter shifts described by generative linguists (e.g., Bruhn de Garavito, 1999; White, 2003), what is clear is that the TLD learners' more steadfast GJ gains and more consistent, targetlike uses of *se* for picture descriptions coincided with qualitative evidence indicating more consistent appeals for attention to the morphosyntactic properties of *se*. Whether these results reflect a profound change in implicit linguistic knowledge or merely an improved explicit memory for instructed forms, the implications for L2 pedagogy are relevant, given an acquisition theory that views attention to L2 form-meaning relationships and any resulting explicit knowledge as at least facilitative of L2 grammatical development (e.g., DeKeyser, 2003; Doughty, 2001; Schmidt, 2001; Terrell, 1991). Thus, despite the presumed more frequent learner turns in LLD and the optimal opportunities for modified output and negotiation that an information gap imparts, there was no advantage for this group when compared to TLD learners engaging in instructor-managed collaborative discourse. Given these results, what indeed can be said about TLD versus LLD in an L2 pedagogy that promotes morphosyntactic development?

Attentional Focus in LLD

To the extent that teachers do not directly manage interactions in small learner groups, it seems fair to say that LLD is indeed more "learner centered" than TLD, which brings both strengths and limitations for target-structure learning outcomes that were apparent in this study. First, it is clear that, with greater possibilities for autonomy and self-selection in turn-taking, learners are indeed freer to focus attention on a broad array of topics, adopt a wide variety of speaking roles, and potentially utilize a greater number of linguistic structures during interaction. Clearly, despite the information-gap design, control over what to say and how to say it is looser. Although not systematically quantified here, a cursory glance at the three LLD transcripts does suggest many more learner-initiated questions and topics than in TLD and a broader array of L2 linguistic issues addressed. Nonetheless, despite ample evidence of collaboration and feedback among learners, the process of producing L2 utterances and reaching a consensus on their acceptability appears to have entailed more protracted negotiations in LLD than in TLD, with each participant having the right to inquire, hypothesize, and give opinions about a variety of issues. Although other research has shown important pedagogical benefits to be derived from such interactions (e.g., Donato, 1994; Foster & Ohta, 2005; Swain & Lapkin, 1995, 1998, 2001; van Lier, 1996), the data here suggest that this might have come at the expense of consistency in attention to the target form for the LLD group, given that requirements to use *se* were manifest only in the task instructions and design.

Although advocates for LLD as essential to task-based pedagogy would argue that such conditions ought to yield maximally "pushed" output and attention to targeted structures (e.g., Fotos, 2002; Loschky & Bley-Vroman, 1993; Long, 1996; Long & Porter, 1985; Pica, 1994; Pica et al., 2006), it appears that LLD participants here inevitably focused on nontargeted task-essential structures as well, most notably lexical items that might not have been sufficiently primed in pretask activities, and other morphosyntactic features that stood at the frontier of their current L2 linguistic competence (i.e., past tense morphology). Thus, when assessments of *se* were administered to learners who had spent significant time directing attention more broadly to the L2 during self-initiated communication, their performance was not as robust as those who had spent equivalent time in teacher-assisted production using the target structure. It would therefore be reasonable to speculate that, given the considerable attention to L2 issues other than the object of instruction that the learners themselves selected as problematic, the assessments in this study might have failed to fully capture the instructional benefits derived from the LLD format. Indeed, a more open-ended assessment, or one that tracked learners more closely after instruction on the L2 structures that emerged in their metatalk, might have demonstrated stronger results. Although documenting learners' posttask performance with issues emerging from LLD can indeed further our understanding of the relationship between learner-learner interactions and L2 development, confirmation of these benefits vis-à-vis TLD would require a comparison with TLD learners on those same LLD-initiated issues as well as a teacher-selected object of instruction. In this way, one could discern whether the LLD-generated attention to L2 structures that are of concern to learners benefits morphosyntactic development in the same way as TLD-generated attention to structures that are of concern to the instructor.

Optimal Teacher-Led Discourse, Attention to Form, and Procedural Assistance

Turning to the TLD results, the transcript data suggest that this group might have experienced an optimal instantiation of this discourse format that avoided many of the potential pitfalls discussed in the literature. In particular, there was no evidence of the "local lexical chaining" in grammar practice described by Hall (1995, 2004) or any of the incoherently wandering closed questions documented by Lee (2000) and Leemann-Guthrie (1984) during "class discussions." Instead, as per instructions, the teacher in Examples 5, 6, and 7 used links between the target structure and the task goals as the organizing feature for discourse (i.e., identifying differences between the two pictures) and avoided the incongruent exchanges that would have resulted had she sought production of all the reflexive pronouns or all of the uses of *se* via "meaningful" and "communicative drills" (Paulston, 1972) that fail to cohere to a broader discourse purpose. In addition, elicitation via task instructions and open-ended rather than closed questions appeared to maximize learner output, given that natural responses entailed sentence-level rather than single-word utterances (e.g., "Describe the differences in these pictures" and "What happened in the picture?" rather than "Did the window open?"). Finally, the solicitation of multiple learner responses before new questions were posed created a discourse space where several learners could experience task performance and feedback before subsequent questions should change the discourse focus. This feedback was optimal in that it provided elaborated subsequent input to learners and focused on key grammatical contrasts. Although the design of this study does not permit definitive causal links to be made between these qualitative observations and TLD's quantitative results, their coincidence does suggest a facilitative impact on L2 development, given current views on the role of attention, scaffolded output, and language processing in acquisition.

For example, one likely benefit of eliciting multiple learner responses for each teacher question is that previous teacher input and feedback would have been directly relevant to anyone speaking after the first respondent. In light of Ohta's (2000, 2001) finding that TLD listeners often actively reflect on feedback to others, the benefit of being able take one's own turn after that of others cannot be underestimated, as the value of instructor support becomes cumulative over the course of the task. Indeed, in Toth's (2004) study, lower achieving L2 Spanish learners reported that they often depended on the previous answers of peers in order to both comprehend teacher questions and formulate appropriate responses. Such benefits are lost, however, when only one response is elicited before the topic/task changes to a new question, given that learners must then disregard as irrelevant the feedback provided for the first question and think up new appropriate answers for the second. Thus, the strategy of maintaining a single task/question's relevance over several learner turns might have created an optimally cohesive context for engaging learners in meaningful production while assisting them in target structure use. Also, to the extent that non-turn-takers were still cognitively engaged, the hypothesis-testing, gap-noticing, and metalinguistic functions of output proposed by Swain (1995, 1998, 2000) might have been maximally realized here as a collective *mental* effort with cumulative effects that would offset the fewer output turns per learner in TLD than in LLD.

Within this context, the qualitative data suggest that the teacher's consistency in highlighting the instructional object was achieved in four important ways: (a) modeling *se* in her input, (b) cueing and eliciting it as output, (c) focusing feedback on ungrammatical omissions or overgeneralizations, and (d) actively assisting learners in articulating utterances. As noted in the transcripts, this latter goal was often accomplished via a sentence-building "fill-in-the-blank" technique that provided a syntactic frame for linking words together while isolating missing or problematic elements in what had been said so far. These turns, which will here be dubbed "procedural assistance" moves, were often inserted between the lines of a typical IRF sequence as a unique feature of L2-oriented TLD, given that they were designed not to facilitate analysis of a concept or clarification of a previous utterance but to help the learner map L2 form onto meaning online, during utterance formulation.

Although it is relevant to cite Wood et al.'s (1976) original exposition of the ways that teachers "scaffold" learners toward instructional goals via moves that simplify tasks and identify key performance features, the procedural assistance observed here is nonetheless unique to the L2 context in that it supports an articulatory task made complex by the linguistic structures involved rather than a conceptual one made complex by demands for critical thinking. Furthermore, this procedural assistance differs from the clarification requests, comprehension checks, recasts, and other feedback identified as useful for L2 development in small-group contexts, given that it is made directly to the learner while he or she formulates an utterance, rather than as an indication afterward that a communication breakdown has occurred. Instead, this assistance is more consistent with Johnson's (1996) proposal that teachers might facilitate the development of fluent communication in learners through strategically targeted "hints" that support the "proceduralization" of subcomponents of the linguistic task (p. 108–109). However, as noted previously, it is doubtful that interaction roles outside of TLD, whether among LLD peers or in nonclassroom settings, would allow interlocutors to offer such assistance. Indeed, Buckwalter's (2001) finding that LLD participants strongly prefer self-correction to other-correction not only supports this conclusion but also concurs with findings from analysts of discourse in noninstructional settings (Seedhouse, 2004). Thus, TLD might be a unique context for providing procedural assistance in L2 utterance formulation.

Procedural Assistance and Output Processing

If indeed L2 procedural assistance is licensed within TLD but generally dispreferred elsewhere, then how can they be theoretically justified as beneficial to

L2 acquisition? Recent work on instructed L2 development has proposed that pedagogical interventions might be most effective when they assist learners in language processing or, rather, pushing them to correctly encode specific form-meaning relationships in the L2 while using the language meaningfully (e.g., Carroll, 2001; Sharwood-Smith, 2004; VanPatten, 1996, 2004b). Current models for how learners process L2 form-meaning links suggest that hierarchical semantic and syntactic relationships might be mentally computed online while comprehending or producing an utterance rather than after an utterance is concluded (Harrington, 2001; Pritchett, 1992). Thus, the cognitive complexity of an utterance's linguistic structure has been shown to affect communicative task performance (Juffs, 1998, 2004; Juffs & Harrington, 1995; VanPatten, 1990, 2004b). To date, L2 processing research has focused primarily on how parsing crashes and/or misinterpretations of L2 input are triggered by the appearance of specific morphemes in the input, such as case-marked pronouns (VanPatten, 1990, 2004b) or inflected verbs in subordinate clauses (Juffs, 1998, 2004; Juffs & Harrington, 1995). VanPatten has proposed "processing instruction" as a means of addressing these difficulties via explicit attention to troublesome L2 form-meaning relationships that appear in the input. Meanwhile, where output is concerned, current models of speech production have ascribed an important role to preverbal message "monitoring" as an accompaniment to lexical and grammatical encoding, such that the potential exists for explicit knowledge of L2 form-meaning relationships to affect the content of speech output (Izumi, 2003; Levelt, 1989; Scovel, 1998). It follows, then, that when the structural complexity of one's usable metalinguistic knowledge exceeds that of the extant implicit L2 grammar, L2 development might be helped if such knowledge can be employed online to guide lexical selection and grammatical encoding during communicative task performance (deBot, 1996; Kormos, 1999; Toth, 2006).

    If through procedural assistance instructors facilitate not only the use of metalinguistic information but also the assembly of structurally more complex utterances to represent learners' intended meanings, then such assistance might indeed be useful as a form of "pushed output" (Swain, 1985), given that part of the cognitive burden associated with the utterance's linguistic structure is borne by the teacher and the production work left to the learner focuses only on those elements that pertain to the instructional object. The strongest support here for this idea appears in Example 7, where metalinguistic feedback first led Student 8 to retreat from overgeneralization and then the teacher's procedural assistance helped her construct not only the intended transitive sentence but also an intransitive one correctly using the target form. In this way, not only were contrastive examples of *se*'s use and nonuse provided—both as output for Student 8 and input provided to other learners—but the full burden of managing the syntax of each utterance as they emerged online was shared by both participants. Although further investigation is surely needed to confirm these ideas, it might be that such assistance in "output processing" constitutes an important initial step in developing the complexity of the learner's linguistic repertoire.

In making a case for output during LLD-based collaborative tasks, Swain (2000) has asserted the possibility that "output pushes learners to process language more deeply—with more mental effort—than does input" (p. 99), especially given the learner's ability to select and encode his or her own intended meaning. The benefits of such autonomy notwithstanding, it might be that although there are still fewer turns per learner in successful TLD, a collective *mental* effort in processing output is nonetheless achieved, as teacher prompts and feedback focus learners' attention on the L2 target and a sense that all are sufficiently enfranchised to take a turn makes nonparticipants into engaged listeners when others are taking theirs.

Limitations of the Study and Directions for Future Research

Although this study has shown that L2 grammar instruction given as TLD can yield stronger learning outcomes than LLD for target forms, it clearly should not to be taken as evidence that TLD in all cases constitutes a better classroom option than LLD. Not only might it be that this study failed to fully capture the advantages of LLD, but also it is certain that the observed benefits of TLD greatly depend on a variety of individual and contextual factors, including the skill of the instructor in managing interactions effectively and a positive class rapport. Indeed, the recordings of both TLD classes suggest that prior to the study, each instructor had established a setting in which learners felt comfortable offering unsolicited support to peers and initiating uncued requests for teacher assistance (e.g., Example 5, line j; Example 7, line l and line n). Although such positive group dynamics were also evident in the LLD classes, they probably more greatly enhanced the TLD treatment, given the centrality of the teacher in building a sense of collaboration and support among learners during whole-group tasks.

Still, the fact that the TLD group engaged in one to two additional tasks per day while the LLD group performed posttask follow-ups raises the issue of time management within the lesson as a possible factor affecting these results, in addition to the discourse format. It also remains for future research to determine whether the successful discourse management shown here for TLD can be reproduced with learners belonging to other social, cultural, and age groups and whether similar results can be obtained for other teacher-selected objects of instruction. This will surely be a crucial aspect for future study, given the intuitive advantage of allowing learners to set their own attentional focus on the L2 during LLD and the transcript evidence here and elsewhere indicating that this is indeed what they do when working on tasks with peers.

By showing stronger learning outcomes for an instructional object via task-based, teacher-led discourse, vis-à-vis learner-led, small-group discourse, this study provides evidence against a common pedagogical belief that learner groups are necessarily a preferable format for achieving development with target L2 structures via a communicative focus on form. Instead, the data here suggest that although there are identifiable advantages to both formats, the teacher's provision of input models, focused elicitation, procedural assistance, and form-focused feedback might have more greatly benefited whole-class learners' performance with the instructional object than the linguistic support provided among learners in small groups. Clearly, some of the problems that have been documented for TLD stem not simply from the teacher's greater control over discourse but rather from ineffective choices in the exercise of that control during classroom interactions.

In the first Spiderman movie of the American series starring Tobey Maguire (Lee & Caracciolo, 2002), the superhero's father warns him that "with great power comes great responsibility." Far be it for Hollywood to have any relevance in applied linguistics, but when assessing the teacher's potential to build a beneficial discourse for learners' linguistic development, it is clear that so much depends on wise moment-by-moment choices and an overall technique that takes morphosyntactic complexity and discourse cohesion into account. Rather than categorically eschewing teacher-led discourse as antithetical to the principles of a "learner-centered curriculum," L2 teacher education programs must, for the sake of learners, do a more adequate job of training teachers to effectively and responsibly conduct whole-class interactions. Nonetheless, rather than urging a pendulum swing to the opposite extreme, with TLD the hero and LLD the villain, it appears that the best approach to facilitating L2 development comes from a careful analysis of the strengths and limitations of each as a discursive pedagogical tool, and from a sound training in maximizing their respective potentials. Clearly, an optimal L2 pedagogy would call for the principled integration of both formats into classroom practice, matching instructional goals with the benefits that either format provides.

Revised version accepted 13 August 2007

Notes

1 Loschky and Bley-Vroman (1993, pp. 140–141) argue that making target structures "essential" on production tasks is difficult, given learners' freedom to use alternate structures. This will indeed be evident in the qualitative data of the present study.

2 The larger study (Toth, 1997) also included an output-free, teacher-led "processing instruction" group, as described in Lee and VanPatten (2003), in addition to the LLD and TLD groups described here. This group's results are reported in Toth (1997, 2000, 2003, 2006).

3 Note that Pica's (1987) study comparing an "information exchange" activity in both a small-group and teacher-led format does not indicate how many students were involved in the whole-class interaction. There, each learner was given a unique piece of visual information about where a flower ought to be planted in a garden, and by pooling each learner's information, a complete picture of the garden emerged. For the present study, this design was unfeasible, given the large class sizes and the fact that such complex interactional planning would have had to be sustained for a full week of instruction rather than a single instructional activity.

4 All materials given to instructors are available upon request.

5 In the Version A picture description, the middle-voice verbs were *romper* (to break) and *mojar* (to wet); in Version B, they were *cocinar* (to cook) and *descomponer* (to break down). The passive or impersonal verbs in Version A were *traer* (to bring) and *destruir* (to destroy); in Version B, they were *oír* (to hear) and *ver* (to see).

6 A number of recent studies have incorporated a picture interpretation component within GJ tasks to ensure that learner judgments are tied to knowledge of L2 form-meaning connections (Bley-Vroman & Yoshinaga, 2000; Montrul, 1999, 2000). Although the lack of picture interpretation on this task means that some learners could have answered without understanding an item's meaning, the statistically reliable distinctions made by these learners between different verb classes and grammatical versus ungrammatical items, as reported in Toth (1997, 2000, 2003), suggest that such blind answering did not occur on a large scale. All test items used vocabulary prominently appearing in the curriculum prior to the test, and learners were instructed to ask for any lexical help they needed. The goal of the GJ task was thus only to have learners indicate whether sentences using familiar vocabulary were possible in Spanish with or without *se*. In order to reduce the impact of explicit "monitoring" on task performance, a 25-min limit was set for the entire test and learners were instructed to answer "by feel" on the GJ task.

7 In Version A of the GJ task, middle-voice verbs were *cocinar, relajar,* and *llenar* (to cook, relax, and fill); in Version B, they were: *descomponer, romper,* and *encender* (to break down, break, and turn on). The passive or impersonal verbs in Version A were *poner, comprar, ver, fumar,* and *comer* (to put, buy, see, smoke, and eat); in Version B, they were: *traer, hacer, llevar, entrar,* and *decidir* (to bring, make, wear, enter, and decide).

8 The high standard deviation for the NS group reflects their frequent use of alternatives to *se*. The most common were transitive sentences for externally caused events (e.g., *Ellos destruyeron la casa* [They destroyed the house]) and resultant-state passives for inchoative ones (*El vaso está roto* [The glass is broken]). Within Pustejovsky's (1995) analysis of transitivity, this distribution of alternatives to *se* is to be expected, given the varying prominence of external agents in the two verb types. Because the task was open-ended, the frequency of nontarget responses was not taken to indicate a lack of validity. Instead, high standard deviations resulted from the necessity of imposing binary scoring on a task that yielded multiple answer categories. The NS performance is indeed intended only to provide a basis for comparison with the learners.

9 The Fisher PLSD simply considers each possible group pairing, whereas the Tukey HSD does so after adjusting the threshold of significance for multiple comparisons. The rationale for using Fisher is that the Tukey adjustment is not necessary, given that the pairwise comparisons occur after reaching a significant ANOVA. Generally, the Fisher is recommended if one simply wants to know which group is more likely to have an effect, whereas the Tukey is preferred if one wants to be sure that a given group will yield an effect (Hilton & Armstrong, 2006).

10 This recording was chosen over that of the other class due principally to sound quality.

References

Adair-Hauck, B., & Donato, R. (1994). Foreign language explanations within the Zone of Proximal Development. *Canadian Modern Language Review, 50*, 532–557.

Antón, M. (1999). The discourse of a learner-centered classroom: Sociocultural perspectives on teacher-learner interaction in the second-language classroom. *Modern Language Journal, 83*, 303–318.

Austin, J. L. (1962). *How to do things with words*. Oxford: Oxford University Press.

Bley-Vroman, R., & Yoshinaga, N. (2000). The acquisition of multiple *wh*-questions by non-native speakers of English. *Second Language Research, 16*, 3–26.

Breen, M. P., & Candlin, C. N. (1980). The essentials of a communicative curriculum in language teaching. *Applied Linguistics, 1*, 89–112.

Brooks, F. B. (1993). Some problems and caveats in "communicative" discourse: Toward a conceptualization of the foreign language classroom. *Foreign Language Annals, 26*, 231–242.

Brooks, F. B., Donato, R., & McGlone, J. V. (1997). When are they going to say "it" right? Understanding learner talk during pair-work activity. *Foreign Language Annals, 30*, 524–541.

Bruhn de Garavito, J. (1999). Adult SLA of SE constructions in Spanish. *Spanish Applied Linguistics, 3*, 247–296.

Buckwalter, P. (2001). Repair sequences in Spanish L2 dyadic discourse: A descriptive study. *Modern Language Journal, 85*, 380–397.

Carroll, S. E. (2001). *Input and evidence: The raw material of second language acquisition*. Philadelphia: Benjamins.

Cazden, C. B. (2001). *Classroom discourse: The language of teaching and learning* (2nd ed.). Portsmouth, NH: Heinemann.

Cullen, R. (1998). Teacher talk and the classroom context. *ELT Journal, 52*, 179–187.

deBot, K. (1996). The psycholinguistics of the output hypothesis. *Language Learning, 46*, 529–555.

DeKeyser, R. (2003). Implicit and explicit learning. In C. J. Doughty & M. H. Long (Eds.), *The handbook of second language acquisition* (pp. 311–348). Oxford: Blackwell.

Dobrobie-Sorin, C. (1998). Impersonal *se* constructions in Romance and passivization of unergatives. *Linguistic Inquiry, 29*, 399–437.

Donato, R. (1994). Collective scaffolding in second language learning. In J. Lantolf & G. Appel (Eds.), *Vygotskian approaches to second language learning*. Norwood, NJ: Ablex.

Donato, R., & Brooks, F. B. (2004). Literary discussions and advanced speaking functions: Researching the (dis)connection. *Foreign Language Annals, 37*(2), 183–199

Doughty, C. (2001). Cognitive underpinnings of focus on form. In P. Robinson (Ed.), *Cognition and second language instruction* (pp. 206–257). Cambridge: Cambridge University Press.

Doughty, C., & Pica, T. (1986). "Information gap" tasks: Do they facilitate second language acquisition? *TESOL Quarterly, 20*, 305–325.

Doughty, C., & Williams, J. (1998a). Issues and terminology. In C. Doughty & J. Williams (Eds.), *Focus on form in classroom second language acquisition* (pp. 1–12). Cambridge: Cambridge University Press.

Doughty, C., & Williams, J. (Eds.). (1998b). *Focus on form in classroom language acquisition*. Cambridge: Cambridge University Press.

Ellis, R. (1997). *SLA research and language teaching*. Oxford: Oxford University Press.

Ellis, R. (2003). *Task-based learning and teaching*. Oxford: Oxford University Press.

Foster, P., & Ohta, A. S. (2005). Negotiation for meaning and peer assistance in second language classrooms. *Applied Linguistics, 26*, 402–430.

Fotos, S. (1993). Consciousness raising and noticing through focus on form: Grammar task performance versus formal instruction. *Applied Linguistics, 14*, 385–403.

Fotos, S. (1994). Integrating grammar instruction and communicative language use through grammar consciousness-raising tasks. *TESOL Quarterly, 28*, 323–351.

Fotos, S. (2002). Structure-based interactive tasks for the EFL grammar learner. In E. Hinkel & S. Fotos (Eds.), *New perspectives on grammar teaching in second language classrooms* (pp. 135–154). Mahwah, NJ: Erlbaum.

Gass, S. (2003). Input and interaction. In C. J. Doughty & M. H. Long (Eds.), *The handbook of second language acquisition* (pp. 224–256). Malden, MA: Blackwell.

Hall, J. K. (1995). "Aw man, where you goin'?": Interaction and the development of L2 interactional competence. *Issues in Applied Linguistics, 6*, 37–62.

Hall, J. K. (2004). "Practicing speaking" in Spanish: Lessons from a high school foreign language classroom. In D. Boxer & A. D. Cohen (Eds.), *Studying speaking to inform second language learning* (pp. 68–87). Clevedon, UK: Multilingual Matters.

Harrington, M. (2001). Sentence processing. In P. Robinson (Ed.), *Cognition and second language instruction* (pp. 91–124). Cambridge: Cambridge University Press.

Hilton, A., & Armstrong, R. (2006, September). Stat note 6: Post hoc ANOVA tests. *Microbiologist, 7*, 34–36.

Hymes, D. (1972). On communicative competence. In J. B. Pride & J. Holmes (Eds.), *Sociolinguistics*. Harmondsworth, UK: Penguin Books.

Izumi, S. (2003). Comprehension and production processes in second language learning: In search of the psycholinguistic rationale of the output hypothesis. *Applied Linguistics, 24*, 168–196.

Jacobs, G. M. (1998). Cooperative learning or just grouping students: The difference makes a difference. In W. A. Renandya & G. M. Jacobs (Eds.), *Learners and language learning* (pp. 145–171). Singapore: SEAMEO.

Johnson, K. (1996). *Language teaching and skill learning*. Oxford: Blackwell.

Johnson, K. E. (1995). *Understanding communication in second language classrooms*. Cambridge: Cambridge University Press.

Juffs, A. (1998). Main verb vs. reduced relative clause ambiguity resolution in second language sentence processing. *Language Learning, 48*, 107–147.

Juffs, A. (2004). Representation, processing, and working memory in a second language. *Transactions of the Philological Society, 102*, 199–225.

Juffs, A., & Harrington, M. (1995). Parsing effects in second language sentence processing: Subject and object asymmetries in *Wh*-extraction. *Studies in Second Language Acquisition, 17*, 483–516.

Kormos, J. (1999). Monitoring and self-repair in L2. *Language Learning, 49*, 303–342.

Krashen, S., Sferlazza, V., Feldman, L., & Fathman, A. (1976). Adult performance on the SLOPE test: More evidence for a natural sequence in adult second language acquisition. *Language Learning, 26*, 145–151.

Larsen-Freeman, D. (1975). The acquisition of grammatical morphemes by adult ESL students. *TESOL Quarterly, 9*, 409–430.

Lee, J. F. (2000). *Tasks and communicating in language classrooms*. New York: McGraw-Hill.

Lee, J. F., & VanPatten, B. (2003). *Making communicative language teaching happen* (2nd ed.). New York: McGraw-Hill.

Lee, S., & Caracciolo, J. M. (Producers), D. Koepp (Writer), & S. Raimi (Director). (2002). *Spider-Man* [Motion picture]. United States: Columbia Pictures.

Leeman, J. (2003). Recasts and second language development: Beyond negative evidence. *Studies in Second Language Acquisition, 25*, 37–64.

Leemann-Guthrie, E. (1984). Intake, communication, and second-language teaching. In S. Savignon & M. Berns (Eds.), *Initiatives in communicative language teaching: A book of readings* (pp. 35–54). Reading, MA: Addison-Wesley.

Levelt, W. J. M. (1989). *Speaking: From intention to articulation.* Cambridge, MA: MIT Press.

Levin, B., & Rappaport-Hovav, M. (1995). *Unaccusativity: At the syntax-lexical semantics interface.* Cambridge, MA: MIT Press.

Long, M. H. (1981). Input, interaction and second language acquisition. In H. Winitz (Ed.), *Native language and foreign language acquisition.* Annals of the New York Academy of Sciences: Vol. 379 (pp. 259–278). New York: New York Academy of Sciences.

Long, M. H. (1985). A role for instruction in second language acquisition: Task-based language teaching. In K. Hyltenstam & M. Pienemann (Eds.), *Modeling and assessing second language acquisition* (pp. 77–99). Clevedon, UK: Multilingual Matters.

Long, M. H. (1991). Focus on form: A design feature in language teaching methodology. In K. deBot, D. Coste, R. Ginsberg, & C. Kramsch (Eds.), *Foreign language research in cross-cultural perspectives* (pp. 39 52). Amsterdam: Benjamins.

Long, M. H. (1996). The role of the linguistic environment in second language acquisition. In W. C. Ritchie & T. K. Bhatia (Eds.), *Handbook of second language acquisition* (pp. 413–468). New York: Academic Press.

Long, M. H., & Crookes, G. (1993). Units of analysis in syllabus design: The case for task. In G. Crookes & S. Gass (Eds.), *Tasks in a pedagogical context: Integrating theory and practice* (pp. 9–54). Clevedon, UK: Multilingual Matters.

Long, M. H., & Porter, P. A. (1985). Group work, interlanguage talk, and second language acquisition. *TESOL Quarterly, 19*, 207–228.

Loschky, L., & Bley-Vroman, R. (1993). Grammar and task-based methodology. In G. Crookes & S. Gass (Eds.), *Tasks and language learning: Integrating theory and practice* (pp. 123–163). Clevedon, UK: Multilingual Matters.

Lyster, R. (2001). Negotiation of form, recasts, and explicit correction in relation to error types and learner repair in immersion classrooms. In R. Ellis (Ed.), *Form-focused instruction and second language learning* (Vol. 51, pp. 265–301). Malden, MA: Blackwell.

Mackey, A. (1999). Input, interaction, and second language development. *Studies in Second Language Acquisition, 21*, 557–587.

McCormick, D. E., & Donato, R. (2000). Teacher questions as scaffolded assistance in an ESL classroom. In J. K. Hall & L. S. Verplaetse (Eds.), *Second and foreign language learning through classroom interaction* (pp. 183–202). Mahwah, NJ: Erlbaum.

Mehan, H. (1979). *Learning lessons: Social organization in the classroom.* Cambridge, MA: Harvard University Press.

Montrul, S. (1999). Causative errors with unaccusative verbs in L2 Spanish. *Second Language Research, 15*, 191–219.

Montrul, S. (2000). Causative psych verbs in Spanish L2 acquisition. In R. Leow & C. Sanz (Eds.), *Spanish applied linguistics at the turn of the millennium* (pp. 97–118). Somerville, MA: Cascadilla Press.

Montrul, S. (2004). *The acquisition of Spanish: Morphosyntactic development in monolingual and bilingual L1 acquisition and adult L2 acquisition.* Philadelphia: Benjamins.

Morris, F. A. (2002). Negotiation moves and recasts in relation to error types and learner repair in the foreign language classroom. *Foreign Language Annals, 35*, 395–404.

Musumeci, D. (1996). Teacher-learner negotiation in content-based instruction: Communication at cross-purposes? *Applied Linguistics, 17*, 286–325.

Myles, F., Mitchell, R., & Hooper, J. (1999). Interrogative chunks in French L2: A basis for creative construction? *Studies in Second Language Acquisition, 21*, 49–80.

National Standards in Foreign Language Learning Project. (1999). *Standards for foreign language learning in the 21st century including Chinese, Classical Languages, French, German, Italian, Japanese, Portuguese, Russian, and Spanish.* Lawrence, KS: Allen Press.

Norris, J. M., & Ortega, L. (2000). Effectiveness of L2 instruction: A research synthesis and quantitative meta-analysis. *Language Learning, 50*, 417–528.

Nunan, D. (1987). Communicative language teaching: Making it work. *ELT Journal, 41*, 136–145.

Nunan, D. (1989). *Designing tasks for the communicative classroom.* Cambridge: Cambridge University Press.

Nunan, D. (1990). The questions teachers ask. *JALT Journal, 12*, 187–202.

Ohta, A. S. (2000). Rethinking recasts: A learner-centered examination of corrective feedback in the Japanese language classroom. In J. K. Hall & L. S. Verplaetse (Eds.), *Second and foreign language learning through classroom interaction* (pp. 47–72). Mahwah, NJ: Erlbaum.

Ohta, A. S. (2001). *Second language acquisition processes in the classroom: Learning Japanese.* Mahwah, NJ: Erlbaum.

Paulston, C. B. (1972). The sequencing of structural pattern drills. *TESOL Quarterly, 5*, 197–208.

Pica, T. (1987). Second-language acquisition, social interaction, and the classroom. *Applied Linguistics, 8*, 3–21.

Pica, T. (1994). Research on negotiation: What does it reveal about second language learning, processes and outcomes? *Language Learning, 44*, 493–527.

Pica, T. (2005). Classroom learning, teaching, and research: A task-based perspective. *Modern Language Journal, 89*, 339–352.

Pica, T., & Doughty, C. (1985). Input and interaction in the communicative language classroom: A comparison of teacher-fronted and group activities. In S. Gass & C. Madden (Eds.), *Input in second language acquisition* (pp. 115–132). Cambridge, MA: Newbury House.

Pica, T., Holliday, L., Lewis, N., & Morgenthaler, L. (1989). Comprehensible output as an outcome of linguistic demands on the learner. *Studies in Second Language Acquisition, 11*, 63–90.

Pica, T., Kanagy, R., & Falodun, J. (1993). Choosing and using communication tasks for second language acquisition. In G. Crookes & S. Gass (Eds.), *Tasks and language learning: Integrating theory and practice* (pp. 9–34). Clevedon, UK: Multilingual Matters.

Pica, T., Kang, H.-S., & Sauro, S. (2006). Information gap tasks: Their multiple roles and contributions to interaction research methodology. *Studies in Second Language Acquisition, 28*, 301–338.

Porter, P. A. (1986). How learners talk to each other: Input and interaction in task-centered discussions. In R. R. Day (Ed.), *Talking to learn: Conversation in second language acquisition* (pp. 200–222). Rowley, MA: Newbury House.

Prabhu, N. S. (1987). *Second language pedagogy*. Oxford: Oxford University Press.

Pritchett, B. L. (1992). *Grammatical competence and parsing performance*. Chicago: University of Chicago Press.

Pustejovsky, J. (1995). *The generative lexicon*. Cambridge, MA: MIT Press.

Raposo, E., & Uriagereka, J. (1996). Indefinite *SE*. *Natural Language and Linguistic Theory, 14*, 749–810.

Samuda, V. (2001). Guiding relationships between form and meaning during task performance: The role of the teacher. In M. Bygate, P. Skehan, & M. Swain (Eds.), *Researching pedagogic tasks: Second language learning, teaching, and testing* (pp. 119–140). Harlow, UK: Longman.

Samuda, V., & Bygate, M. (2008). *Tasks in second language learning*. Basingstoke, UK: Palgrave Macmillan.

Schmidt, R. W. (2001). Attention. In P. Robinson (Ed.), *Cognition and second language instruction* (pp. 3–32). Cambridge: Cambridge University Press.

Scovel, T. (1998). *Psycholinguistics*. Oxford: Oxford University Press.

Searle, J. (1969). *Speech acts*. Cambridge: Cambridge University Press.

Seedhouse, P. (1999). Task-based interaction. *ELT Journal, 53*, 149–156.

Seedhouse, P. (2004). *The interactional architecture of the language classroom: A conversation analysis perspective*. Malden, MA: Blackwell.

Sharwood-Smith, M. (2004). In two minds about grammar: On the interaction of linguistic and metalinguistic knowledge in performance. *Transactions of the Philological Society, 102*, 255–280.

Sinclair, J. M., & Coulthard, R. M. (1975). *Toward an analysis of discourse: The English used by teachers and pupils*. London: Oxford University Press.

Skehan, P. (1996). A framework for the implementation of task-based instruction. *Applied Linguistics, 17*, 38–62.

Skehan, P. (1998). *A cognitive approach to language learning.* Oxford: Oxford University Press.

Skehan, P., & Foster, P. (1999). The influence of task structure and processing conditions on narrative retellings. *Language Learning, 49*, 93–120.

Swain, M. (1985). Communicative competence: Some roles of comprehensible input and comprehensible output in its development. In S. Gass & C. Madden (Eds.), *Input in second language acquisition.* Cambridge, MA: Newbury House.

Swain, M. (1995). Three functions of output in second language learning. In G. Cook & B. Seidlhofer (Eds.), *Principle and practice in applied linguistics: Studies in honour of H. G. Widdowson* (pp. 125–144). Oxford: Oxford University Press.

Swain, M. (1998). Focus on form through conscious reflection. In C. Doughty & J. Williams (Eds.), *Focus on form in classroom second language acquisition* (pp. 64–82). Cambridge: Cambridge University Press.

Swain, M. (2000). The output hypothesis and beyond: Mediating acquisition through collaborative dialogue. In J. Lantolf (Ed.), *Sociocultural theory and second language learning* (pp. 97–114). Oxford: Oxford University Press.

Swain, M., & Lapkin, S. (1995). Problems in output and the cognitive processes they generate: A step towards second language learning. *Applied Linguistics, 16*, 371–391.

Swain, M., & Lapkin, S. (1998). Interaction and second language learning: Two adolescent French immersion students working together. *Modern Language Journal, 82*, 320–337.

Swain, M., & Lapkin, S. (2001). Focus on form through collaborative dialogue: Exploring task effects. In M. Bygate, P. Skehan, & M. Swain (Eds.), *Researching pedagogic tasks: Second language learning, teaching, and testing* (pp. 99–118). Harlow, UK: Longman.

Terrell, T. (1991). The role of grammar instruction in a communicative approach. *Modern Language Journal, 75*, 52–63.

Terrell, T., Andrade, M., Egasse, J., & Muñoz, E. M. (1994). *Dos Mundos* (3rd ed.). New York: McGraw-Hill.

Tharp, R. G., & Gallimore, R. (1988). *Rousing minds to life: Teaching, learning, and schooling in social context.* Cambridge: Cambridge University Press.

Toth, P. D. (1997). *Linguistic and pedagogical perspectives on acquiring second-language morpho-syntax: A look at Spanish* se. Unpublished doctoral dissertation, University of Pittsburgh, Pittsburgh.

Toth, P. D. (2000). The interaction of instruction and learner-internal factors in the acquisition of L2 morphosyntax. *Studies in Second Language Acquisition, 22*, 169–208.

Toth, P. D. (2003). Psych verbs and morphosyntactic development in instructed L2 Spanish. In S. Montrul & F. Ordóñez (Eds.), *Linguistic theory and language development in Hispanic languages: Papers from the 5th Hispanic linguistics symposium and the 4th conference on the acquisition of Spanish and Portuguese* (pp. 468–497). Somerville, MA: Cascadilla Press.

Toth, P. D. (2004). When grammar instruction undermines cohesion in L2 Spanish classroom discourse. *Modern Language Journal, 88*, 14–30.

Toth, P. D. (2006). Processing Instruction and a role for output in second language acquisition. *Language Learning, 56*, 319–385.

Van den Branden, K. (1997). Effects of negotiation on language learners' output. *Language Learning, 47*, 589–636.

Van den Branden, K. (2000). Does negotiation of meaning promote reading comprehension? A study of multilingual primary school classes. *Reading Research Quarterly, 35*, 426–443.

Van Den Branden, K. (Ed.). (2006). *Task-based language education: From theory to practice*. Cambridge: Cambridge University Press.

van Lier, L. (1996). *Interaction in the language curriculum: Awareness, autonomy, and authenticity*. London: Longman.

VanPatten, B. (1990). Attending to form and content in the input. *Studies in Second Language Acquisition, 12*, 287–301.

VanPatten, B. (1996). *Input processing and grammar instruction in second language acquisition: Theory and research*. Norwood, NJ: Ablex.

VanPatten, B. (2004a). Input and output in establishing form-meaning connections. In B. VanPatten, J. Williams, S. Rott, & M. Overstreet (Eds.), *Form-meaning connections in second language acquisition* (pp. 29–47). Mahwah, NJ: Erlbaum.

VanPatten, B. (Ed.). (2004b). *Processing Instruction: Theory, research, and commentary*. Mahwah, NJ: Erlbaum.

Varonis, E. M., & Gass, S. (1985). Non-native/non-native conversations: A model for negotiation of meaning. *Applied Linguistics, 6*, 71–90.

Wells, G. (1993). Reevaluating the IRF sequence: A proposal for the articulation of theories of activity and discourse for the analysis of teaching and learning in the classroom. *Linguistics and Education, 5*, 1–37.

Wells, G. (1998). Some questions about direct instruction: Why? To whom? How? and When? *Language Arts, 76*(1), 27–35.

White, L. (2003). *Second language acquisition and Universal Grammar*. Cambridge: Cambridge University Press.

Williams, J. (1999). Learner-generated attention to form. *Language Learning, 49*, 583–625.

Wood, D., Bruner, J. S., & Ross, G. (1976). The role of tutoring in problem solving. *The Journal of Child Psychology and Psychiatry, 17*, 89–100.

Language Learning   ISSN 0023-8333

Task-Based Interactions in Classroom and Laboratory Settings

Susan Gass
Michigan State University

Alison Mackey
Georgetown University

Lauren Ross-Feldman
Georgetown University

This study was originally motivated by claims by a few classroom researchers (e.g., Foster, 1998, see Foster & Ohta, 2005) that the findings of laboratory-based studies of second-language interaction cannot automatically be applied to classroom language learning settings. Instead of simply accepting this assumption, we treated it as an empirical question. Our study was designed to examine the impact of setting—classroom and laboratory—on task-based interactions. We worked with learners of Spanish as a foreign language. Seventy-four university-level learners in dyads completed three interactive tasks. The tasks were designed in partnership with their instructors to be consistent with activities that these learners would do as part of their regular instruction. They were also consistent with activities that second language researchers typically use to elicit data in experimental work. Half of the learners worked in the classroom with their regular teacher and the other half met in a laboratory and were supervised by a researcher. Our findings indicated that there were significant differences in the incidence

---

Susan Gass, Department of Linguistics and Germanic, Slavic, Asian and African Languages; Alison Mackey, Department of Linguistics; Lauren Ross-Feldman, Department of Linguistics.

Funding for this project was provided by federal grants (nos. P229A990012 and P229A020001) from the U.S. Department of Education to the Center of Language Education and Research (CLEAR) at Michigan State University. We would like to thank Carolina Holtheuer and Maria Alvarez-Torres for help with data gathering and transcription and Maria Alvarez-Torres and Rebecca Adams for help with coding. We are grateful to Rusan Chen for statistical guidance. An earlier version of this article was presented at the Second Language Research Forum at the University of Arizona in Tucson in October 2003.

Correspondence concerning this article should be addressed to Susan Gass, English Language Center, A-714 Wells Hall, Michigan State University, East Lansing, MI 48824. Internet: gass@msu.edu

of interactional modifications among tasks. Interestingly, however, these differences were found in *both* the classroom and laboratory settings. No significant differences in interactional patterns were found between the two settings. Our finding that there were no significant differences between classroom and laboratory settings has been widely cited in publications on task-based language learning (e.g., Bygate & Samuda, 2009; Eckerth, 2009; Ellis, 2010; Fujii, Obata, Takahashi, & Tanabe, 2008; Jenks, 2009; Johnstone, 2006; Nassaji, 2007; Philp, Oliver, & Mackey, 2006; Révész, 2009). Subsequent work in the field has continued to find similar task effects on interaction in other learner populations and instructional settings (e.g., Eckerth, 2009; Fujii & Mackey, 2009; Gilabert, Baron, & Llanes, 2009). In summary then, a major contribution of our study was to raise awareness that the effects of setting on interactional processes cannot simply be assumed and claimed but should be empirically demonstrated. The onus is on both classroom and laboratory researchers to determine whether setting has influenced their findings, and if so, how and to what degree.

Keywords laboratory settings; classroom settings; interaction; communicative tasks; Spanish

Within the context of second language acquisition (SLA), the interaction hypothesis suggests that receiving comprehensible input and interactional feedback (Gass, 1997; Long, 1996; Pica, 1994b), being pushed to make changes in output (Swain, 1995, 2005), and negotiating for meaning (Gass, 2003) are all helpful for second language (L2) learning. To date, many of the empirical studies that support the interaction hypothesis have been carried out in laboratory settings, and some researchers have suggested that the same patterns may not occur in L2 classroom settings (Foster, 1998). The current study examines this suggestion by comparing interactional patterns in classroom and laboratory settings.

Claims About the Benefits of Conversational Interaction

According to the interaction hypothesis, interaction, particularly when it involves negotiation for meaning and feedback, facilitates SLA.[1] The factors beneficial for L2 learners arising from interaction are said to include receiving comprehensible input and interactional feedback (Gass, 1997; Long, 1996; Pica, 1994b), as well as being pushed to make changes in their output (Swain, 1995, 2005). There have been a number of claims about how interaction works to facilitate L2 learning. For example, interaction may provide opportunities for learners to test target language hypotheses and to "notice the gap" (Schmidt & Frota, 1986) between their interlanguage and the target language. As Long (1996) explains:

while correct form-meaning associations are strengthened both by positive evidence and negative feedback that contains positive evidence, incorrect associations are weakened and in some cases ultimately relinquished altogether as a result both of negative evidence and prolonged absence of support in the input. (p. 430)

Pica (1994a) describes negotiation for meaning as being an activity "in which learners seek clarification, confirmation, and repetition of L2 utterances they do not understand" (p. 56). She emphasizes the negotiation that occurs as a result of interaction, saying that "the twofold potential of negotiation—to assist L2 comprehension and draw attention to L2 form—affords it a more powerful role in L2 learning than has been claimed so far" (Pica, 1994b, p. 508). In terms of output, Swain (1995) argues that metalinguistic reflection is one of the benefits of output resulting from interaction. She suggests that "under certain task conditions, learners will not only reveal their hypotheses, but reflect on them, using language to do so" (p. 132). Finally, the capacity of negotiation to connect input and output is an important benefit of interaction.

Although the interaction research area began by considering various aspects of the role of negotiation in comprehension (see early studies by Gass & Varonis, 1984, 1985; Hatch, 1978; Long, 1981, 1983, 1985; Pica, 1985, 1988, 1989, 1992; Pica, Holliday, Lewis, & Morgenthaler, 1989; Pica & Long, 1986; Pica, Young, & Doughty, 1987; Varonis & Gass, 1985), research of the past decade has progressed beyond interaction-comprehension links. A number of studies have now convincingly demonstrated a relationship between various types of interaction and L2 learning (see, for example, recent empirical work by Ayoun, 2001; Braidi, 2002; Iwashita, 2003; Leeman, 2003; Long, Inagaki, & Ortega, 1998; Mackey, 1999; Mackey & Philp, 1998; McDonough, 2005; Muranoi, 2000; Philp, 2003; as well as work reviewed in Gass, 2003; Long, in press; and Mackey, 2007). In summary, a number of researchers have made claims about the benefits of conversational interaction. These claims have been supported by empirical work showing that there is a relationship between interaction and L2 learning. But as noted above, much of the empirical work demonstrating an interaction-learning relationship has been conducted in laboratory settings. The extent to which the findings from these studies would hold in a classroom context has been questioned by some researchers, and it is this debate that we turn to now.

Interaction in the L2 Classroom

Foster (1998) has questioned the extendibility of laboratory results on negotiation for meaning in L2 classrooms based on her research findings that negotiation did not occur in the classroom she studied. In Foster's words, her research

> call[s] into question the typicality of previous research into the incidence of negotiation of meaning and the justification therefore of constructing an SLA theory upon it. . . . teachers can be expected to show little interest in research that tells them negotiation of meaning flourishes under narrowly controlled conditions, especially conditions that would be very unusual in a classroom. (p. 19)

She goes on to say, on the basis of her classroom findings, that "learners appear to choose not to negotiate for meaning" (p. 20). Nunan (1991) has also argued that experimental findings may not be applicable in classroom settings if the studies are based on tightly controlled experimental variables, because the environment in the classroom is not as easily controlled as that in the laboratory. There are reasons why we might expect interactional patterns to be different in classrooms and laboratories. One reason is that classrooms, at least many English as a second language (ESL) classrooms, are often focused on meaning rather than L2 form and in such classrooms, "responses to learner utterances are even more likely to be interpreted as reactions to meaning" than to L2 form (Nicholas, Lightbown, & Spada, 2001, p. 721). Another reason why we might expect the interactional patterns of classrooms and laboratories to differ comes from the work of Ellis, Basturkmen, and Loewen (2001a), who examined learner uptake in a communicative ESL classroom. Defining "uptake" as an optional move that "occurs in episodes where learners have demonstrated a gap in their knowledge ... [and] occurs as a reaction to some preceding move in which another participant (usually the teacher) either explicitly or implicitly provides information about a linguistic feature" (p. 286), Ellis et al. found that "successful uptake was more likely when students were focused on linguistic problems that they perceived as important and when they had the chance to negotiate extensively around a problem" (p. 313). Thus, differences between classroom settings and laboratory settings may reflect what learners perceive as important or not important in terms of gaps in their knowledge, which may, in turn, affect their interactional patterns. In other words, it is possible to interpret previous findings as suggesting that in some settings, classrooms learners may believe that meaning is primary, whereas learners who are taking part in laboratory studies are attending more to form.

Naturally, claims about research in classroom contexts require us to decide what is meant by a classroom.[2] There are important differences between specific classrooms, as well as broader differences among numerous types of classrooms. For example, ESL classrooms might be different from English as a foreign language (EFL) classrooms; EFL classrooms might differ depending on geographical context; foreign language classrooms and immersion classrooms probably provide additional differences. This fact is brought to light by differences in findings by Lyster (1998a, 1998b; Lyster & Ranta, 1997) in immersion settings, and by Ellis, Basturkmen, and Loewen (2001a, 2001b) in ESL settings. Sheen's (2004) study of different classrooms also illustrates these points. Further, work by Loewen (2003) has shown that there is variation in the extent to which there is incidental focus on form even in classes within the same school. Quite clearly, there is not a "prototypical" classroom, any more than there is a "prototypical" laboratory, and claims about laboratory findings not applying in classroom contexts must be carefully operationalized and tested.

In her study of negotiation for meaning in the ESL classroom, Foster (1998) found little evidence of negotiation in her data and interpreted her findings as suggesting that there is a difference between laboratory and classroom settings with regard to the amount of negotiation produced. Because of the small amount of negotiation in any of her tasks, she concluded that "uncoached negotiation for meaning" (p. 19) does not occur in the classroom. However, other interpretations of Foster's data may be tenable. In her data, dyads carrying out information exchange tasks were the most successful in producing negotiation for meaning, with more of the negotiation incidences in her data occurring in a picture differences task than in a grammar task, suggesting that it may be worthwhile to investigate task types further.[3] It is also possible that the data used in Foster's analysis do not represent the full range of negotiation patterns that would exist in an entire class period. As in other studies of negotiation (Oliver, 1998, 2000, 2002), Foster examined only the first 10 min of data from her map task and the first 5 min of data from her remaining tasks. Although data-sampling practices like this are often necessary for comparability, it is possible that using only the first 5 min of the interaction in the majority of tasks may have obscured other patterns, since students might be "warming up" during the first few minutes of any activity (Aston, 1986, p. 132, cited in Shehadeh, 2001). It is thus possible that Foster's results may not paint a complete picture of the classroom setting.

Of course, classrooms are not as easily controlled as laboratories, and Foster (1998) makes an interesting point when she claims that if "language acquisition research wants to feed into teaching methodology, the research environment has to be willing to move out of the laboratory and into the classroom" (p. 21).

In summary, whereas some researchers have documented benefits for interactional feedback in L2 classrooms (Ellis, 2000; Mackey, 2000; Oliver, 2000; Samuda, 2001; Williams, 1999), others have argued that learners provide and make use of interactional feedback in laboratory settings more than is the case in classroom settings. Some researchers point to differences in settings to explain differential experimental results; for example, Foster (1998) notes that "the setting of the study within a classroom as opposed to a venue especially arranged for data collecting, is suggested as a significant variable" (p. 1).

The relevance and applicability of laboratory research to L2 classroom settings is clearly an important issue in interaction research. To this end, the current study takes a first step toward investigating the differences between classrooms and laboratories by examining the extent to which interaction is present in two highly comparable settings. This was done by comparing a traditional, controlled laboratory setting, in which learners worked in dyads to carry out tasks, with a foreign language classroom, in which learners from the same population carried out the same tasks as in the laboratory setting, but as part of their regular classroom instruction. In other words, we compared task-based interactions in everyday classes and in a laboratory setting.[4] The tasks were typical of materials that have been used as instructional tools and research instruments and, thus, were not unique to either setting (see Pica, Kang, & Sauro, 2006).

Research Questions

This study addressed two research questions. Our primary interest was to compare task-based interaction in the classroom with task-based performance in laboratory settings; thus we asked two related questions:

1. How does task-based interaction in the classroom compare to task-based interaction in a laboratory setting?
2. How do different tasks influence interaction in classrooms and laboratories?

Method

Participants

The participants ($N = 74$)[5] in this study, 55 females and 19 males, ranged in age from 17 to 25, with an average age of 19.2. All were students enrolled in 3rd-semester university-level Spanish courses. The classes met 4 days a week for 50 min. At the time of data collection, the students had been taking the class for 11 weeks. To the best of our knowledge, all participants were native speakers of English (7 participants did not respond to the question about native language). The number of years that the learners reported on a bio-data form for previous instruction in Spanish varied from 1.5 to 8 years,[6] with a mean of 4.42 years. No participant reported spending time on Spanish outside of class other than for her regular homework activities and class assignments. Only 2 participants had spent more than a few weeks in a Spanish-speaking country, and with the exception of 3 participants, none had ever lived or worked in a predominantly Spanish-speaking environment.

Materials

Three tasks were used in the current study. One task was an optional information exchange task (consensus), and two were required information exchange tasks (picture differences and map), with all tasks being performed by all dyads in the laboratory and in the classroom. The tasks were selected or adapted from materials appearing in popular commercially available textbooks, and all materials were of the type typically used in the students' language classrooms.[7] When necessary, the tasks were adapted and translated by an experienced language instructor and native speaker of Spanish and checked by a second native-speaking Spanish instructor to ensure that the language of the tasks was at an appropriate level for the participants in this study.

Picture Differences Task

The set of pictures used in the picture differences task depicted identical park scenes with differences between the pictures; for example, in one picture, a girl is drinking water from a water fountain; in the other picture, the girl is missing (see Appendix A). These pictures describe real-life scenes and are, thus, contextualized and communicative, allowing students to use and learn "authentic" and meaningful language, the value of which is well documented in the literature (e.g., Brown, 2001; Ellis, 2003; Nunan, 1989). Interactants are instructed to find 10 differences between their pictures.

Consensus Task
The text used in the consensus task consisted of descriptions in Spanish of several Spanish universities (i.e., number of students and professors, description of facilities, etc.) with the premise that a college student has been accepted to all four of them and needs the participants' help in deciding which school to attend (see Appendix B). The interactants have to agree on a ranking of the universities from most to least desirable.

Map Task
In the map task, a map is provided for both participants, along with a different list of street properties (for example, one road is one-way, another is closed) for each of them (see Appendix C). The first goal of the task is for participants to share their knowledge of the street conditions and cooperate with each other to successfully locate them on the map. Once the map is complete with the street information, interactants are instructed to draw a driving route from a starting point to where a friend is waiting.

Procedure
Intact classes were randomly assigned to either classroom or laboratory settings. Forty-four students in two classes (22 dyads) completed the tasks during their regular class time in their classroom with their regular instructor; 30 students from two classes (15 dyads) completed the tasks in a laboratory setting with a research assistant. Each session lasted between 50 and 55 min. The researchers and the teachers had collaborated to ensure that the tasks were typical of activities presented by the point in the semester when the sessions occurred and that the teachers' behavior was typical of their regular instructional styles.

All tasks completed in the classroom setting were presented by the teacher as part of regular classroom instruction.[8] Teachers were asked to do nothing different from what they would ordinarily do in their classrooms when using the same sort of activities. At the beginning of each task, teachers gave brief directions before students worked together with their peers. They also reminded students that they were to talk only in the target language. While the students were engaged in tasks, teachers circulated among the students as was their common practice, keeping the students on task where necessary and responding to any queries that arose. All interactions during tasks were audiotaped. A research assistant was present in[9] or immediately outside the classroom to monitor the recording equipment (mini audio tape recorders were placed between each pair of participants). In the laboratory setting, a Spanish native speaker met with each dyad separately, as is typical in laboratory settings. Participants faced each other at a table where a mini audio tape recorder was placed. For each task, participants were first provided with the required materials. The native speaker then read the instructions in Spanish and answered questions. Once all questions had been clarified, the native speaker left the room, although participants were reminded that if they had any further questions regarding instructions, they could request assistance. All interactions during tasks were audiotaped.

Coding

We selected three commonly studied interactional features for analysis. These three features have been found to be facilitative of SLA and/or to have been used in the literature in relation to interaction studies:[10] (a) negotiation for meaning (Ellis, Tanaka, & Yamazaki, 1994; Foster, 1998; Gass & Varonis, 1985; Long, 1983, 1996; Oliver, 1998, 2000, 2002; Van den Branden, 1997; Varonis & Gass, 1985); (b) language-related episodes (LREs; Kowal & Swain, 1994; Swain, 1998; Swain & Lapkin, 1998; Williams, 1999, 2001); and (c) recasts (Braidi, 2002; Leeman, 2003; Lyster, 1998a, 1998b; Lyster & Ranta, 1997; Mackey & Philp, 1998; Nicholas et al., 2001; Philp, 2003). Definitions and examples of each of these features are provided below.

Negotiation for Meaning

Negotiation for meaning was used as a major category following Foster (1998, p. 11) and was operationalized, following Long (1983) and Foster, as confirmation checks, clarification requests, and comprehension checks. Definitions and examples (all taken from data collected for the current study) are provided below. Confirmation checks are "any expressions ... immediately following an utterance by the interlocutor which are designed to elicit confirmation that the utterance has been correctly heard or understood by the speaker" (Long, 1983, p. 137). Example 1 illustrates a confirmation check from data collected for the current study, in which Learner 2 confirms that she has heard Learner 1 correctly regarding the number of birds in Learner 1's picture.

Example 1. Confirmation Check

Learner 1: En mi dibujo hay un pájaro.
            In my drawing there is a bird.
→ Learner 2: **¿Solamente un?** Tengo, uh, cinco pájaros con un hombre, en sus hombros.
            Only one? *I have, uh, five birds with a man, on his shoulders.*

Learner 1: Oh, oh, sí, sí.
            Oh, oh, yes, yes.
            [Dyad L82–77, Picture Differences Task]

A clarification request is "any expression . . . designed to elicit clarification of the interlocutor's preceding utterance(s)" (Long, 1983, p. 137). Example 2 illustrates a clarification request, in which Learner 2 needs more information in order to understand Learner 1's question about what is important to the character in the task.

Example 2. Clarification Request

Learner 1: ¿Qué es importante a ella?
            What is important to her?
→Learner 2: **¿Cómo?**
            What?
Learner 1: ¿Qué es importante a la amiga? ¿Es solamente el costo?
            What is important to the friend? Is it just the cost?
            [Dyad M02–09, Consensus Task]

A comprehension check is an attempt "to anticipate and prevent a break-down in communication" (Long, 1983, p. 136). In Example 3, Learner 1 asks if Learner 2 needs him to repeat what he has just said, basically checking to see if Learner 2 has understood the previous utterance.

Example 3. Comprehension Check

Learner 1: La avenida siete va en una dirección hacia el
            norte desde la calle siete hasta la calle ocho.
→   **¿Quieres que repita?**
            Avenue Seven goes in one direction towards the north from Street Seven to Street Eight.
            Do you want me to repeat?
Learner 2: Por favor.
            Please.
Learner 1: La avenida seven, uh siete, va en una dirección hacia el norte
            desde la calle siete hasta la calle ocho.
            Avenue Seven, uh Seven, goes in one direction towards the north from Street Seven to Street Eight.
            [Dyad A46–41, Map Task]

LREs

Swain and Lapkin (1998) have defined an LRE as "any part of a dialogue in which students talk about the language they are producing, question their language use, or other-or self-correct" (p. 70). This includes instances of students asking for glosses of individual words or phrases. Example 4 illustrates an LRE in which students discuss the gender of the word for "map."

Example 4. LRE

Learner 1: Los nombres en el mapa. ¿Es el mapa o la mapa?
            The names on the map. Is it the (m.) map or the (f.) map?
Learner 2: El mapa
            The (m.) map
            [Dyad A33–104, Map Task]

Recasts

The final coding category was recasts. According to Nicholas et al. (2001), a recast is a "correct restatement of a learner's incorrectly formed utterance" (p. 721). Example 5 shows a recast in which Learner 2 corrects Learner 1's pronunciation of the word meaning "forest."

Example 5. Recast

Learner 1: No tiene flores . . . uh un bosco.
            It doesn't have flowers . . . uh, a forest
            [mispronunciation]
→ Learner 2: **Bosque**.
            Forest. [correct pronunciation]
Learner 1: Bosque.
            Forest. [correct pronunciation]
            [Dyad L70–69, Picture Differences Task]

All interactions were transcribed by a native Spanish speaker. Interactions were then coded by three individuals, one researcher (a proficient speaker of Spanish) and two research assistants (one native and one proficient speaker of Spanish). Because of the level of detail involved in the coding, each rater coded two thirds of the data and then engaged in a joint coding session with one other rater. Data about which there were disagreements were not included in the analysis. (This amounted to less than 5% of the data set.)

Table 1 Descriptive statistics for negotiation for meaning by task

	Setting	Mean	Standard deviation	95% confidence interval	
				Lower bound	Upper bound
Picture differences task	Classroom	7.09	3.91 (2–14)	5.03	9.15
	Laboratory	8.53	5.78 (3–24)	6.04	11.02
Consensus task	Classroom	1.36	1.25 (0–3)	0.85	1.88
	Laboratory	1.07	1.10 (0–4)	0.44	1.69
Map task	Classroom	8.23	4.61 (2–16)	6.17	10.29
	Laboratory	9.00	4.98 (1–18)	6.50	11.50

Note. Numbers in parentheses indicate the range per dyad.

Analysis

To address our primary research question, "How does task-based interaction in the classroom compare to task-based interaction in a laboratory setting?" repeated-measures analyses of variance (ANOVAs) were performed to compare the settings and the tasks and to explore whether there were any significant interactions between the settings and the tasks.[11] When significant differences were found among the tasks, post hoc Bonferroni analyses were conducted to determine the relationships.

Results

Negotiation for Meaning

Table 1 provides descriptive statistics for the amount of negotiation in the classroom and the laboratory on each task (see Figure 1 for a graphical representation of the mean amount of negotiation on each task in each setting). Repeated-measures ANOVAs revealed that there were no significant interactions between setting and task, $F(2, 70) = 0.57, p = .57$, nor were there significant differences between the classroom and the laboratory on the total amount of negotiation, $F(1, 35) = 0.48, p = .49$. However, there were significant differences among the tasks for the total amount of negotiation, $F(2, 70) = 49.16$, $p = .00, \eta^2 = .58$, as can be seen in Table 2. Post hoc Bonferroni analyses

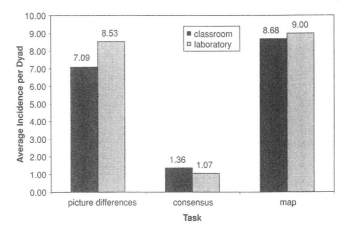

Figure 1 Mean amount of negotiation by task.

Table 2 Results of repeated-measures ANOVAs for negotiation by task

ANOVA	df	F	η^2
Setting	1	0.48	.01
Task	2	49.16*	.58
Setting × Task	2	0.57	.02

*$p < .05$.

revealed that there was more negotiation on the picture differences task, $t(36)$ = 8.15, $p = .00$, and the map task, $t(36) = -9.28$, $p = .00$, than on the consensus task, with no significant differences between the picture differences and map tasks.

Table 3 provides descriptive statistics for the amount of each type of negotiation (confirmation check, clarification request, comprehension check) for each task (picture differences, consensus, map) in the classroom and the laboratory. Figure 2 combines the data for the tasks, presenting the mean amount of each type of negotiation in the classroom and laboratory. As can be seen in Table 4, repeated-measures ANOVAs revealed that there were no significant interactions between setting and task for any of the three types of negotiation, nor were there significant differences between the classroom and the laboratory on the incidence of any of the three types. However, there were significant differences among the tasks for both confirmation checks, $F(2, 70) = 26.71$, $p = .00$, $\eta^2 = .43$, and clarification requests, $F(2, 70) = 29.07$, $p = .00$, $\eta^2 = .45$, but not for comprehension checks, $F(2, 70) = 2.30$, $p = .11$. This may be due

Table 3 Descriptive statistics for negotiation of meaning by type

	Setting	Mean	Standard deviation	95% confidence interval	
				Lower bound	Upper bound
Confirmation check					
Picture differences task	Classroom	4.05	2.65 (1–10)	2.29	5.80
	Laboratory	5.93	5.52 (0–23)	3.81	8.06
Consensus task	Classroom	0.77	0.92 (0–3)	0.34	1.20
	Laboratory	0.73	1.10 (0–4)	0.21	1.26
Map task	Classroom	4.18	2.82 (0–10)	2.71	5.66
	Laboratory	5.07	4.13 (0–13)	3.28	6.58
Clarification request					
Picture differences task	Classroom	3.00	2.53 (0–11)	2.03	3.97
	Laboratory	2.60	1.76 (1–7)	1.42	3.78
Consensus task	Classroom	0.59	0.85 (0–2)	0.26	0.92
	Laboratory	0.33	0.62 (0–2)	−0.69	0.74
Map task	Classroom	3.91	2.89 (0–11)	2.71	5.11
	Laboratory	3.87	2.59 (0–8)	2.41	5.32
Comprehension check					
Picture differences task	Classroom	0.05	0.23 (0–1)	−0.03	0.12
	Laboratory	0.00	0.00 (0)	−0.09	0.09

(Continued).

Table 3 Continued

	Setting	Mean	Standard deviation	95% confidence interval	
				Lower bound	Upper bound
Consensus task	Classroom	0.00	0.00 (0)	0.00	0.00
	Laboratory	0.00	0.00 (0)	0.00	0.00
Map task	Classroom	0.14	0.35 (0–1)	0.00	0.27
	Laboratory	0.07	0.31 (0–1)	−0.10	0.23

Note. Numbers in parentheses indicate the range per dyad.

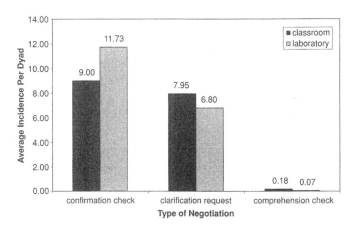

Figure 2 Mean amount of negotiation by type.

in part to the low overall incidence of comprehension checks in these data. Post hoc Bonferroni analyses revealed that there were more confirmation checks on the picture differences task, $t(36) = 5.97$, $p = .00$, and the map task, $t(36) = -6.45$, $p = .00$, than on the consensus task, with no significant differences between the picture differences and map tasks. There were more clarification requests on the picture differences task, $t(36) = 6.35$, $p = .00$, and the map task, $t(36) = -7.88$, $p = .00$, than on the consensus task, and more clarification requests on the map task than on the picture differences task, $t(36) = -2.03$, $p = .05$.

Table 4 Results of repeated-measures ANOVAs for negotiation by type

ANOVA	df	F	η^2
Confirmation checks			
Setting	1	1.56	.04
Task	2	26.71*	.43
Setting × Task	2	1.126	.03
Clarification requests			
Setting	1	0.25	.01
Task	2	29.07*	.45
Setting × Task	2	0.08	.00
Comprehension checks			
Setting	1	4.58	.12
Task	2	2.30	.06
Setting × Task	2	0.25	.01

*$p < .05$.

LREs

Table 5 provides the means and standard deviations for the number of LREs in the classroom and the laboratory on each task (see Figure 3 for a graphical representation of the mean incidence of LREs on each task). Repeated-measures ANOVAs revealed that there were no significant interactions between setting and task, $F(2, 70) = 0.83$, $p = .44$, nor were there significant differences between the classroom and the laboratory on the total number of LREs, $F(1, 35) = 0.04$, $p = .84$. However, there were significant differences among the

Table 5 Descriptive statistics for language-related episodes

				95% confidence interval	
	Setting	Mean	Standard deviation	Lower bound	Upper bound
Picture differences	Classroom	2.09	2.56 (0–9)	1.03	3.15
task	Laboratory	1.87	2.29 (0–7)	0.58	3.15
Consensus task	Classroom	0.36	0.90 (0–4)	−0.06	0.78
	Laboratory	1.00	1.07 (0–3)	0.49	1.51
Map task	Classroom	1.32	1.36 (0–6)	0.75	1.89
	Laboratory	1.13	1.24 (0–4)	0.44	1.82

Note. Numbers in parentheses indicate the range per dyad.

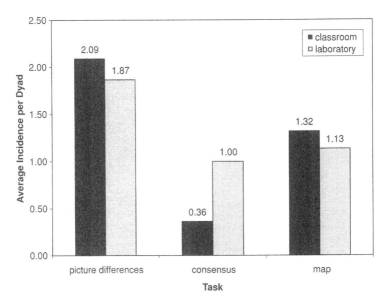

Figure 3 Mean incidence of LREs by task.

tasks for the total number of LREs, $F(2, 70) = 5.93$, $p = .00$, $\eta^2 = .15$, as can be seen in Table 6. Post hoc Bonferroni analyses revealed that there were more LREs on the picture differences task, $t(36) = 3.85$, $p = .00$, and the map task, $t(36) = -2.28$, $p = .03$, than on the consensus task, with no significant ndifferences between the picture differences and map tasks.

Recasts
As can be seen in Table 7, in these data there were fewer than four recasts per dyad across all three tasks in each context (see Figure 4 for a graphical representation of the average incidence of recasts per task). Clearly, then, the results we report here should be interpreted with caution in view of these low numbers. As can be seen in Table 8, repeated-measures ANOVAs revealed that

Table 6 Results of repeated-measures ANOVAs for LREs

ANOVA	df	F	η^2
Setting	1	0.04	.00
Task	2	5.93*	.15
Setting × Task	2	0.83	.02

$^*p < .05$.

Table 7 Descriptive statistics for recasts

	Setting	Mean	Standard deviation	95% confidence interval	
				Lower bound	Upper bound
Picture differences	Classroom	0.64	0.79 (0–2)	0.21	1.07
task	Laboratory	1.13	1.24 (0–4)	0.61	1.66
Consensus task	Classroom	0.32	0.79 (0–3)	0.03	0.60
	Laboratory	0.20	0.41 (0–1)	−0.15	0.55
Map task	Classroom	0.32	0.72 (0–3)	0.02	0.61
	Laboratory	0.47	0.64 (0–2)	0.11	0.83

Note. Numbers in parentheses indicate the range per dyad.

there were no significant interactions between setting and task, $F(2, 70) = 1.30$, $p = .28$, nor were there significant differences between the classroom and the laboratory on the total number of recasts, $F(1, 35) = 1.38$, $p = .25$. Consistent with the patterns in the other interactional data, there were significant differences by task for the total number of recasts, $F(2, 70) = 5.59$, $p = .00$, $\eta^2 = .15$. According to post hoc Bonferroni analyses, there were more recasts in the picture differences task than in either the consensus task, $t(36) = 2.90$,

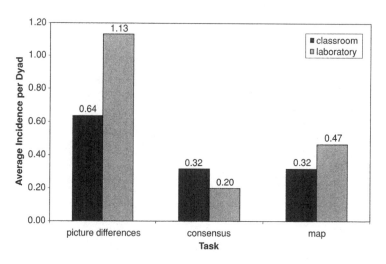

Figure 4 Mean incidence of recasts by task.

Table 8 Results of repeated-measures ANOVAs for recasts

ANOVA	df	F	η^2
Setting	1	1.38	.04
Task	2	5.95*	.15
Setting × Task	2	1.30	.04

*$p < .05$.

$p = .01$, or the map task, $t(36) = 2.26$, $p = .03$, with no other significant relationships among tasks.

Summary of Results
The analysis suggests that in terms of amount and type of negotiation for meaning, LREs, and recasts, whether learners interacted in classroom or laboratory settings had very little impact on the interactional patterns. However, the type of task learners carried out did affect their interactions (although the relative values of the effect sizes[12] indicate that the type of task may have been a more important factor in accounting for the incidence of negotiation for meaning than in accounting for the incidence of LREs and recasts).

Discussion

The results of this study indicate that, at least for this population of students and in this classroom context, there were very few differences in the classroom and laboratory contexts in terms of the interactional features examined. As we noted earlier, the generalizability of these findings is clearly limited given the wide range of classrooms that can be examined. Classrooms have a number of social and contextual features that were not focused on in this study because the varying effects of these features on interaction was beyond the scope of our research questions. We compared a typical foreign language classroom and a typical interaction laboratory experiment, with a comparable population.

The features we focused on were total amount and different types of negotiation of meaning and total incidence of LREs and recasts. As noted in the summary above, there were differences in the use of these features depending on the type of task the learners worked on, regardless of whether these tasks were carried out in classrooms or laboratories. Our results are not consistent with Foster's (1998) assertions that negotiation occurs infrequently in the L2 classroom. She claimed that negotiation is uncommon and unevenly distributed and pointed out the need to look at learners themselves rather than pooled data.

In Appendix D, we present a scatter plot based on raw data that shows our results by individual dyads of learners as opposed to the group data shown earlier. This scatter plot was developed by matching laboratory and classroom dyads by the number of negotiation moves on the picture differences task. We carried out the same analysis for each task as well as for the number of LREs and recasts for each task. In all cases but one, the laboratory scores and classroom scores were matched[13] using the criterion that they differ by no more than two.[14]

In the current study, not only was negotiation for meaning used in the L2 classroom, but so were two other interactional features, LREs and recasts, both of which have also been empirically demonstrated to facilitate SLA (see Iwashita, 2003; Mackey, 1999; Mackey & Philp, 1998; Philp, 2003; Williams, 1999). Again, the incidences of LREs and recasts in the classroom interactions were highly comparable to those in the laboratory. Example 6 illustrates interaction in the classroom in which the participants from one of the classroom dyads focus on the meanings and pronunciation of two words (*pareja*, 'pair/couple,' and *pajaro*, 'bird'), demonstrating that interaction in the classroom can be rich, incorporating negotiation, LREs, and recasts within one exchange.

Example 6. Classroom Interaction

Learner 1: ¿Cuántas personas tienes?
How many people do you have?
Learner 2: (counting) Trece.
Thirteen.
Learner 1: ¿Trece? Tengo uh diecisiete ... ¿Cuántos **parejas?**
Thirteen? I have uh seventeen... How many **pairs?**
Learner 2: ¿Parejas de amores? ←clarification request
Pairs of lovers?
Learner 1: ¿Qué es **parejas?**   ←LRE
What is 'parejas'?
Learner 2: **Pairs.**
Learner 1: Oh
Learner 2: No tiene el merry-go-round.
It doesn't have the merry-go-round.
Learner 1: Hmm. ¿Cómo se dice **bird?**   ←LRE
*How do you say **bird?***
Learner 2: **Pájaro**
Bird

Learner 1: Oh! That's what I was trying to say.
             ¿Cuántos **pájaros**?
             *How many **birds**?*

Learner 2: Uhm cinco. ¿Cuántos tienes?
             Uhm, five. How many do you have?

Learner 1: Tengo nueve, tengo más **parejos**,
             ¿parejos ?¿parejas?
             I have nine, I have nine more [trouble with pronunciation of 'birds']

Learner 2: **Pájaros**
             Birds [correct pronunciation]   ←recast

Learner 1: **Pájaros**   ←uptake
             Birds [correct pronunciation]

In summary, the claim by Foster (1998) that there is a lower incidence of negotiation of meaning in a classroom setting than in a laboratory setting was 'not supported in our data. Example 6 and the patterns in our data resonate well with findings by a range of researchers who have reported on intact classrooms (e.g., Ellis et al., 2001a, 2001b; Samuda, 2001; Williams, 1999). In our data and those of others, negotiation and other forms of interaction are "alive and well" in many types of L2 classrooms. For example, Williams (1999) found that learners working together in her meaning-centered classroom spontaneously focused on matters of form. Ellis et al. (2001a) found that student-initiated focus-on-form episodes not only occurred in communicative ESL classrooms but resulted in more successful uptake than teacher-initiated focus-on-form episodes. This finding was underscored by a second study by Ellis et al. (2001b), this one focusing on preemptive focus on form. Samuda's (2001) study, although targeted more to the role of the teacher than the students, shows that both teachers and students attend to matters of form together in the context of meaningful communication. Sheen's (2004) comparative study also shows interactional feedback in operation in French immersion, Canadian ESL, New Zealand ESL, and Korean EFL classrooms, with recasts being the most frequent form of feedback; indeed in French immersion "recasts were primarily used for negotiation for meaning" (p. 292). Taken together, these research findings, when combined with the results of the current study, support the contention that interactional feedback, whether operationalized as negotiation for meaning, LREs, or recasts, occurs in a range of classrooms as well as in controlled laboratory settings.

What we found were some interesting differences in interactional processes according to the task (but not the setting). In both settings, there were differences between the two required information exchange task (picture differences and map) and the optional information exchange task (consensus) in terms of the interactional patterns produced. This points to the need to carefully examine task types in any investigation of interaction. Gass and Varonis (1985) point to a number of variables that need to be considered when looking at negotiation (they did not deal with LREs or recasts in their study) in a classroom context, among them, one-way versus two-way flow of information, the role of the interlocutors (i.e., who is receiving information and who is giving), task familiarity, and gender. Pica's (2002) study of subject matter content has also pointed to the need to examine tasks as a variable when considering classroom interaction. There are many other potentially important variables that need to be considered when conducting or implementing research in a classroom context. The current study was able to focus only on one variable, setting, showing that the setting was not in and of itself a significant variable in our data in determining the extent to which negotiation for meaning, LREs, and recasts did or did not occur.

Conclusions, Limitations, and Future Research

We believe our results support what seems to be an ongoing practice by some SLA researchers, which is to make cautious generalizations about laboratory-based research findings to L2 classroom settings, based on a careful assessment of research designs. We think our findings point to the inadvisability of making the automatic assumption (as Foster did) that findings will be different in different settings. However, it must be understood that we did not take into account the various complexities of the classroom context, for example, in terms of participants and their social relationships. As we stated earlier, classrooms can vary tremendously, and not all laboratories are equivalent either. When considering generalization, researchers and teachers need to consider what makes sense in their contexts. This study was carried out in a foreign, rather than an L2, classroom, unlike Foster's (1998) research, although it could be argued that there may be even more potential for negotiation in L2 classrooms, where learners do not share a common L1 (see Varonis & Gass, 1985). Also, in future research, it might be interesting to bring in other considerations, such as gender differences, and examine this in light of who initiates interactional modifications and what the length and linguistic target of the interactional feedback is, as well as other qualitative information. Replication studies are obviously advisable in order to permit greater confidence in the results. Nevertheless, on the basis of these data, it is possible to suggest that interaction may not be as context-dependent as some researchers have claimed and may not vary depending on whether the participants are in the classroom or the laboratory. Rather, interaction may be more task-dependent, varying in each context from task to task.

Revised version accepted 20 April 2005

Notes

1 It is not our intent in this article to review the many studies that have empirically demonstrated interaction-driven learning in respect to interactional feedback, including negotiation of meaning and recasts.

2 We are grateful to an anonymous *Language Learning* reviewer for pointing out that an explicit discussion of different types of classrooms would be interesting.

3 Foster compared task types and dyads versus groups, finding the most negotiation from dyads during a required information exchange task. However, it is important to point out that in her research design, the dyads and the groups did not perform the same tasks. The dyads performed (a) a grammar-based task in which the students had to compose questions and (b) a picture differences task, whereas the groups performed (a) a consensus task and (b) a map task. This limits comparability.

4 As an anonymous *Language Learning* reviewer has noted, these settings were defined by the participants and the roles and relationships that are typical of these two settings.

5 There were originally 80 participants in the study. One dyad was eliminated because of a malfunctioning tape recorder, and two dyads were eliminated because of extensive exposure to another Romance language (French or Portuguese) on the part of 1 participant in each dyad. All participants were paid 20 U.S. dollars for their participation in the study.

6 These numbers conflate years of study of Spanish in high school versus years of study of Spanish at the postsecondary level. Given the average age of the participants, we assume that most of these years reflect years of high school study. The level of proficiency of the students was comparable; there were no indications from their teachers that any of the students were grossly misplaced.

7 Prior to the onset of data collection, one of the researchers spent time visiting Spanish-language classrooms to ensure that the type of materials and the mode of

presentation (i.e., group/pair work as opposed to teacher-fronted) were typical of the Spanish curriculum.

8 We have not included an analysis of the teacher-student or teacher-dyad exchanges because these issues are beyond the scope of the current article. However, our ongoing research investigations are exploring this important issue.

9 When in the classroom, the researcher sat in the corner of the classroom unobtrusively.

10 It should be noted that coding categories were not completely mutually exclusive: there was some partial overlap among categories. Fewer than 1% of the utterances could clearly be classified as an incidence of more than one coding category, and these were coded twice, once in each category. Another way of coding the data would be to use utterances or c-units. We opted not to do this because we held time constant. In other words, both groups had the same amount of time to complete the tasks (approximately 50–55 min).

11 As part of the process of our analysis, we used several statistical tests, including chi-square, t-tests, and ANOVAs, obtaining the same results regardless of the test.

12 Cohen (1988) defines effect sizes as small (0.2), medium (0.5), and large (0.8).

13 The data are presented for dyads because our purpose was to match dyads in the classroom with those in the laboratory.

14 Because there were seven more classroom dyads than laboratory dyads, in Appendix D, seven classroom dyads are unmatched.

References

Ayoun, D. (2001). The role of negative and positive feedback in the second language acquisition of the passé composé and imparfait. *Modern Language Journal, 85*, 226–243.

Braidi, S. M. (2002). Reexamining the role of recasts in native-speaker/ nonnative-speaker interactions. *Language Learning, 52*, 1–42.

Brown, H. D. (2001). Teaching by principles: An interactive approach to language pedagogy (2nd ed.). White Plains, NY: Longman.

Bygate, M., & Samuda, V. (2009). Creating pressure in task pedagogy: The joint roles of field, purpose, and engagement within the interaction approach. In A. Mackey & C. Polio (Eds.), *Multiple perspectives on interaction in second language acquisition: Research in honor of Susan M. Gass* (pp. 90–116). New York: Routledge.

Cohen, J. (1988). Statistical power analysis for the behavioral sciences (2nd ed.). Hillsdale, NJ: Erlbaum.

Eckerth, J. (2009). Negotiated interaction in the L2 classroom. *Language Teaching, 42*, 109–129.

Ellis, R. (2000). Task-based research and language pedagogy. *Language Teaching Research, 4*, 193–220.

Ellis, R. (2003). *Task-based language learning and teaching.* Oxford, UK: Oxford University Press.

Ellis, R. (2010). Second language acquisition, teacher education and language pedagogy. *Language Teaching, 43,* 182–201.

Ellis, R., Basturkmen, H., & Loewen, S. (2001a). Learner uptake in communicative ESL lessons. *Language Learning, 51,* 281–318.

Ellis, R., Basturkmen, H., & Loewen, S. (2001b). Preemptive focus on form in the ESL classroom. *TESOL Quarterly, 35,* 407–432.

Ellis, R., Tanaka, Y., & Yamazaki, A. (1994). Classroom interaction, comprehension and the acquisition of L2 word meanings. *Language Learning, 44,* 449–491.

Foster, P. (1998). A classroom perspective on the negotiation of meaning. *Applied Linguistics, 19,* 1–23.

Foster, P., & Ohta, A. S. (2005). Negotiation for meaning and peer assistance in second language classrooms. *Applied Linguistics, 26,* 402–430.

Fujii, A., & Mackey, A. (2009). Interactional feedback in learner-learner interactions in a task based EFL classroom. *IRAL, 47,* 267–301.

Fujii, A., Obata, M., Takahashi, S., & Tanabe, S. (2008). Training learners to negotiate for meaning: An exploratory case study. *Language Research Bulletin, 23,* 1–15.

Gass, S. M. (1997). Input, interaction, and the second language learner. Mahwah, NJ: Erlbaum.

Gass, S. M. (2003). Input and interaction. In C. Doughty & M. H. Long (Eds.), *The handbook of second language acquisition* (pp. 224–255). Oxford, UK: Blackwell.

Gass, S. M., & Varonis, E. (1984). The effect of familiarity on the compre-hensibility of nonnative speech. *Language Learning, 34,* 65–89.

Gass, S. M., & Varonis, E. (1985). Task variation and nonnative/nonnative negotiation of meaning. In S. M. Gass & C. Madden (Eds.), *Input in second language acquisition* (pp. 149–161). Rowley, MA: Newbury House.

Gilabert, R., Baron, J., & Llanes, A. (2009). Manipulating cognitive complexity across task types and its impact on learners' interaction during oral performance. *IRAL, 47,* 367–395.

Hatch, E. (1978). Discourse analysis and second language acquisition. In E. Hatch (Ed.), *Second language acquisition* (pp. 401–435). Rowley, MA: Newbury House.

Iwashita, N. (2003). Negative feedback and positive evidence in task-based interaction: Differential effects on L2 development. *Studies in Second Language Acquisition, 25,* 1–36.

Jenks, C. J. (2009). Exchanging missing information in tasks: Old and new interpretations. *Modern Language Journal, 93,* 185–194.

Johnstone, R. (2006). Review of research on language teaching, learning and policy published in 2004 and 2005. *Language Teaching, 39,* 1–27.

Kowal, M., & Swain, M. (1994). Using collaborative language production tasks to promote students' language awareness. *Language Awareness, 3,* 73–93.

Leeman, J. (2003). Recasts and second language development: Beyond negative evidence. *Studies in Second Language Acquisition, 25,* 37–63.

Loewen, S. (2003). Variation in the frequency and characteristics of incidental focus on form. *Language Teaching Research, 7,* 315–345.

Long, M. H. (1981). Input, interaction and second language acquisition. In H. Winitz (Ed.), *Native language and foreign language acquisition: Annals of the New York Academy of Sciences* (Vol. 379, pp. 259–278).

Long, M. H. (1983). Native speaker/non-native speaker conversation and the negotiation of comprehensible input. *Applied Linguistics, 4,* 126–141.

Long, M. H. (1985). Input and second language acquisition theory. In S. M. Gass & C. Madden (Eds.), *Input in second language acquisition* (pp. 377–393). Rowley, MA: Newbury House.

Long, M. H. (1996). The role of the linguistic environment in second language acquisition. In W. C. Ritchie & T. K. Bhatia (Eds.), *Handbook of research on language acquisition* (Vol. 2, pp. 413–468). New York: Academic Press.

Long, M. H. (in press). *Task-based language teaching.* Oxford, UK: Blackwell.

Long, M. H., Inagaki, S., & Ortega, L. (1998). The role of implicit negative feedback in SLA: Models and recasts in Japanese and Spanish. *Modern Language Journal, 82,* 357–371.

Lyster, R. (1998a). Negotiation of form, recasts, and explicit correction in relation to error types and learner repair in immersion classrooms. *Language Learning, 48,* 183–218.

Lyster, R. (1998b). Recasts, repetition and ambiguity in L2 classroom discourse. *Studies in Second Language Acquisition, 20,* 51–81.

Lyster, R., & Ranta, L. (1997). Corrective feedback and learner uptake: Negotiation of form in communicative classrooms. *Studies in Second Language Acquisition, 19,* 37–66.

Mackey, A. (1999). Input, interaction, and second language development: An empirical study of question formation in ESL. *Studies in Second Language Acquisition, 21,* 557–587.

Mackey, A. (2000, October). *Feedback, noticing and second language development: An empirical study of L2 classroom interaction.* Paper presented at the annual meeting of the British Association for Applied Linguistics, Cambridge, UK.

Mackey, A. (2007). Interaction as practice. In R. DeKeyser (Ed.), *Practice in a second language: Perspectives from applied linguistics and cognitive psychology* (pp. 85–110). New York: Cambridge University Press.

Mackey, A., & Philp, J. (1998). Conversational interaction and second language development: Recasts, responses, and red herrings? *Modern Language Journal, 82,* 338–356.

McDonough, K. (2005). Identifying the impact of negative feedback and learners' responses on ESL question development. *Studies in Second Language Acquisition, 27,* 79–103.

Muranoi, H. (2000). Focus on form through interaction enhancement: Integrating formal instruction into a communicative task in EFL classrooms. *Language Learning, 50,* 617–673.

Nassaji, H. (2007). Elicitation and reformulation and their relationship with learner repair in dyadic interaction. *Language Learning, 57,* 511–548.

Nicholas, H., Lightbown, P. M., & Spada, N. (2001). Recasts as feedback to language learners. *Language Learning, 51,* 719–758.

Nunan, D. (1989). *Designing tasks for the communicative classroom.* Cambridge, UK: Cambridge University Press.

Nunan, D. (1991). Methods in second language classroom research: A critical review. *Studies in Second Language Acquisition, 13,* 249–274.

Oliver, R. (1998). Negotiation of meaning in child interactions. *Modern Language Journal, 82,* 372–386.

Oliver, R. (2000). Age differences in negotiation and feedback in classroom and pairwork. *Language Learning, 50,* 119–151.

Oliver, R. (2002). The patterns of negotiation for meaning in child interactions. *Modern Language Journal, 86,* 97–111.

Philp, J. (2003). Constraints on "noticing the gap": Nonnative speakers' noticing of recasts in NS-NNS interaction. *Studies in Second Language Acquisition, 25,* 99–126.

Philp, J., Oliver, R., & Mackey, A. (2006). The impact of planning time on children's task-based interactions. *System, 34,* 547–565.

Pica, T. (1985). The selective impact of classroom instruction on second language acquisition. *Applied Linguistics, 6,* 214–222.

Pica, T. (1988). Interlanguage adjustments as an outcome of NS-NNS negotiated interaction. *Language Learning, 38,* 45–73.

Pica, T. (1989). Research on language learning: How can it respond to classroom concerns? *Working Papers in Educational Linguistics, 5,* 1–27.

Pica, T. (1992). Communication with second language learners: What does it reveal about the social and linguistic processes of second language learning? In J. Alatis (Ed.), *Georgetown University Round Table on Languages and Linguistics* (pp. 435–464). Washington, DC: Georgetown University Press.

Pica, T. (1994a). Questions from the language classroom: Research perspectives. *TESOL Quarterly, 28,* 49–79.

Pica, T. (1994b). Research on negotiation: What does it reveal about second-language learning conditions, processes, and outcomes? *Language Learning, 44,* 493–527.

Pica, T. (2002). Subject-matter content: How does it assist the interactional and linguistic needs of classroom language learners? *Modern Language Journal, 86,* 1–19.

Pica, T., Holliday, L., Lewis, N. E., & Morgenthaler, L. (1989). Comprehensible output as an outcome of linguistic demands on the learner. *Studies in Second Language Acquisition, 11,* 63–90.

Pica, T., Kang, H.-S., & Sauro, S. (2006). Information gap tasks: Their multiple roles and contributions to interaction research methodology. *Studies in Second Language Acquisition, 28,* 301–338.

Pica, T., & Long, M. H. (1986). The linguistic and conversational performance of experienced and inexperienced teachers. In R. R. Day (Ed.), *Talking to learn: Conversation in second language acquisition* (pp. 85–98). Rowley, MA: Newbury House.

Pica, T., Young, R., & Doughty, C. (1987). The impact of interaction on comprehension. *TESOL Quarterly, 21*, 737–758.

Révész, A. (2009). Task complexity, focus on form, and second language development. *Studies in Second Language Acquisition, 31*, 437–470.

Samuda, V. (2001). Guiding relationships between form and meaning during task performance: The role of the teacher. In M. Bygate, P. Skehan, & M. Swain (Eds.), *Researching pedagogic tasks: Second language learning, teaching and testing* (pp. 119–140). London: Longman.

Schmidt, R., & Frota, S. (1986). Developing basic conversational ability in a second language: A case study of an adult learner of Portuguese. In R. R. Day (Ed.), *Talking to learn: Conversation in second language acquisition* (pp. 237–326). Rowley, MA: Newbury House.

Sheen, Y. (2004). Corrective feedback and learner uptake in communicative classrooms across instructional settings. *Language Teaching Research, 8*, 263–300.

Shehadeh, A. (2001). Self and other-initiated modified output during task-based interaction. *TESOL Quarterly, 35*, 433–457.

Swain, M. (1995). Three functions of output in second language learning. In G. Cook & B. Seidlhofer (Eds.), *Principle and practice in applied linguistics: Studies in honour of H. G. Widdowson* (pp. 125–144). Oxford, UK: Oxford University Press.

Swain, M. (1998). Focus on form through conscious reflection. In C. Doughty & J. Williams (Eds.), *Focus on form in classroom second language acquisition* (pp. 64–81). Cambridge, UK: Cambridge University Press.

Swain, M. (2005). The output hypothesis: Theory and research. In E. Hinkel (Ed.), *Handbook of research in second language teaching and learning* (pp. 471–483). Mahwah, NJ: Erlbaum.

Swain, M., & Lapkin, S. (1998). Interaction and second language learning: Two adolescent French immersion students working together. *Modern Language Journal, 82*, 320–337.

Van Den Branden, K. (1997). Effects of negotiation on language learners' output. *Language Learning, 47*, 589–636.

Varonis, E., & Gass, S. M. (1985). Non-native/non-native conversations: A model for negotiation of meaning. *Applied Linguistics, 6*, 71–90.

Williams, J. (1999). Learner-generated attention to form. *Language Learning, 49*, 583–625.

Williams, J. (2001). The effectiveness of spontaneous attention to form. *System, 29*, 325–340.

Appendix A

Picture Differences Task

Picture differences - Park scene

© *University of Sydney & NLLIA. 1994*

Picture differences - Park scene

© University of Sydney & NLLIA, 1994

Appendix B

Consensus Task

Instructions **[English translation]:**
Your friend wants to study Electrical Engineering at a university in Spain. She has been accepted to six universities and you need to help her decide which one to attend.

Example of a University Description **[English translation]**
University of Granada

- 19,900 students; 1,050 teachers
- Electrical Engineering department: Rated #76 in Spain
- Climate: Hot and humid in the summer, cold in the winter
- Cost of living: Low
- Cost of tuition: Low
- Advantage: Your friend's cousin attends this university

Appendix C

Map Task

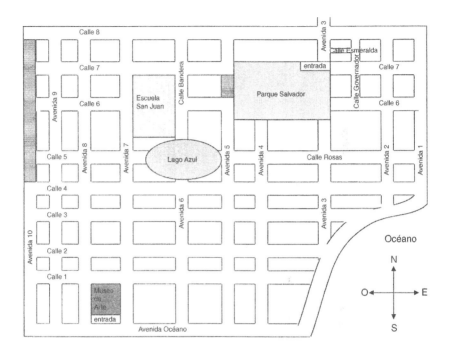

Example of Instructions

Participant 1

La avenida 10 está cerrada entre la calle 4 y la calle 8.

Avenue 10 is closed between Street 4 and Street 8.

La calle 5 está cerrada desde el Lago Azul hasta la avenida 10.

Street 5 is closed from the Blue Lake to Avenue 10.

La avenida Oceano va en una sola dirección hacia el oeste.

Ocean Avenue goes in a single direction towards the west.

Participant 2

La avenida 5 está cerrada entre la calle 6 y la calle 7.

Avenue 5 is closed between Street 6 and Street 7.

La avenida 8 va en una sola direccion hacia el sur.

Avenue 8 goes in a single direction towards the south.

La avenida 2 estará cerrada todo el día.

Avenue 2 will be closed all day.

Appendix D

Negotiation Moves per Dyad

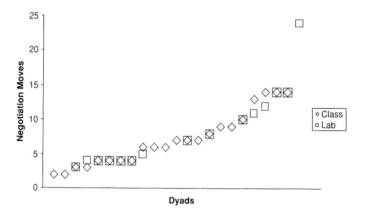

Figure D1 Negotiation moves per dyad on the picture differences task

Subject Index

Printed in the USA/Agawam, MA
March 7, 2013

573436.023